ASSASSINATED!

ASSASSINATED!

Assassinations that shook the world:
from Julius Caesar to JFK

STEVEN PARISSIEN

Quercus

CONTENTS

THE LONG HISTORY OF ASSASSINATION

Political assassinations have been a part of history since records began. *Assassinated!* begins with the killing of Julius Caesar in 44 BC – but it could have begun with any one of the gruesome political murders that litter the political history of the ancient world. The word 'assassination' may have only come into general use in the 12th century (see the chapter on Conrad of Montferrat, page 20), but the motives, ambitions and goals that the act encompasses have existed since communities were first organized and their leaders were first appointed.

The potential field is therefore dizzyingly large, and I have attempted to contain it here in manageable proportions, selecting what seemed to me some of the most interesting, unusual and significant examples. I have interpreted an 'assassination' here as a premeditated and politically inspired killing. (Therefore, cultural and essentially non-political figures, such as John Lennon, are excluded.) I have also attempted to distinguish assassinations from contract killings – albeit a slender distinction – and from executions of political figures in custody, whether quasi-judicial or otherwise. Thus, there is no retelling here of the tale of England's imprisoned King Edward II and the alleged application of the fatal poker, nor of the Bolshevik execution of the last Tsar of Russia, nor of the death in prison of the South African martyr Steve Biko – to name but three. But even excluding these categories, the potential field remains very large.

Assassinations have inevitably changed history. As the following stories will demonstrate, assassinations have caused governments to fall, countries to collapse, wars to erupt and populations to become oppressed. The moral status of the assassination victims varies hugely, of course: how can one compare a cold, genocidal Nazi such as Reinhard Heydrich to a civil rights leader such as Martin Luther King or Medgar Evers? Occasionally, in the aftermath of the assassination of a particularly inspiring figure, it seems as if the last hope of freedom or liberty has been extinguished. Nevertheless, as this book will show, communities are resilient things, and they invariably bounce back from even the most tragic loss.

Not all assassination attempts have succeeded, of course. Benjamin Jones and Benjamin Olken recently published a Harvard University paper (entitled

Hit or Miss?), looking at the statistics of assassination. They point out that of the 298 assassination attempts that they record between 1875 and 2004, only 59 resulted in the target's death. Our lives would certainly have been dramatically altered had many of these near-misses actually succeeded.

Indeed, contemplating what would have happened if a particular politician or sovereign had died, rather than survived, is one of the great 'what-ifs' of bar-room history. What if Hitler had left a Munich beer hall 13 minutes later than he did in 1939, or had sat a few inches to his left at his conference of 20 July 1944? On both occasions he narrowly escaped death by a bomb. What if John F. Kennedy, or Abraham Lincoln, or Robert Kennedy – or, for that matter, Julius Caesar – had lived? What if Archduke Franz Ferdinand of Austria had not perished in 1914 – and, but for his driver taking a wrong turn, that might well have been the case. Would the First World War have been averted or merely postponed? These are fantasies that, sadly, we must leave for another book.

The assassination is, depressingly, still very much with us. (Astonishingly, government-sponsored assassination was not made illegal in the United States until the Carter administration changed policy in 1976.) Indeed, the assassination, rather than dying out, is becoming an increasingly common feature of modern political life. As Jones and Olken observe, across the globe 'a national leader has been assassinated in nearly two of every three years since 1950'. The recent 2006 murder of Alexander Litvinenko by the secret application of a radioactive poison reminds us that, all too often, governments, sects and factions are – perhaps now more than ever – still prepared to waive elementary rules of social responsibility, personal integrity, democratic accountability and freedom of speech in order to eliminate political opponents. And the 2007 extinguishing of Pakistan's leading secular politician, Benazir Bhutto, reminds us – if we need to be reminded – that for some on the fundamentalist extremes, God and politics have been reconnected to deadly effect in the 21st century. In such a savage and predatory environment, who is really safe?

Steven Parissien

Julius CAESAR

100–44 BC, ROMAN GENERAL AND DICTATOR

ASSASSINS	Brutus, Cassius and other Senators
DATE	15 March 44 BC
PLACE	Rome, Italy

The assassination of Gaius Julius Caesar in 44 BC – on the 'Ides of March' (the 15th of the month, the 'ides' being the midway point) – is surely one of the best-known political murders in history. It not only ended the life of one of the most successful generals of the Roman Republic; its brutal aftermath also laid the foundation for the mighty Roman Empire that was to last four centuries. In this sense, it was one of the most profoundly influential of all historical assassinations.

In 44 BC the Roman Senate named this 55-year-old politician-general 'dictator for life'. He had certainly struggled hard to reach that position. By 55 BC he had pacified the Gauls and subdued the Belgae (who inhabited an area similar to modern France), conquered Armorica (present-day Brittany) and invaded Britain. All this had not been achieved through a softly-softly approach. Recent estimates suggest that as many as 1 million people in Gaul – approximately one in four of the population – died as a result of Caesar's 'pacification', while the 1st-century historian Plutarch recorded that another 1 million were enslaved, 300 tribes subjugated and 800 cities destroyed. It is hardly surprising, then, that Julius Caesar's name is not venerated in France today, the French preferring to commemorate that vigorously anti-Roman comic-book creation, Asterix the Gaul.

Caesar had made enemies at home as well as abroad. In 50 BC the Senate, led by his arch-rival Pompey (Gnaeus Pompeius Magnus), ordered Caesar to return to Rome and disband his army on the expiration of his term as proconsul. Caesar judged – probably correctly – that if he entered Rome without the immunity enjoyed by a consul, or without the power of his army behind him, he would be at best politically neutered and at worst imprisoned or even murdered. Pompey publicly accused Caesar of insubordination and treason, making an accommodation between Caesar and his senatorial critics look impossible. Accordingly, the following year Caesar crossed the River Rubicon at Italy's northern boundary (with Cisalpine Gaul) with one legion at his back – an illegal act for a Roman subject – and lit the touchpaper of Rome's first civil war in decades.

Nervous of plunging the republic into bloody anarchy, Pompey – a brave but somewhat intellectually challenged general – allowed Caesar, with just his one legion, to seize the initiative. Pompey was ultimately forced to flee by sea to Spain, where Caesar followed after leaving Italy in the hands of his allies Marcus Aemilius Lepidus and Mark Antony. In Spain, Caesar defeated Pompey's army, but the elusive general himself escaped to Greece and subsequently to Egypt. Having ensured his appointment as dictator in Rome, Caesar pursued Pompey to Alexandria, where he arrived to find that Pompey had been murdered on the orders of the slippery Egyptian pharaoh Ptolemy XIII.

> 'The die is cast'
>
> Caesar, crossing the Rubicon, 49 BC

Caesar then plunged himself into the local civil strife between Ptolemy and one of history's legendary figures of the classical world – Ptolemy's sister, wife and co-ruler, Cleopatra VII. Caesar not only defeated the Ptolemaic forces and installed Cleopatra as sole ruler, but pursued a passionate affair with the wily (though not, apparently, particularly handsome) Egyptian queen, with whom he had a son, Caesarion. In the event, Caesar and Cleopatra never married – they were forbidden to do so under Roman law. Nevertheless, their relationship lasted 14 years.

Meanwhile, Caesar crushed Pompey's remaining supporters in Africa and Spain. Returning to Italy in 45 BC, with the known world seemingly at his feet, Caesar was

IOO BC Born into a Roman patrician and aristocratic family.

81–61 BC Serves Rome and its provinces in military and civil capacities. Governor of the Spanish province Hispania Ulterior (61 BC).

60 BC Elected consul and forms the First Triumvirate to lead Rome with Crassus and Pompey.

58–50 BC Conducts military campaigns to impose Roman authority on vast areas of Gaulish territory, and invades Britain twice (55 and 54 BC).

50–48 BC After the death of Crassus and the collapse of the triumvirate, competes for power with Pompey and his armies from Italy to Egypt.

47–45 BC Appointed dictator and (again) consul, both for a year, and establishes his personal and political alliance with Cleopatra. Quells rebellions by Pompey's sons in Spain.

45 BC Appointed dictator for life, and a consul for 10 years; achieves honour of deification and the naming of the month 'Julius' (July) after him.

44 BC Assassinated (15 March) by Senators fearing his growing power.

acclaimed dictator for life. He was not idle: he made a new will, naming his great-nephew and adopted son Octavian (Gaius Octavius) as his sole heir; he overhauled the old Roman calendar, creating a regular year and bringing the months roughly into line with seasonal changes; he initiated far-reaching economic reforms, regulating the price of grain to prevent rampant inflation and instituting a land-for-veterans scheme for retired legionaries; and he launched a massive programme of public works, centred on Rome itself – which soon had the formidable Forum of Caesar at its heart.

However, to many neutral observers, as well as to his numerous political enemies, the honours heaped on Caesar in recent years seemed to have gone to his head. The Senate delegates despatched to inform Caesar of his new dictatorial title were indignant that, rather than rise to meet them in the customary Roman patrician manner, Caesar had remained sitting as they approached – more in the fashion of an eastern potentate (or, indeed, an autocratic Egyptian pharaoh) than a servant of the republic. (One commentator subsequently wrote that Caesar had been incapacitated by a sudden attack of diarrhoea, but other sources observed that he had subsequently walked home unaided and unperturbed.)

The Senators were also deeply worried that Caesar might respond positively to the increasingly frequent popular acclamations of the general as their *rex* – king. The Romans had dispensed with kings many centuries before, and the Senate was fearful of an overmighty subject leaning that way. Some Senators thus began to conspire to try and halt what they perceived as a headlong rush towards a personal seizure of power. Caesar's former close friend and one-time heir, Marcus Junius Brutus, together with his brother-in-law Cassius, led a group calling themselves the 'Liberators', and this quixotic but loosely knit outfit resolved to murder Caesar before he could effect his alleged popular coup.

On 15 March 44 BC, a group of Senators led by Brutus called Caesar into the forum to read a petition demanding that he hand power back to the Senate. However, the petition itself was a fake. Caesar's ally Mark Antony had effectively learned as much the night before, having overheard the over-confident rantings of one of the plotters, Servillius Casca. Fearing the worst, Antony went to warn Caesar on the steps of the forum, but was too late. The group of Senators intercepted Caesar just as he was passing Pompey's Theatre – a venue laden with heavy irony – and directed him into a loggia behind the building's eastern portico. Here one of the Senators, Tillius Cimber, presented him with the bogus petition.

As Caesar began to read, Cimber pulled down Caesar's tunic and produced a dagger, ineffectively stabbing at the dictator's neck. Caesar spun around and caught Casca's arm, demanding to know what he was doing. The petrified Casca shrieked for help, and within moments the entire group, including Brutus, had produced their daggers and were knifing the general indiscriminately. Caesar attempted to escape, but tripped and fell on the portico steps, and his assassins continued to stab him as he lay there. Altogether, Caesar was stabbed 23 times. A physician later opined, however, that the second wound – to his chest – had proved the lethal blow.

Caesar's last words – as with the final words of so many historical celebrities – are not known for certain. In the 16th century Shakespeare paraphrased the historian Suetonius in suggesting 'et tu, Brute?' – 'you too, Brutus?' Plutarch, however, reported that Caesar had said nothing at all and that, once Caesar was dead, Brutus had stepped forward as if to make a speech, but that his fellow Senators had fled in all directions. Brutus and his immediate companions then attempted to rouse the mob, marching to the Capitol while crying out 'People of Rome! We are once again free!' They were, however, met in stony silence. Once rumours of Caesar's assassination had begun to spread, Rome's people preferred to lock themselves in their houses to avoid any ensuing bloodshed. While the feared rising failed to materialize, an angry mob did set fire to the forum, and the city itself only narrowly escaped immolation.

Caesar had been highly popular with the middle and lower classes, and it was this popularity that Octavian and Mark Antony, Caesar's heir and right-hand man respectively, now sought to harness. Mark Antony did not actually give the speech that Shakespeare penned for him 16 centuries later ('Friends, Romans, countrymen, lend me your ears …'), but he did orate a dramatic eulogy that won over the Roman crowds. His ensuing hold on the citizenry made many Senators fear that one would-be king had simply been replaced by another.

The subsequent months and years were, unsurprisingly, plagued with civil war. Caesar's assassins were declared enemies of the state, and many of them were hunted down and executed. Octavian and Mark Antony soon fell out, however, making the political and military landscape even more confusing. The former consolidated his hold on Italy, while Antony attempted to establish a power-base in Caesar's old stamping-ground, Gaul. Yet two years after Caesar's death, Brutus still remained at large. With a sizeable army of 17 legions behind him, and encouraged by the rift between Octavian and Mark Antony, he decided to march on Rome. Although initially successful against Octavian's forces, Brutus's radical republicanism temporarily healed the disputes between Caesar's self-styled avengers, and the combined legions of Antony and Octavian overcame Brutus's army at Philippi in 42 BC. Brutus evaded capture, but committed suicide rather than submit to the inevitable show-trial and execution. In a belated gesture of aristocratic respect, Antony had Brutus's corpse cremated, clad in a cloak of patrician purple. What Antony failed to realize, however, was that with Marcus Junius Brutus died the last hopes for the Roman Republic.

BIRTH OF THE ROMAN EMPIRE

THE DIRECT RESULT OF CAESAR'S MURDER, impossible to foresee by Brutus and his fellow-assassins, was that the dictator's death would precipitate the end of the Roman Republic.

Caesar's heir, Octavian, was immensely ambitious. Although only 19 at the time of Caesar's assassination, he had designs far beyond Caesar's senatorially gifted dictatorship. Having helped to defeat Brutus, he formed a ruling triumvirate of consuls with Mark Antony and Lepidus, and also saw to it (with half an eye on his own future prospects) that Caesar was deified.

Over the next decade, Octavian successfully marginalized Lepidus and drove Antony into a self-imposed exile with his *inamorata*, the same Cleopatra who had bewitched Caesar, in Egypt. In 31 BC the combined fleets of Antony and Cleopatra were crushed by Octavian's naval forces at the Battle of Actium, and the ill-starred lovers subsequently followed Brutus's example and committed suicide.

Four years later, in 27 BC, Octavian was declared 'Augustus' (Sacred), was confirmed as the 'son of a god' despite his relatively distant blood-connection to Caesar, and was accorded powers that far exceeded those of his illustrious predecessor. Augustus, as *princeps*, had effectively become Rome's first emperor.

CALIGULA

AD 12–41, ROMAN EMPEROR

ASSASSINS Praetorian Guards led by Cassius Chaerea
DATE 24 January AD 41
PLACE Rome, Italy

Historical judgements are constantly being reassessed, and for centuries historians have been using documentary sources, new evidence and their personal insights to reconsider individuals' reputations. The result is often a strikingly different, and possibly fairer, portrait; and all manner of past villains have, in this way, been more positively reinterpreted, while some much-celebrated heroes have been toppled from their pedestals.

Not every historical celebrity, however, is capable of being rehabilitated. While alleged tyrants such as Richard III of England and Ivan IV of Russia, for example, are now seen in a far more favourable light than they were a few decades ago, some rulers' reputations resist improvement by historical revisionism. One such example is Rome's Emperor Caligula: while the solid evidence for his life and character is rather slim, he has received a universally bad press since the earliest historical accounts. If anyone in this book can be said to have deserved their violent death, it is surely him.

Caligula was born Gaius Julius Caesar Germanicus in AD 12. The third of six surviving children born to Emperor Augustus's adopted grandson, Germanicus, he was much feted as a small boy. The son of an immensely popular general – who might himself conceivably have become Augustus's heir – he accompanied his parents on military campaigns in Germany, during which time he became the mascot of his father's army and was often dressed in a miniature soldier's uniform. In this way he acquired his affectionate nickname 'Caligula' – from *caligae*, literally 'little boots', after the military footwear that he wore on these occasions.

Little Caligula's upbringing, however, was far from merry. His father was poisoned – by, Germanicus claimed, agents of his rival, Augustus's son Tiberius – and he grew up as a hostage in the home of Tiberius's mother, the Machiavellian schemer Livia, and later his grandmother Antonia. In both of these houses he was deliberately kept away from the world; indoors, however, he was allowed to indulge himself liberally. It is from these years that accusations originate of his incest with his three sisters – his sole companions during this period. Caligula's morals took a further nosedive in AD 31, when he was given over to the personal care of Tiberius on the Mediterranean island of Capri. Here, the historian Suetonius would have us believe, Caligula was encouraged to indulge in any perversion he desired.

With Tiberius's death, Caligula was acclaimed emperor in AD 37. (Suetonius writes that Macro, the prefect of the Praetorian Guard, actually smothered the dying Tiberius with a pillow to hasten Caligula's accession.) In his first weeks and months, Caligula took care to keep public opinion on his side. Tiberius's hated lieutenant Sejanus was executed, as were many of his allies and appointees. Caligula brought a swift end to Tiberius's treason trials, reformed the tax system, revived free elections and (in what was later to be seen as an appalling irony) banished sex offenders from the empire.

> 'Make him feel that he is dying'
>
> Caligula's way with executions, according to Suetonius

Caligula was also keen to stage lavish spectacles for the public. Soon after his accession, he ordered the construction of a temporary two-mile floating bridge across the Bay of Naples, using ships as pontoons, from the resort of Baiae to the neighbouring port of Puteoli. Ever the consummate actor, he then proceeded to ride his favourite horse,

Caligula in brief

AD 12 Born Gaius Julius Caesar Germanicus in Antium, into Rome's Julio-Claudian dynasty.

AD 15—19 Accompanies his father Germanicus on expeditions in German territories and the Middle East.

AD 37 On the death of Tiberius, becomes Rome's emperor. A serious illness possibly exacerbates his mental instability.

AD 38 Executes Macro, head of the Praetorian Guard, and Tiberius's grandson Tiberius Gemellus. Deifies his dead sister Drusilla.

AD 39 Quells a revolt in the Upper Rhine region.

AD 40 Takes an army to the northern coast of Gaul, but decides against invading Britain.

AD 41 Assassinated (along with his wife and daughter) by Cassius Chaerea, tribune of the Praetorian Guard.

Incitatus, across the straits, wearing the breastplate of Alexander the Great – both to rival the Persian King Xerxes' crossing of the Hellespont and to defy a recent prophecy that he had 'no more chance of becoming emperor than of riding a horse across the Gulf of Baiae'.

After recovering from a serious illness in AD 37, however, Caligula's personality began to show a marked change for the worse. His behaviour grew more arbitrary, and more violent. Thus, in AD 39 Caligula removed and replaced Rome's consuls without consulting the Senate, and he publicly humiliated several Senators by forcing them to run alongside his chariot in their full robes. He subsequently dressed Gauls up as German prisoners, to provide 'proof' of a vast (but fictional) military victory; on another occasion, veteran Roman troops were ordered to collect sea-shells – 'spoils of the sea' – to illustrate the emperor's victory over Neptune, the god of the sea. (Sources suggest that this task was a deliberate face-saver after mutinous troops had refused to embark on the Channel coast for an invasion of Britain.)

Back in Rome, Caligula – declaring himself now a living god – ensured that Augustus's Cult of the Deified Emperor now centred only on himself. He would appear at the Temple of Castor and Pollux on the forum, dressed as a god, and demand that those in his presence worship him. In other Roman temples, the heads of the gods' statues were replaced with Caligula's own likeness – even those of female deities.

Numerous stories of Calgula's increasingly deranged behaviour circulated around the empire. Many focused on his alleged incestuous relationships with his sisters, especially Drusilla. (However, the story of her death at Caligula's hands – while the emperor tried to deliver, by caesarian section, the baby he had fathered – was invented by Robert Graves for his splendidly colourful novel *I Claudius* of 1934.) He is also said to have named his favourite horse, Incitatus, as a priest, and to have given the beast a house to reside in – complete with a marble stable, golden manger and jewelled necklaces. The tale that he intended to make the same horse a member of the Senate, though, was most likely a lame senatorial joke.

There was wide testimony of Caligula's frequent public exposure of his impressively sized genitalia, which he happily manipulated at public games. More seriously, he was said to have opened a brothel in his palace and populated it with Senators' wives, who were required to perform while the hapless patricians looked on in horror.

Caligula's behaviour grew more unpredictable by the week. When there were not enough convicts to fight the lions and tigers in the arena, he threw in some spectators to make the numbers up. He is said to have made it a crime to look down on him from above, and to refuse to leave him everything in one's will.

For years, the increasingly insane Caligula was protected by his German bodyguards and by the Roman Praetorian Guard. It was only when the latter finally decided they could not stomach the emperor's excesses that his days were truly numbered. One of the Praetorians' senior commanders, Cassius Chaerea, had received a serious wound to his groin during his long years of unsullied service. According to Suetonius, Caligula had often mocked Chaerea for his injury, decreeing that the guards' watchword for the day should be insulting terms such as 'priapus' (erection) or 'Venus' (Roman slang for a eunuch) whenever Chaerea was on duty. On 24 January AD 41, Chaerea and other guardsmen accosted Caligula while he was addressing an acting troupe of young men during a series of games held in honour of the Divine Augustus. Chaerea requested the day's watchword from Caligula, at which Chaerea shouted 'So be it!' and attacked him. After the first blow, Caligula cried for help, prompting Chaerea's fellow conspirators to strike as well. Suetonius records a total of at least 30 wounds, several of them delivered to the despised emperor's genitals.

Another of Chaerea's soldiers sought out and murdered Caligula's wife and daughter. Back at the arena, Caligula's enraged German bodyguards arrived at the scene of the assassination too late: stricken with grief and rage, they responded with a vicious attack on innocent Senators and arena spectators. In the ensuing mayhem, Caligula's half-forgotten uncle, Claudius, was dragged from his hiding-place and spirited out of the city to a nearby Praetorian camp, where the guards declared him emperor.

The Senate, supported by Chaerea, attempted to use Caligula's death as an opportunity to restore the republic that Augustus had dissolved. The legions, however, remained loyal to the office of the emperor. The Roman mob, meanwhile, demanded that Caligula's murderers be brought to justice.

In the event, it was the legions and the mob that carried the day. The Senate demanded that Claudius be delivered to them so that his office could be ratified; Claudius and the Praetorians, however, rightly sensed that this would inexorably lead to the diminution, if not the abolition, of imperial authority, and Claudius refused. In return, the new emperor agreed to pardon all of the assassins except the brave Chaerea. Sentenced to death, he requested to be executed with the same words that had assassinated Caligula.

In the ensuing days, Claudius made sure that his rule – one that would witness imperial expansion – was swiftly legitimized. To that end, he adopted the illustrious name 'Caesar' as a cognomen, and added the name 'Augustus', as the two previous emperors had done at their accessions. Meanwhile, he kept the honorific 'Germanicus', in order to remind his subjects of the connection with his heroic and much-loved brother. In the Roman Empire, a name could mean everything.

THE INVASION OF BRITAIN

UNDER CALIGULA'S SUCCESSOR, CLAUDIUS (ruled AD 41–54), the Roman Empire underwent its first major expansion since the reign of Augustus. Thrace, Judea and many other territories were added to the empire at the eastern end of the Mediterranean. In North Africa, Caligula's annexation of Mauretania was completed. But the most important new conquest, in both political and economic terms, was that of Britain – Britannia – at the empire's northern extremity.

In AD 43, Claudius sent Aulus Plautius with four legions to Britain after an appeal from an ousted tribal ally. Britain was wealthy, and also a safe haven for Gallic malcontents. It had been invaded by Julius Caesar in 55 BC, but no permanent Roman settlement had followed.

Now Claudius intended to claim this rich plum for his empire. Aulus's conquest was relatively straightforward. The disunited British tribes failed to ally against the Roman legions, allowing Aulus to pick them off one by one.

Claudius himself sailed to Britain, bringing with him additional legions and, to the astonishment of the Britons, a squadron of elephants. (The elephants were used in the capture of Camulodunum – Colchester – but they perished soon afterwards.)

When the only British general who offered any real opposition, Caractacus, was finally captured by the Romans in AD 50, Claudius granted him clemency, and the vanquished Briton lived out his days as a captive curiosity, on land provided by the Roman state.

Thomas BECKET

c.1118–1170, ARCHBISHOP OF CANTERBURY

ASSASSINS Reginald Fitzurse, Hugh de Moreville, William de Tracy and Richard le Breton

DATE 29 December 1170

PLACE Canterbury, England

The story of England's King Henry II and Thomas Becket is a classic tragedy. Friendship and support turned to envy and enmity, as the best of friends became sworn enemies. The results were dramatic: an Archbishop of Canterbury fleeing abroad; international disputes and threats of war; and, ultimately, a cold-blooded murder at a cathedral altar.

Thomas Becket was born c.1118 in Cheapside, London, to good, reasonably well-off parents from a Norman background. As a boy, he attracted the attention of the then Archbishop of Canterbury, Theobald. In the 12th century, social mobility was really possible only through the patronage of the Church. This the clever young Thomas quickly won, and his subsequent rise was meteoric. Theobald sent him abroad on missions, employed him as his clerk, and ultimately appointed him Archdeacon of Canterbury.

Becket's next appointment brought him into the king's orbit. Henry II had assumed the throne in 1154 after almost two decades of bitter civil war between the rival claimants Stephen and Henry's mother, Matilda. Predictably, Henry's primary aim was thus to establish strong and stable government. To that end he wanted a reliable lord chancellor who would be accepted by most, if not all, of the powerful vested interests in the kingdom. This he found in Archbishop Theobald's nominee: Thomas Becket. Thomas's close links with the City of London oligarchs, and the wholehearted support of the Church that he brought with him, highly recommended him to Henry. What the king did not expect was that his relationship with Thomas would grow into a close friendship.

Becket soon became known as Henry's mail-fisted right-hand. Using unashamedly brutal methods, he enforced Henry's authority in the extensive French territories – the Angevin Empire – that came from the king's marriage to Eleanor of Aquitaine in 1152. He also repaired the English tax system, much to the fury of the nobles who now had to pay the first full tax imposition for 20 years. And he became one of Henry's most indispensable courtiers, advising Henry on social events and palace etiquette as well as legal, fiscal and military issues. King Henry even sent his eldest son and heir, Prince Henry (subsequently called the 'Young King'), to live in Becket's household. The eventual outcome of this (by no means unusual) fostering, however, was to drive a wedge between Henry II and Becket and between the king and his heir. The Young King was later reported to have said that Becket had showed him more fatherly love in a day than his father did his entire life.

In 1161 Archbishop Theobald died, and Henry – after some hesitation – installed his friend Thomas as Theobald's successor in May 1162. This, however, proved the end of the friendship between the king and his chancellor. Becket was reputedly unhappy at being removed from the king's inner counsels, and saw his promotion to the primacy of England as a means of neutralizing his political influence. He sulked in Canterbury and turned to the pope for support – just at the time when Henry was seeking to reduce papal influence over the English Church. He was unnecessarily provocative, opposing the king's new tax proposals, insisting that barons do homage to him for land connected with the Archdiocese of Canterbury, and upholding the Church's independent legal system (thereby preventing the secular authorities from prosecuting clergy who had committed crimes). In short, Becket metamorphosed from a royal political fixer into a self-appointed defender of the Church. Henry had clearly mistaken his man: he had expected his loyal chancellor to rally

'Will no one rid me of this turbulent priest?'

Henry II's rash outburst, in popular tradition, December 1170

the Church behind the throne, and had instead found an archbishop who preferred to distance the Church from the state and to publicly challenge the king's authority.

The first tangible expression of the growing void between Henry and Becket came when the latter unilaterally resigned his chancellorship in 1163, claiming, with false modesty, that he was not man enough for one of his two jobs, let alone both. Henry was astounded. The Holy Roman Emperor's chancellor was also an archbishop; why should not the same happen in England? Henry had been busy with his French dominions for years, and he had been unaware of the full scale of Becket's estrangement. Now he knew.

The showdown between the two came in 1164, at the (now long-disappeared) New Forest palace of Clarendon. The purpose of the assembly was to enable Henry to tighten his control of the Church at the pope's expense. (The timing of this move was propitious: Pope Alexander III, currently a wandering exile in France, had been ousted from Rome by Imperial troops.) Henry assumed that his Church would obediently fall into line. His proposed 'Constitutions of Clarendon' appeared to be fair and reasonable, yet Becket chose to interpret them as unwarranted encroachments on ecclesiastical jurisdiction and encouraged his bishops to resist them.

Henry II – notorious for his violent temper – was enraged at Becket's opposition, and resolved to remove him as archbishop and to ensure that he was utterly humiliated. Becket was (rightly) arraigned for contempt of court over a land dispute, and when Becket went to Northampton Castle for a royal council meeting in October 1164, the king refused to see him. Becket then applied to the king to leave England. But before the king gave his judgement – according to the Constitutions of Clarendon, no cleric could leave England without the king's express permission – Becket fled the castle, and the country.

Becket's flight swiftly became an international incident. He arrived at the court of Henry II's greatest enemy, the French king Louis VII, who was already harbouring the pope. His typically melodramatic appeal to Alexander III won the pope over and guaranteed his support. By 1165 Alexander was denouncing Henry's actions, and the following year he appointed Becket as his papal legate for England.

Meanwhile, Henry did his cause no favours by mean-spiritedly dismissing all of Becket's allies and appointees. More positively, he allied himself with the pope's enemies in the Holy Roman Empire. However, in order to consolidate his mighty empire – and Henry's Angevin territories then covered all of what is now western France – Henry wanted to have the Young King, Prince Henry, crowned as joint-king. And a legitimate coronation could only be conducted by an Archbishop of Canterbury.

By 1168 Becket's presence in France was becoming an embarrassment to Louis VII, preventing him from putting out peace feelers in the wake of recent defeats by Henry's armies. Even Pope Alexander, far more of a diplomat than his ambitious Archbishop of Canterbury, restrained Becket from more intemperate action while trying secretly to heal the breach with his king. Accordingly, Louis and Alexander brokered a series of wide-ranging negotiations at Montmirail in January 1169. Both Henry II and Thomas Becket were invited – and both accepted. However, the attempted mediation ultimately failed because of Becket's pride, and Henry went ahead with his coronation of the Young King in his archbishop's absence.

Pressured by the French, Becket finally agreed to an ostensible reconciliation with Henry in July 1170. Nothing was said about the Constitutions of Clarendon, and no kiss of peace – a major sticking-point the previous year – was proffered or received.

On 1 December 1170 Becket's ship docked at Sandwich, in Kent. But Becket had already scored a major own-goal. Before leaving France, he had, with the pope's connivance, excommunicated the Archbishop of York (the other province of the English Church) as well as the bishops of Salisbury and London for officiating at the Young King's coronation. The timing of this deed was spectacularly poor: it would ultimately cost Becket his life. To an enraged Henry, it seemed to indicate that nothing had changed: Becket was still the same self-centred, over-proud and vain prelate. In the end, the tension between the two men would only be solved by an act of violence.

We don't know if Henry really uttered the words traditionally ascribed to him, 'Will no one rid me of this turbulent priest?' However, it is likely that he muttered something of this sort, possibly as an aside. He is known to have said something similar four years earlier, when the Bishop of Salisbury reported that 'he said they were all traitors who could not summon up the zeal and loyalty to rid him of the harassment of one man'. This time, however, there were four knights of the household who took their king's words seriously.

On 29 December 1170 Reginald Fitzurse, Hugh de Moreville, William de Tracy and Richard le Breton – eager to win the king's favour but not, it has been said, over-endowed with intelligence – set out to confront the archbishop in his cathedral. At Canterbury they were actually offered dinner by Becket, but angry exchanges followed, during which Fitzurse accused the archbishop of breaking the peace and of wanting to deprive the Young King of his crown. The four then considered murdering Becket with his own processional cross, but thought better of it. They called for support – many onlookers believed, possibly correctly, that the four knights were drunk – but none came, and Becket went into his cathedral to celebrate vespers. The knights armed themselves, raced into the cathedral, and confronted the archbishop. One struck Becket on the shoulder with the flat of his sword, declaring: 'Fly, you are a dead man!' But the archbishop faced them with calm dignity and resignation, and challenged them to do their worst. This they duly did, and Becket fell to the ground in a rain of sword blows. The life of a man ended; but the afterlife, of a saint and a remorseful king, was to begin.

ST THOMAS

THE INDICATIONS ARE THAT Thomas Becket expected martyrdom, and when the occasion arose even welcomed it. Undoubtedly, though, his story and murder touched a chord with contemporary Europe, who interpreted Becket merely as a humbly born subject defending the Church's liberties against the depredations of a powerful king, and he was soon being venerated all over the continent.

Becket was, accordingly, propelled to an unusually swift canonization, in March 1173. Fourteen months later, Henry II (who had already agreed with the pope to repeal the Constitutions of Clarendon) humbled himself in a public penance at Becket's tomb in Canterbury Cathedral. In 1220, Becket's remains were decanted from this tomb into a formal shrine in the recently completed

Trinity Chapel. This became one England's most popular pilgrimage sites until the Reformation of the 1530s, when the shrine was demolished. (A lighted candle today marks the pavement where the shrine once stood.) It was to Becket's shrine that Chaucer's 14th-century pilgrims of the *Canterbury Tales* were making their way.

Many local legends grew up around his death: the alleged absence of nightingales in the Kentish village of Otford was ascribed to Becket, who is said to have been so disturbed in his devotions by the song of a nightingale that he commanded that none should sing in the town ever again, while in the nearby town of Strood Becket was said to have caused the inhabitants' descendants to be born with tails.

CONRAD of Montferrat

*c.*1145–1192, CRUSADER LEADER

ASSASSINS Two members of the 'Assassin' sect
DATE 28 April 1192
PLACE Jerusalem, Palestine

The word 'assassin' derives from the Arabic *hashishi* or *hashsash* and literally denotes someone who has ingested the plant-drug *cannabis sativa* (often today known simply as 'hash'). However, the numerous ancient stories in which groups of Muslim *hashashin* or 'assassins' were fed cannabis, shown an earthly paradise, and then exhorted to go out and murder in order to attain this heaven-on-earth have been proven to be old wives' tales, invented to explain their grim determination and, for a while, their astonishing success.

The term *hashashin*, westernized to 'assassin', actually seems to have been simply a dismissive nickname for an Islamic sect whose predilection for political murder made them notorious as early as the 12th century. Only a reliance on mind-altering drugs, it was believed, could have encouraged the Assassins to such foolhardy and often suicidal attacks.

The Assassins were, in truth, an offshoot of the Ismaili community, itself a sect of Shia Islam. The Assassins first appeared at the end of the 11th century in Persia and Syria, led by their charismatic revolutionary leader, Hasan-i Sabbah. Having seized a series of castles in eastern Persia, they used their bases to erode the integrity of the Seljuk Empire to the west. The targeted murders of leading Seljuk commanders and other prominent members of the Sunni Muslim faith, initially at Hasan's behest, began around 1100. But it was their murder of a Western potentate in 1192 that brought them to the attention of the wider world.

Conrad of Montferrat appeared to have it all. He was rich, famously handsome and prodigiously well-connected – cousin to the Holy Roman Emperor, Frederick I 'Barbarossa', to King Louis VII of France and to Duke Leopold V of Austria. Celebrated across Europe as the epitome of chivalry and courage, he was one of Christendom's most illustrious warriors. He was trained as a diplomat, but became a skilled military commander, defeating Emperor Frederick's army at Camerino in 1179. When he appeared at the Byzantine court in 1180, an observer wrote that he was 'of beautiful appearance, comely in life's springtime, exceptional and peerless in manly courage and intelligence, and in the flower of his body's strength'.

In 1187 this picture of perfection set off to join his father in the kingdom of Jerusalem, which had been established by crusaders in 1099 but was currently threatened with extinction at the hands of the Seljuk Turks, led by their immensely able ruler, the legendary Kurdish-born Sultan Saladin. Conrad arrived to find that the crusader army had been crushed by Saladin at the Battle of Hattin; that the King of Jersualem, Guy of Lusignan, was Saladin's prisoner, along with Conrad's own father, Duke William V of Montferrat; and that the city of Jerusalem and the fortress of Acre had already fallen to Saladin's forces. He thus sailed to the besieged port of Tyre, with the aim of rescuing the city.

> '**A man of extraordinary bravery**'
>
> Contemporary chronicler Ibn al-Athir's verdict on Conrad

Saladin assaulted Tyre by land and sea, and, the story goes, offered to release Conrad's father if Conrad would give up Tyre. The old man supposedly told his son to stand firm, even when threatened with death; Conrad replied to the Seljuk leader that his father had already lived a long life and aimed his own crossbow at him – prompting Saladin to the reported (though unlikely) comment that 'This man is an unbeliever and very cruel.' Whatever the real details of the exchange, the Seljuks agreed to release William V to the custody of his son. At the end of December 1187 Conrad launched a bold counter-attack against the besieging Seljuks, and routed both Saladin's Egyptian navy and his landward troops. Tyre was saved, at least for now.

Conrad was now the only Christian general who appeared to offer any hope of saving the embattled kingdom of Jerusalem. Saladin released Guy of Lusignan, who duly appeared at Tyre and demanded that Conrad owe him fealty as king and that he hand over the keys of the city to him. Unsurprisingly, Conrad – whose impressive record of military achievement entirely eclipsed Guy's miserable résumé – refused, declaring that Guy had effectively lost his throne at the Battle of Hattin. Conrad even refused permission for Guy and his queen to enter the city until the matter had been arbitrated by a panel comprising the Holy Roman Emperor and the kings of France and England, who had bankrolled much of the current expedition. Conrad then cemented his own claim to the kingdom by marrying the only major claimant after Guy, Isabella of Jerusalem. Isabella happened to be happily married at the time, but Conrad and Isabella's ambitious mother cheerfully colluded to have her marriage annulled on the spurious grounds that Isabella had been under-age. The less-than-happy couple were thus joined in matrimony on 24 November 1190.

Guy of Lusignan did not take this lying down. He travelled across Europe to the court of Richard I, newly installed as King of England on the death of his father and a renowned warrior, whose eyes were firmly set on restoring Christian fortunes in the Middle East. Guy won Richard's support, the English king pledging to restore Guy's throne and to remove Conrad, and Richard himself set sail for the Holy Land. Meanwhile, Conrad had further strengthened his hand by wining back the key fortress of Acre, which had been taken after a two-year siege. The two sides thus came to an uneasy compromise: Guy was reconfirmed as King of Jerusalem, while Conrad was made his sole heir as well as governor of the cities of Tyre, Beirut and Sidon.

The shrinking kingdom of Jerusalem was, nevertheless, not big enough to embrace two military prima donnas. It was inevitable that Conrad and Richard – the latter now recognized as the senior crusader commander – would fall out, which they promptly did. In 1191 a dispute over the ownership of Seljuk hostages captured by French forces led to Richard I having all the hostages killed and Conrad taking refuge in Tyre, in fear of his life.

Saladin did not have to move against the Christian armies when their bitter infighting could do the job for him equally well. Early in 1192 Saladin was surprised to find Conrad opening direct negotiations with him, aimed at creating a coalition against Richard. (Saladin, meanwhile, had already approached Richard, suggesting a marriage alliance between his brother and Richard's widowed sister.) In the event, all this intriguing came to nought. Weary of the internecine strife, the crusader barons pressed for a rapid solution to the power vacuum in the kingdom, and in April 1192 the crown of Jerusalem was put to the vote: to Richard's horror, the nobles unanimously elected Conrad. Richard arbitrarily awarded Guy of Lusignan the island of Cyprus as a consolation prize, which he ruled as nominal king until his death in 1194.

Conrad's triumph was tragically shortlived. Returning from the house of his kinsman and friend, the Bishop of Beauvais, he was attacked by two Assassins, who stabbed him at

THE DEATH OF THE LION

RICHARD THE LIONHEART, given his reputation, could have expected a bloody but glorious finale in the thick of battle. But it was not quite like that.

Barely had the ransomed Richard returned to England when he was off fighting once more. This time, though, the cause was more justifiable and pressing: Philip II of France was threatening to seize the choicest parts of Richard's vast and lucrative Angevin Empire, comprising so much of western France.

Richard's campaigns went well. After the Battle of Fréteval in 1194, Philip fled the field so rapidly that he left much of his treasury and administration behind. However, while besieging the relatively minor castle of Chalus-Chabrol in 1199, Richard was struck by a crossbowman's lucky shot. He tried to pull the arrow out in the privacy of his tent, but failed; a surgeon then removed it but mangled Richard's arm in the process. The wound

swiftly became gangrenous, and Richard the Lionheart died on 6 April in the arms of his formidable mother, Eleanor of Aquitaine.

It was a bathetic and unnecessary death for such a celebrated warrior; as a chronicler later wrote, 'the Lion by the Ant was slain'. Even his last act of chivalry was shortlived. His assassin had been captured, but the king pardoned him on his deathbed; yet immediately on Richard's death the mercenary captain had the crossbowman skinned alive and hanged.

Richard's remains were strewn all over his mighty empire. His brain was buried at the Charroux Abbey in Poitou; his heart was buried at Rouen in Normandy; and the rest of his body was buried at the feet of his father at Fontrevaud in Anjou. Barely five years after his death, most of these Angevin lands had been lost to the French by his inept brother, King John.

least twice in the side and back. His guards killed one of his attackers and captured the other, but Conrad died either at the scene of the attack or shortly afterwards. He was, most appropriately, buried in Tyre, in the Church of the Hospitallers.

Under torture, the surviving Assassin claimed convincingly that Richard I was behind the killing. It is certainly quite unlikely that Saladin was the perpetrator: the Assassins had already targeted a number of Saladin's senior officials, and the sultan was no friend to the Assassins. Other Western princes have been suggested as the possible perpetrator, but with inconclusive evidence and the passing of eight centuries, it is doubtful whether the real story will ever be uncovered.

Much of Europe believed in Richard's guilt, though, and as a result he became a marked man. Returning home from the Middle East overland, supposedly in disguise, he was recognized by a nephew of Conrad, and duly captured and imprisoned by one of the late King of Jeruslaem's many well-placed cousins, Leopold V of Austria. Accused of Conrad's murder, Richard requested that the Assassins vindicate him. A letter that purportedly came from the Assassins' leader, Rashid al-Din Sinan, appeared to do just that; but evidence both then and since suggests that the letter was forged. Leopold certainly did not believe it and instead he handed his illustrious prisoner over to the new Holy Roman Emperor, Henry VI, who demanded an enormous ransom for Richard's release. Swingeing taxes decimated clergy and laity in England and Richard's Angevin Empire to pay the sum, but eventually the 150,000 marks were raised and (despite a more generous counter-offer by the King of France to keep Richard in captivity) Richard was released in February 1194.

The Assassins thrived for another eighty or so years. In the 1270s, assassination attempts on Western European crusaders such as the Count of Tripoli and Prince Edward of England (later King Edward I), together with the murder of Philip de Montfort in Tyre in 1270, were all attributed to the Assassins. But while their reputation lived on in myth and legend for centuries, their political power was extinguished by the invading Mongols, who swept over their Persian homelands and erased their mountain strongholds.

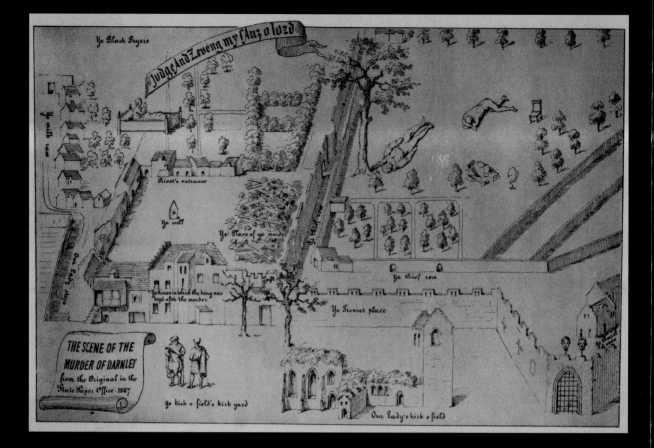

The scene of the murder of Darnley, from the original in the State Paper Office, 1567.

Lord DARNLEY

1545–1567, CONSORT TO MARY, QUEEN OF SCOTS

ASSASSINS Unverified
DATE 9/10 February 1567
PLACE Edinburgh, Scotland

Henry Stewart (or Stuart), Lord Darnley, was born in 1545, the son of the 4th Earl of Lennox. His life may have passed relatively uneventfully, and lasted rather longer, were it not for the fact that before his 20th birthday he had married his relative and the most eligible woman in Scotland – and thereby entered the turbulent personal and political dramas that constituted the life of Mary Stuart, Queen of Scots. Before two years were out, Darnley fell victim to an assassination plot, but not before conspiring in a murder plot of his own.

Mary Stuart, the eye of the storm to which Darnley contributed, was born in 1542, the daughter of James V of Scotland and his French wife, Mary of Guise. The six-day-old princess became Queen of Scotland when her father died at the age of thirty, and she was crowned the following year. There could not have been a worse time for monarchical instability: the Scottish army had recently been routed at the Battle of Solway Moss, and Scotland was ripe for English intervention. In July 1543, when Mary was a mere six months old, the Treaty of Greenwich betrothed her to Edward, son of Henry VIII of England, enabling their heirs to inherit the kingdoms of both Scotland and England.

When Mary of Guise soon made it clear that she would not abide by the treaty, Henry VIII launched a series of punitive raids on Scottish territory, culminating in a full-scale invasion in 1544. Nevertheless, despite the Scots' overwhelming defeat at the Battle of Pinkie Cleugh in 1547, Mary of Guise ensured that the toddler queen always evaded arrest.

When Mary of Guise turned to the traditional 'Auld Alliance' between Scotland and France, the French King Henry II proposed uniting the two kingdoms by marrying the infant Mary to his newborn son, Francis. On 7 July 1548, while English forces were devastating the Scottish Lowlands, a marriage treaty was signed and Queen Mary was despatched to the French court. For 11 years the young queen's luck held. Vivacious, pretty, and clever, she impressed a French court dismayed by the macho posturing of the king, becoming an accomplished linguist and musician, and mastering horsemanship, falconry, and needlework. However, this was not the right environment in which to learn statecraft, a deficiency that would cost her dearly.

Mary married Francis on 24 April 1558, and on his accession a year later she became Queen of France, as well as the Queen Regnant of Scotland. That same year her cousin, the childless Elizabeth I, acceded to the English throne, and Mary became Elizabeth's notional heir, notwithstanding the objection that Henry VIII's will had explicitly barred the Stuarts from the succession.

'No more tears now. I will think upon revenge'

Attributed to Mary, Queen of Scots, after Rizzio's murder, 1566

However, the horizon quickly clouded. Francis had always been a sickly youth, and he died on 5 December 1560 after only 15 months on the throne. Mary was now diplomatically isolated: five months previously, on her mother's death, the French tamely undertook to withdraw troops from Scotland and to recognize Elizabeth's I sovereignty in England. The 17-year-old Mary, still in France, refused to ratify the treaty. However, with France now wracked by civil strife she had no alternative but to return to Scotland.

Mary arrived in Leith on 19 August 1561. She soon realized that she had merely exchanged one incipient civil war for another. Scotland, like France, was being torn apart between Catholic and Protestant factions, the latter of which was led by Mary's illegitimate half-brother, the Earl of Moray. Much to the Catholics' rage, however, Mary initially chose to follow a compromise path, balancing Catholic and Protestant interests. She also attempted to heal the breach with England. Yet her crude diplomatic gesture of inviting Elizabeth to her restive kingdom backfired: the Queen of England, unsurprisingly, refused, and Mary took grave offence. (Elizabeth proposed that Mary should, instead, journey to England, but the planned meeting never transpired.) Mary's second gambit was even more gauche: she sent an ambassador to the English court to press her case to be recognized as Elizabeth's heir. Once again, the response was predictable: both Elizabeth and her Parliament swiftly rejected her suit. Two years later, in the face of Parliament's growing unease about the succession, Elizabeth did agree to consider Mary's claim, provided that Mary marry a man of Elizabeth's choosing. And her choice was her current favourite, the self-important Protestant aristocrat Robert Dudley, Earl of Leicester. This suggestion was, equally unsurprisingly, dismissed by Queen Mary.

Mary then chose to solve the resulting stalemate with an astonishingly inept diplomatic own-goal. In July 1565 she rashly married the Catholic Lord Darnley, whom she had first met in France. The union infuriated Elizabeth I, who felt she should have been asked permission for the marriage, as Darnley himself held a claim to the English throne on his mother's side. The consequences of the marriage followed swiftly: Elizabeth broke off diplomatic relations, and the Earl of Moray joined with other Protestant nobles in open rebellion.

Mary was never a good judge of men. Darnley was an immature, violent (and possibly syphilitic) 19-year-old, with less political sensitivity even than his wife. He demanded that he be made joint sovereign, but instead had to be content with the role of consort. Mary became pregnant, but even then she was not safe from Darnley's physical attacks. (On one occasion he even tried to force a miscarriage.) Increasingly embittered and estranged from Mary, Darnley focused his jealousy on her private secretary, the Italian-born David Rizzio (born c.1533) and plotted with his former Protestant enemies.

Rizzio had arrived at the Scottish court in 1561 on the staff of the Duke of Savoy's ambassador. He was handsome and, like Mary herself, a good musician. By 1564 he was not only the queen's secretary for relations with France, but also effectively her principal adviser. On 9 March 1566, however, Darnley's thugs stabbed him 57 times in the pregnant queen's presence at the Palace of Holyroodhouse.

Not only Darnley, but also Mary and her whole court were deeply tainted by this appallingly public and clumsy murder. Mary gave birth to their son, James, a few months later, but before the boy's first birthday his father was dead. On 10 February 1567 the bodies of Darnley and his servant were discovered in the garden of an Edinburgh house in which they had been staying (*see* illustration p. 24). Darnley had been recuperating from illness – possibly the advanced stages of syphilis. A violent explosion had occurred that night at the house; yet the evidence pointed to Darnley having escaped that attempted assassination, only to be strangled when he ran outside.

Suspicion immediately fell on Mary's latest bit of rough – the Protestant 4th Earl of Bothwell – and Mary found herself flung from the frying pan into the fire. An enquiry she set up to 'investigate' the murder exonerated Bothwell but convinced no-one. On 24 April she saw her son at Stirling for the last time. Then, the notoriously violent and unprincipled

Bothwell 'abducted' the suspiciously pliant queen and took her to Dunbar Castle where, apparently, he raped her. Under severe duress, Mary agreed to marry him. Thus on 6 May 1567 – barely three months after Darnley's assassination – the unlikely couple returned to Edinburgh and, nine days later, were married according to Protestant rites.

Mary's reputation and authority were now in tatters. Catholic and Protestant nobles immediately made common cause and raised an army to confront the royal forces. To avoid further bloodshed, Mary capitulated, on the proviso that they let Bothwell go. The earl subsequently fled abroad to Norway, where he was imprisoned by the Danish king and subsequently died, insane, in 1578.

By mid-June 1567, mere weeks after her marriage, Mary, found herself imprisoned by the nobles in a castle on an island in the middle of Loch Leven. Having miscarried the twins she had conceived with Bothwell, on 24 July 1567 she was compelled to abdicate the Scottish throne in favour of her one-year-old son, James. And the regent for James was to be the ubiquitous Earl of Moray.

All was not entirely lost. On 2 May 1568 Mary escaped from Loch Leven and managed to raise a small army. Yet this became her last stand, and government forces decimated her army. She fled to England on 19 May, only to be imprisoned at Carlisle.

Elizabeth I refused to try Mary for the murder of Darnley, hoping to protect some of her fellow-sovereign's majesty. However, an inquiry was held, which hinged on the 'Casket Letters', eight letters purportedly written by Mary to Bothwell. Whether or not these were forgeries, the incriminating passages appeared to have the ring of truth. Elizabeth sought to avoid an outright 'guilty' verdict, but Mary was in effect condemned by association. In any case, Mary was considered too much of a risk to set free, at a time when her candidacy for the English throne could be used by the Catholic powers of continental Europe – notably France or Spain – as a pretext for invasion and usurpation. The remaining 18 years of her life were spent in England – under house arrest. To the more extreme sort of disaffected Catholic plotter, Mary remained a tempting potential replacement for Elizabeth on the throne of England, and that was to seal her fate.

THE DEATH OF MARY, QUEEN OF SCOTS

EVEN WHILE A PRISONER, MARY STUART remained a huge liability for the English monarchy. In the aftermath of the Ridolfi Plot – a harebrained Catholic scheme of 1572 to marry Mary and the Duke of Norfolk, England's premier Catholic aristocrat, and put them on the throne in Elizabeth's stead – Parliament introduced a bill explicitly barring Mary from the throne. In the event, Elizabeth unexpectedly refused the bill royal assent.

The discovery of the Catholic Babington Plot in 1586, though, finally forced Elizabeth to act. This plot had centred on a plan to assassinate Elizabeth and install Mary as queen with the help of Philip II of Spain and the Catholic Guise faction (Mary's maternal family) in France. Whether or not the plot was undertaken without Mary's knowledge, Mary was put on trial for treason. She denied the accusation, and was spirited in her defence but ultimately convicted. A reluctant and vacillating Elizabeth was finally persuaded to sign the death sentence, and Mary was beheaded at Fotheringay Castle in Northamptonshire, on 8 February 1587.

Even in death, Mary's luck failed her. The execution was poorly carried out, and it took three blows to hack off her head, the executioner resorting to using his axe as a saw.

The body was embalmed and left unburied at her place of execution for a year after her death. Her remains were then placed in a secure lead coffin – carefully sealed to prevent relic-hunting – and buried at Peterborough Cathedral in 1588. The coffin was exhumed in 1612 when her son, now James I of England, ordered that she be reinterred in great pomp in Westminster Abbey, the same church in which her cousin Elizabeth I already lay.

WILLIAM I, 'the Silent'

1533–1584, RULER OF THE DUTCH UNITED PROVINCES

ASSASSIN	Balthasar Gérard
DATE	10 July 1584
PLACE	Delft, the Netherlands

William of Orange was the Protestant founding father of the modern nation that is the Netherlands. Balthasar Gérard, born in 1557, was a French Catholic zealot caught up in the maelstrom of the Reformation. Attracted by the prospect of eradicating a high-profile enemy of Catholicism and the sizeable cash incentive (25,000 crowns) being offered by Philip II of Spain to kill the 'outlaw' William, Gérard vowed to travel to the Netherlands and do the deed.

Balthasar Gérard served in the Luxembourgeois army for two years, hoping to get close to William when the Dutch and allied armies met; but in the event this conjunction never happened, and Gérard, disillusioned, resigned his commission in 1584. He then went to the Spanish commander, the Duke of Parma, to present his plan of assassination. Parma, sensibly, would have nothing to do with the underhand plot, so Gérard decided that boldness was his only alternative.

In May 1584 Gérard presented himself to William himself, posing as a French nobleman who could guarantee the support of French sympathizers – both the beleaguered French Protestants and those who feared that their country was about to be surrounded by the Spanish. William believed his story, and sent Gérard back to France as an intermediary. Gérard returned in July – having bought pistols on his return voyage – and on 10 July made an appointment with William of Orange at the latter's home in Delft.

On hearing Gérard had arrived, William left his first-floor dining room and descended the stairs to the hall. Barely had he set foot in the hallway when Gérard shot him in the chest at point-blank range, and fled. According to traditional Dutch accounts, William's last words were 'Lord, My Lord, have pity on me and your poor people.' However, as is often the case in these circumstances, it is highly likely that this pious sentiment was concocted after the *stadtholder's* untimely death.

William I's assassination was a grievous setback to the nascent Dutch nation, then fighting bitterly for its independence from its Spanish overlords. It was a blow from which the Dutch almost failed to recover. It was only after 64 more years of intermittent slaughter that the Dutch were finally awarded their complete independence.

William of Orange was born in 1533 at his family seat of Dillenburg in Nassau (then a Dutch province, although today sited across the German border). The son of the Count of Nassau, he was raised as a Lutheran; however, when, aged 11, he inherited the title 'Prince of Orange' (and the vast tracts of land right across the Netherlands that went with it) from his cousin. William's nominal overlord, the Holy Roman Emperor Charles V, was one of Protestantism's most implacable opponents, and he not only imposed himself as the province's regent, but also insisted that William be educated as a Catholic. The young prince obeyed: he rose to be one of Charles V's most trusted Dutch advisers and most effective military commanders.

In 1555 Charles V, to the astonishment of Europe, succumbed to his morbid fears of death and began the process of abdicating from his many lands and titles. In that year the sovereignty of the Netherlands was passed to his eldest son, Philip, who the following year also became Philip II of Spain. Philip, too, relied heavily on William's advice and authority,

> '**My body or wealth altogether I did not spare to help you**'
>
> From the early 'Wilhelmus' (1568), the Netherlands' national anthem glorifying William

and he viewed him as a trusty bulwark against the rising Protestant tide. In 1559 he appointed William as *stadtholder* (effectively, governor under Philip's suzerainty) of the northern Netherlandish provinces of Holland, Zeeland, Utrecht as well as Burgundy (the latter territory an independent dukedom that passed to the Habsburgs in 1477).

Philip II, however, chose to rule the Netherlands from Madrid, and in his absence the tensions caused by the rapid spread of Protestantism and the heavy tax burden imposed by the Spanish escalated into widespread violence. Full-scale warfare erupted in 1568, a date which the Dutch regard as the first year of the Eighty Years War, the titanic conflict that led finally to Dutch independence in 1648.

William had already signalled sympathy with the Protestant cause, but in 1565 he stood aloof from the nobles (including his brother Louis) who presented Philip's regent, Margaret of Parma, with a petition demanding toleration for Protestants. He also distanced himself from the iconoclasm of 1566, when Calvinist mobs ransacked churches and shrines. Guided by William and his fellow moderates, Margaret's inclinations were to compromise; however, she soon found her authority undermined by Philip's Spanish hawks, who strenuously opposed any concessions to the Protestants. With order deteriorating throughout the province, Philip II announced the despatch there of the fanatically Catholic Spanish general, the Duke of Alva. William astutely recognized that the time for compromise or his characteristic circumspection (one possible reason for his nickname 'the Silent') had passed, and he withdrew to his Nassau seat.

Alva's administration was as disastrous as William had predicted. After his arrival in August 1567, the duke established the Council of Troubles – known to the Dutch as the 'Council of Blood' – to assess those suspected of involvement with the Protestant violence. In an act of crass stupidity, which demonstrated his utter lack of political understanding, Alva successfully alienated William by including him in the list of 10,000 to be summoned before the council. Wisely, William chose not to appear. As a result, the *stadtholder* was deprived of his title and properties and declared an outlaw by Philip.

Almost overnight, William successfully transformed himself from an austere pillar of the Spanish establishment into the feisty, pragmatic leader of the Dutch rebels. He used his considerable wealth to fund the Protestant naval groups who raided the coastal settlements and he helped to raise an army, led by his brother Louis, in the northern provinces. In May 1568 the Orangist army defeated a Spanish force under the new *stadtholder*, the Duke of Aremberg (who was killed in the fighting), at Heiligerlee. Alva countered by executing the Dutch noblemen he had assembled as hostages, including the important counts of Egmont and Hoorn. He then assumed personal command of his army, and annihilated Louis's Dutch troops at the Battle of Jemmingen in July 1568. With his back now to the wall,

FATHER OF THE FATHERLAND

AFTER WILLIAM'S DEATH, HIS SECOND SON Maurice led the Dutch to a very favourable 12-year armistice in 1609. When fighting was renewed in 1621, it was William's youngest son, Frederick Henry, who successfully resisted the Spanish. Frederick Henry died in March 1647, and was buried alongside William in Delft. A year later the Netherlands became formally independent by the Treaty of Westphalia, and by 1700 the new powerful nation was dominating the politics of Europe and the world's maritime trade.

Gérard's bullets may have ended William I's prospects, but they could not prevent the rise of a dynasty that would rule the Dutch Republic and then, in the shape of the House of Orange-Nassau, reign over the Netherlands to this day. William I's legacy still permeates the modern country. The red, white and blue flag of the Netherlands is derived directly from the colours displayed on the Orange coat of arms. The country's national anthem, the 'Wilhelmus', was originally a propaganda song for William's followers. And the colour worn by Dutch sporting teams is orange, in commemoration of William's family name. Truly can William I be termed the *Vader des Vaderlands*, 'Father of the Fatherland'.

William led a second army into the south, but it soon disintegrated.

By 1572 it looked as if the Dutch Revolt was finally crushed. William was restricted to issuing anti-Spanish pamphlets from across the German border. In April of that year, however, the rebels' cause was reignited by the Protestant pirates' unexpected capture of the coastal garrison of Brielle. Oppressed by Alva's heavy-handed retribution, other cities in the Northern Netherlands cheerfully opened their gates to the Protestant rebels. Once more, William had a cause to lead. The rebel States General met and acclaimed William as the *stadtholder* of Holland and Zeeland.

Over the next few years, the tide of battle went one way then the other. William's low point was reached in 1573 when the new Spanish regent, Don Luis de Requesens, decisively defeated the Orangists at the Battle of Mookerheyde, and William's brothers Louis and Henry were killed. The Protestants staved off complete defeat only by breaching the dykes to save the city of Leiden. Thereafter, the Spanish forfeited moderate support when unpaid soldiers went on the rampage in what became known as the 'Spanish Fury'. Starved of cash, the new regent, Don John of Austria, signed the Perpetual Edict in 1577, which seemed to assure religious toleration and the departure of Spanish troops. But it proved a false dawn: Don John retook the offensive, capturing Namur, while William took the capital, Brussels. The fighting went on.

In 1579 the religious schism that William had long feared split the province asunder. Alarmed by the radical Calvinism of some of William's northern followers, the more Catholic provinces of the Southern Netherlands surrendered to the Spanish at the Treaty of Arras. In response, the predominantly Protestant provinces signed the Union of Utrecht, binding themselves to continue the struggle. William had no choice but to back the Union, but for the rest of his life he still hankered after reuniting all of the provinces of the former Spanish Netherlands under his rule.

> 'Lord, My Lord, have pity on me and your poor people'
>
> By popular tradition, William's last words

The conclusion of the Union by no means guaranteed victory. William was desperate for foreign support, and turned to the sympathetic French prince Francis, the Duke of Anjou and Alençon, brother of Henry II of France. In 1581 the duke was, in his absence, declared 'Protector of the Liberty of the Netherlands' – effectively installed as sovereign of the Netherlands in place of Philip II. The listless and superficial Anjou was hardly an inspiring figure, however, and did little to further the Dutch cause before his ignominious flight back to France in June 1583, following the failure of his attempt to take Antwerp by force. He narrowly escaped with his life from the city.

Danger arrived on William's doorstep on 18 March 1582 when a deranged Spanish soldier, Juan de Jáuregui, fired a pistol at his head while offering him a petition. William was lucky to survive: a bullet pierced the neck below the right ear and passed out at his left jaw-bone. Nursed by his wife, Charlotte, William recovered; but Jáuregui himself was killed by William's bodyguard.

Two years later, though, William was not so lucky. Gérard's pistol shots ensured that he died almost instantaneously. Mourned by the whole of the Netherlands, William of Orange was buried in the impressive 'New Church' in Delft. In 1623 his original, sober tomb was replaced with a more effusive composition by Hendrik de Keyser, befitting the father of the modern Dutch nation. From the 17th century onwards, nearly all Dutch monarchs and members of the ruling House of Orange have been buried beside him.

Gérard himself was caught before he could flee Delft. He was tortured before his trial, at the culmination of which he was sentenced to an elaborate death: to be burned with a red-hot iron, lacerated with pincers in six different places, quartered and disembowelled (while still alive), have his heart torn out and flung in his face and, finally, to be decapitated.

The TWO HENRIES

Henry, Duke of Guise

ASSASSINS Royal servants of Henry III
DATE 23 December 1588
PLACE Castle of Blois, France

Henry III, King of France

ASSASSIN Friar Jacques Clément
DATE 1 August 1589 (died 2 August)
PLACE St Cloud, France

Henry III of France had the world at his feet. The handsome, athletic favourite son of the chivalrous Henry II (who had died from a jousting wound in 1559) and his scheming queen, Catherine de' Medici, Henry was elected King of Poland before inheriting the throne of France in 1574. His two elder brothers, Francis II and Charles IX, had been sickly children, whose reigns were short and whose policies were dominated by their overbearing mother. Henry, though, appeared a marked contrast to his sibling predecessors. His emphatic victories over the French Protestants – the Huguenots – at the battles of Jarnac and Montcontour in 1570 had given him the aura of an invincible and virile military leader. In 1570, while still Duke of Anjou, he was promoted as a natural match for Elizabeth I of England – a scheme that failed ostensibly because of Henry's Catholicism. Now his mother was content to take a back seat: Henry was surely the monarch to crush the Huguenots and save France from the coruscating religious civil war which had wracked the country since the early 1560s.

The reality, however, was sadly different. Henry had been his mother's favourite child and the effects on his personality were all too evident in adult life. Fond of dressing up in women's clothing, the effeminate atmosphere of his court was a far cry from the chivalric idealism of his father's, as Henry surrounded himself with acolytes of indeterminate sexuality, all made up to the nines. His blatant homosexuality was a major factor in the failure of marriage negotiations with Queen Elizabeth in 1570; it also ensured that his marriage of 1575 to Louise de Lorraine-Vaudemont remained childless, and that Henry would be the last of the Valois kings.

Despised and mistrusted by both the Catholic and Huguenot factions, Henry ultimately became a powerless spectator of the internecine religious struggles. He had connived at his mother's anti-Protestant campaign of 1572, ignited by the Massacre of St Bartholomew's Day of 23–24 August, when Catherine attempted to have all the principal Huguenot leaders murdered. Thereafter, both Henry and his mother remained objects of implacable hatred to the Huguenot camp. In 1576 Henry III granted concessions to the Huguenots, but this failed to win them over and merely served to antagonize the Catholic League, led by the extremely powerful Henry, Duke of Guise.

Guise was everything that Henry II was not. A notoriously tough and dashing military commander – he was nicknamed (though not to his face) *le balafré*,

Henry III:

'My Lord of Guise, we understand that you Have gathered a power of men. What your intent is yet we cannot learn, but we presume it is not for our good.'

'scarface', after a wound he had received in battle in 1575 – he was also the mainspring of the ultra-Catholic opposition to the Huguenot cause. He had helped Catherine de' Medici perpetrate the Massacre of St Bartholomew's Day, and in 1576 he founded the Catholic League to resist any further concessions to the Huguenot minority. Many of France's Catholics looked to him rather than Henry III to lead France out of the mire of civil war and into the welcoming arms of the Counter-Reformation. Guise's stature was certainly not harmed by his assertion that he was directly descended from Charlemagne, a claim that clearly implied designs on the French throne.

The stakes of the religious wars were raised still further in 1584, when the king's youngest brother and heir-presumptive Francis, Duke of Anjou and Alençon, died. This meant that the new heir was Henry III's cousin, the king of the small Pyrenean kingdom of Navarre – also, confusingly, called Henry. Yet Navarre was a Protestant and *de facto* leader of the Huguenots. This was just the pretext that the Catholic League had been waiting for, and all-out war – the 'War of the Three Henries' – ensued, with Henry III vainly attempting to influence events from the sidelines. Three regimes now ran France simultaneously: one Catholic, one Huguenot, and one an enfeebled royal administration. The result was, predictably, chaos and disorder.

> *Duke of Guise:*
>
> ## 'Why I am no traitor to the crown of France. What I have done 'tis for the Gospel's sake.'
>
> From Christopher Marlowe's play *The Massacre at Paris* (c.1592), Act I sc. xvii

In 1584 Guise did the unthinkable and concluded the secret Treaty of Joinville – named after his family's ancestral home – with the Spanish. Philip II of Spain committed himself to support the Catholic League with arms and money (though not, for the time being at least, with men); in return, Guise pledged that he would eradicate heresy in France, by exterminating the Huguenots, and install his elderly relative the Cardinal of Bourbon on the throne in the place of the rightful heir, Navarre.

By 1585 Guise was massively popular, particularly in the Catholic north. Henry III had alienated what few supporters he had by the increasingly bizarre behaviour of his effeminate courtiers, led by the royal favourite the Duke of Epernon. While Epernon and his Gascon friends indulged in the latest fad – playing with yo-yos – Guise was raising an army to crush the Huguenots and any royal forces that happened to stand in their way. In March of that year the League issued the Declaration of Péronne, which, in the name of the Cardinal of Bourbon, denounced royal maladministration and the power of the Huguenots, demanded that all previous concessions to the Protestants should be revoked, and called all loyal Catholics to arms. Returning to Paris, Guise, backed by his growing army, persuaded the weak-willed monarch that the only way to keep his throne was to abide by the Declaration, suppressing Protestantism and duly waiving Navarre's right to the throne. The king, seeing no alternative, duly did so by the terms of the craven Treaty of Nemours and a subsequent edict banning Henry of Navarre from succession – an illegal deed, which was unnecessarily followed by Navarre's excommunication by Pope Sixtus V. It was a crushing humiliation that Henry III would never forget.

In the ensuing conflict, Navarre was by far the abler strategist. He sought to detach moderate Catholic opinion from Guise and the League by emphasizing the principle of legitimacy – he was, after all, the rightful heir – and by downplaying the religious issues. He also cleverly played the patriotic card, by reminding audiences of the French Church's traditional, quasi-independent ('Gallican') liberties and by stressing the strong Spanish ties of Guise's League. In truth, though, both sides were dependent on foreign aid. While Spanish troops began to appear to fight for the Catholic cause, Elizabeth I of England provided the Huguenots with subsidies that bought them Swiss and German mercenaries,

1551 Born into Valois royal family, the 3rd son of Henry II and Catherine de' Medici. Made Duke of Anjou.

1569 Defeats Huguenots at battles of Jarnac and Montcontour.

1573 Elected King of Poland.

1574 On death of his brother Charles IX, becomes King of France (abandoning Poland). Thereafter a weakened monarchy vies with Catholic and Huguenot factions for religious and political upper hand.

1576–7 The Catholic League, under Henry, 3rd Duke of Guise, fights for Catholic interests.

1584–8 Emergence of Huguenot Henry of Navarre as royal heir leads to revival of Catholic League and the 'War of the Three Henries'.

1588 Flees Catholic Paris (May), but has Guise and his brother, Cardinal of Lorraine, assassinated (Oct.).

1589 Forms alliance with Navarre to win back Paris, but is assassinated by Friar Jacques Clément (1 Aug.).

which arrived in Lorraine under Baron von Dohna in August 1587.

Desperate to re-establish the primacy of royal rule, Henry III, hardly for the first time in his life, gravely miscalculated the forces ranged against him. Still under the control of the League, he ordered the Duke of Guise to attack Dohna's troops, expecting Guise to be defeated and (with luck) killed. At the same time, he sent his current favourite, the Duke of Joyeuse, at the head of a royal army to extinguish Navarre's Huguenot force. What transpired, though, was exactly the reverse of his hopes: on 20 October 1587 Joyeuse was defeated and killed at Coutras by Navarre's army, while Guise crushed the Protestant mercenaries at Auneau a month later, returning to Paris as the hero of Catholic France.

France was by now effectively split in two, with the south and west having largely broken away to form a quasi-independent state under the King of Navarre. The predominantly Catholic north was bitter at the high tax burden that resulted, and at the economic dislocation that almost thirty years of civil strife had caused. The two sides were virtually irreconcilable. There was one thing, however, that united them: hatred of a profligate, vacillating and limp-wristed monarch whose court was seen as an unnecessary fiscal and moral burden on an impoverished nation.

Tempers were particularly short in Paris. Food prices were high, and the city was hungry. The League whipped up enthusiasm for their cause by lurid tales of Huguenot excesses and the recent execution of Mary, Queen of Scots, by England's Protestant queen. Henry III imprisoned a few of the more extremist Catholic preachers, but was dissuaded from further action by the spectre of the League's military might.

Guise, meanwhile, had moved even closer to Spain. He supported Philip II's plan for an invasion of England and had promised to secure the Channel ports in the event that the Spanish Armada should need to use them as a haven. In retaliation, Henry III plotted to use royal troops to break the League's stranglehold on Paris, and to send Epernon to the Normandy coast to offer support for England should Spanish troops attempt to land.

In April 1588 King Henry finally asserted his independence by moving 4000 Swiss mercenaries into the heart of Paris. He planned to use these troops to effect a decisive assertion of his authority, capturing Guise and the League's leaders. But once again his judgement and nerve failed him. Guise entered Paris, showing considerable personal bravery: the king could have ordered him killed at any moment. Paying his respects to the king's mother, a startled Catherine de' Medici, Guise then asked for an audience with the king, plunging Henry III into an abyss of indecision. When the Paris mob attacked the Swiss, the king failed to provide his troops with the requisite orders. As a result, they fell back, and it was Guise and his League forces who restored order. Henry III slipped ignominiously away from his capital through an unguarded gate, having effectively given up Paris to the duke.

Henry III was now powerless, his last vestiges of authority having been stripped away. He signed an Edict of Union in July 1588, agreeing to all the League's demands (including nominating the Cardinal of Bourbon as his heir) and creating Guise Lieutenant General of

ENDING THE WARS OF RELIGION

HENRY III WAS MOURNED BY FEW. His mother, the redoubtable Catherine de' Medici, had died in January 1589. Now the bells were rung in Paris as a joyous population celebrated the king's untimely death; the Catholic League proclaimed the Cardinal of Bourbon as King Charles X, and Henry of Navarre, now technically Henry IV, wisely withdrew his besieging army from the gates of Paris.

A few months later, however, the League's position was deteriorating. The old Cardinal of Bourbon died in May 1590, and Spain's Philip II put forward his eldest daughter, Isabella, as his heir – in defiance of the French Salic Law, which declared that no woman could inherit the French throne. The League now appeared to be little more than a Spanish puppet, as Frenchmen – and even the pope – rallied to Henry IV's cause in response to foreign intervention. Having guaranteed the maintenance of the Catholic religion in 1589, Henry IV crushed the League's forces at Ivry in 1590. Spanish troops then invaded France, redefining the conflict entirely. Only one of the most astute and celebrated U-turns in history – Henry IV's pragmatic conversion to Catholicism in 1593 – saved France.

France – regent in all but name. The Duke of Epernon fled from Normandy, enabling League troops to garrison the Channel ports in support of the Spanish fleet. It seemed now that nothing could stop the forces of the Counter-Reformation from gaining ascendancy in France, England and the Netherlands.

Two events in the autumn of 1588, however, gave Henry III hope. The defeat of the Spanish Armada suddenly made Philip II of Spain seem vulnerable after all. And the Spanish committed a strategic error by occupying a Spanish enclave within Piedmont. Now both Henry III and Navarre could justifiably claim that the League had merely been a front for Spanish aggression.

Emboldened by this turn of events, on 23 December 1588 Henry III summoned the Duke of Guise for an audience in the council chamber at the castle of Blois. The duke was told that the king wished to see him in the private room adjoining the royal bedroom; there, however, he was immediately cut down by royal assassins. (Durupt's picture shows a satisfied king checking the body, p. 33.) Guise's brother, the Cardinal of Lorraine, was taken into custody along with the Cardinal of Bourbon and Guise's son; and the next day, Lorraine was also murdered by his guards.

Henry's elation at the assassination of the Guises was shortlived. Parisians rose in revolt when they heard the news, the League declared that the king could now be deposed or slain, while Pope Sixtus V ordered Henry III to Rome to answer for the cardinal's murder. The king had no choice but to turn to Henry of Navarre for help, and Navarre's troops accordingly besieged Paris. The day before Navarre's final assault on the capital, 1 August 1589, a fanatical young Dominican friar, Jacques Clément, approached the king stating that he had a secret message to deliver. The king signalled for his attendants to allow them some privacy and, while whispering in the royal ear, Clément plunged a knife into the king's stomach.

Clément was killed on the spot by the guards; Henry III – the last of the Valois kings – died the following morning. But not before he had named Henry of Navarre as his successor.

HENRY IV

1553–1610, KING OF FRANCE

ASSASSIN François Ravaillac
DATE 14 May 1610
PLACE Paris, France

Henry IV is consistently lauded as one of the most gifted monarchs France ever had. He was brave, personally leading his troops into battle; he was cruel and authoritarian, even flogging his own children; he cut a virile figure – whether in bed, with one of his many mistresses, on the hunting field, or playing his favourite game, tennis. Henry was also clever and politically astute, leading France to an impressive recovery after the haemorrhaging of 30 years of fratricidal religious wars.

Henry IV made peace with the Catholics, ostensibly converting in 1593 when it seemed politically adroit to do so – no religious fanatic he. Yet he continued to guarantee the Huguenots both freedom of worship and generous civil rights. His chief minister, the Duke of Sully, lowered direct taxes and began an enormous programme of public works. When war with the Austrian Habsburgs seemed likely in 1610, Henry's prompt and decisive political and military action – clearing the threatened German area of Habsburg troops while at the same time marrying his eldest son and his daughter to Habsburg heirs – proved an exemplary exercise of military diplomacy. Yet it all came to an end when Henry was stabbed to death in his coach, a monarch at the peak of his powers.

In an age of religious bigotry and savage religious violence, Henry IV was never a martyr to clerical dogmatism. Although baptized as a Catholic, Henry was raised as a Protestant by his mother Jeanne d'Albret, who declared Calvinism the religion of Navarre – the small, landlocked kingdom perched precariously on the Pyrenees between France and Spain. As a mere teenager, Henry left his home town of Pau, the Navarrese capital, and joined the Huguenot forces in the French Wars of Religion, fighting alongside the Prince of Condé and Admiral Coligny during the battles of the late 1560s.

1572 was a significant turning point for Henry. His mother died, leaving him as king – King Henry III – of Navarre. (Navarre had nothing like the Salic Law of France, prohibiting women from assuming the throne; thus Jeanne, though married to Antoine de Bourbon, Duke of Vendôme, had ruled the tiny kingdom in her own right.) On 18 August he married the sister of Charles IX, King of France, in a bid to end the religious fratricide. However, Charles IX's Machiavellian mother, Catherine de' Medici, and her ultra-Catholic supporters, led by the Duke of Guise, had no intention of allowing the marriage to last. Six days after the wedding, on St Bartholomew's Day, the royal family authorized an orgy of violence against the Protestant community, massacring thousands of Huguenots across France. Henry himself narrowly escaped death by pretending to convert to Roman Catholicism. He was imprisoned, but escaped in January 1576, renouncing his enforced 'conversion' and rejoining the Protestant armies in the field.

In 1584 Henry of Navarre became the legal heir to the French throne upon the death of Francis, Duke of Anjou and Alençon, brother and heir to the French king, Henry III. The latter had had no choice but to recognize Navarre as his legitimate successor, as Salic Law disinherited the king's sisters and any others who could claim descent by the female line. Henry of Navarre's claim was slender – he was directly descended on the male line from King Louis IX, who had died in 1270 – but irrefutable. Thus, on the assassination of

> 'I want there to be no peasant so poor that he is unable to have a chicken in his pot every Sunday'
>
> Attributed to Henry IV

THE SALIC LAW

THE SALIC LAW, BANNING ANY ACCESSION to the throne by women or those descended by a female line, was originally framed in the 6th century for the Salian Franks, the branch of the Frankish confederation that had, in the 5th century, defeated the Romans in what was then Gaul. The law was primarily enforced in the Frankish successor-state of France, but it was also adopted by other Central European states, and as late as 1740 the War of the Austrian Succession was ostensibly justified by a pedantic interpretation of the law by the Prussians, who objected to the accession of Empress Maria Theresa.

Salic Law originally incorporated a wide variety of subjects, including policies on theft, crime and murder, but the only element to survive through to the 14th century was the stipulation about inheritance, which prohibited women from inheriting land. The application of the long-defunct Salic Law by French jurists in 1328 – thus barring Edward III of England from the French throne – led ultimately to the outbreak of the Hundred Years War and, in the 15th century, to Henry V's celebrated claim at Agincourt that he was the rightful King of France. During the 16th century, Henry VIII of England was still invoking the Salic dispute to promote his extremely tenuous claim to the French throne, a claim undermined by the bewildering vacillations in his foreign policy. Sixty years later, however, the Catholic League found that they could not apply it in the case of Henry of Navarre: while Henry's succession to the sovereignty of Navarre was derived from his mother, his claim to France was based firmly on direct male succession via his Bourbon father.

Henry III in 1589, Henry of Navarre became Henry IV of France, the first of the Bourbon kings who were to rule France, on and off, for another 141 years.

In 1593, to the delight of moderate Catholics (though to the horror of Elizabeth I of England), he renounced his Protestant faith in favour of Catholicism, allegedly declaring that 'Paris vaut bien une messe' ('Paris is well worth a Mass'). His pragmatism won him the support of most of the war-weary Catholic population, the Catholic cause having been indelibly tarred by its overly close association with the predatory foreign policy of Philip II of Spain, who consistently sought to overturn the Salic Law by installing his daughter Isabella as regnant queen. Henry was crowned at Chartres Cathedral in February 1594; the following month, his forces finally occupied a cowed Paris. Even the ultra-conservative Sorbonne recognized Henry as the legitimate sovereign – though this did not prevent a Jesuit student, Jacques Chastel, from attempting to assassinate the king in December of that year.

In 1595 Henry felt confident enough to declare war on Spain and, in 1596, to ally with the English and Dutch. The sizeable Spanish threat evaporated with the Spanish treasury's bankruptcy of 1596, and negotiations began. On 30 April 1598 Henry issued the Edict of Nantes, guaranteeing limited toleration to the Protestant communities of France. Two days later, his envoys made peace with Spain at Vervins, with Spain agreeing to withdraw her troops from all French and Dutch territory and to withdraw to the borders of Henry II's time.

Henry's programme for the recovery of France after almost forty years of civil war was bold, imaginative and, by the standards of the day, liberal. His goal for his subjects – enshrined in the possibly apocryphal quotation 'every Sunday everyone in my kingdom should be able to enjoy a chicken in his pot' – was to raise standards of living. By the time he died in 1610, France boasted a healthy fiscal surplus (in contrast with the appalling deficit of 1589) and the rule of law and order had been fully re-established.

Trade and agriculture were comprehensively overhauled, and the nation's dependence on the importation of luxury goods was reversed. His first minister, Sully, presided over ambitious programmes to drain swampland in order to create productive areas for agriculture, to protect forests from devastation, to build a new system of tree-lined roads, and to construct new bridges and canals. Paris itself was adorned with the Pont Neuf and grandiose additions to the Louvre palace. France seemed to be entering a new Golden Age.

Abroad, Henry IV wisely preferred to subsidize his allies rather than wage costly and risky wars himself, and to rely on the judicious use of bellicose threats and the power of these alliances to encourage his opponents to climb down. In 1610, however, this policy failed, and Henry found himself on the brink of war with the Holy Roman Emperor, Rudolf II, over the succession to the dukedom of Jülich-Cleves. Never one to shrink from a challenge, Henry mobilized his forces, and on 14 May rode out to take personal command of his army. It was while on his way to this command that he was stabbed to death by François Ravaillac, a fanatical anti-Huguenot who had been rejected by the Jesuits. Ravaillac lay in wait for the king in the Rue de la Ferronnerie in Paris; when Henry's coach passed, it was halted by an obstacle, which Ravaillac had presumably installed. The assassin then leaped at the coach and stabbed the king to death. The king's guard seized him and took him to the nearby Hôtel de Retz to avoid a lynching by the mob.

During the course of his trial, Ravaillac was tortured in an attempt to make him identify his accomplices, but he always declared that he was working alone, and that he had simply sought to stop Henry 'making war on the pope'. The fortuitous combination of knowing the king's route and the timely roadblock, however, caused much feverish speculation as to who the mastermind had been.

Henry IV was buried with great ceremony and much grief at the traditional resting-place of France's sovereigns, the Parisian church of St-Denis. On 27 May 1610 Ravaillac, by contrast, suffered the punishment meted out to regicides in France: he was tortured one last time – publicly scalded with burning sulphur, molten lead, boiling oil and resin, then slashed with steel pincers – before being pulled asunder (see p.38) by four horses. Before his death, Ravaillac declared that 'I have no regrets at all about dying, because I've done what I came to do'. Thereafter his family were forbidden to use the surname 'Ravaillac' ever again.

Henry IV's succession had been complicated by his active love life. His Valois bride of 1572, Margaret, soon tired of Henry's constant affairs – particularly with Gabrielle d'Estrées, who bore the king three illegitimate children and who, by 1590, was living as the king's wife in all but name. In 1599 the marriage was annulled; however, Gabrielle died suddenly, and Henry turned instead to a dynastic marriage with Marie de' Medici (changed to Marie de Médicis by the French). Marie was a famed beauty who also brought a vast dowry of 600,000 crowns to the French exchequer. She was also, however, headstrong and proud, with little of the political astuteness of her husband. When their nine-year-old son was proclaimed as King Louis XIII on the death of his father, she was also installed as regent. Within months she had foolishly engineered Sully's resignation, began building a Spanish alliance and was soon entirely under the influence of her unscrupulous and ambitious Italian favourite, Concini, who was created Marquis d'Ancre (and, ludicrously, a Marshal of France). Only in 1617 did the young Louis XIII finally assert his authority, ordering Concini's assassination and exiling his mother to the fabulous castle of Blois.

Henry in brief

1553 Born in Navarre, and raised as a Calvinist by his mother, Jeanne d'Albret, Queen of Navarre.

1569–70 Gains military experience under the leading Huguenots Prince of Condé and Gaspard de Coligny.

1572 Becomes King of Navarre. Marriage into the royal Valois house is marred by St Bartholemew's Day Massacre of Huguenots.

1572–7 Confined at French court, having superficially converted to Catholicism. Accedes to the Treaty of Bergerac and restrictions on Huguenots (1577).

1584–8 Becomes French 'heir presumptive' on the death of Henry III's brother Francis, but has to fight a revived Catholic League as well as Henry III: 'The War of the Three Henries'.

1589–94 Proclaimed King of France by the dying Henry III, but spends next few years fighting for control of France against the League until his conversion to Catholicism (1593).

1594 Finally controls Paris.

1595 His excommunication is rescinded by the pope.

1598 Signs the Edict of Nantes, ending the French Wars of Religion.

1599–1610 Pursues polices to rebuild France's economy, stability and international status.

1610 Assassinated (14 May) by François Ravaillac, a Catholic extremist.

1st Duke of
BUCKINGHAM

1592–1628, ENGLISH ROYAL FAVOURITE

ASSASSIN	John Felton
DATE	23 August 1628
PLACE	Portsmouth, England

George Villiers, who was created 1st Duke of Buckingham in 1623 at the age of 31, had it all. He was tall, strikingly handsome, an accomplished linguist and dancer, and possessed of great charm, wit and – by now – wealth. And all from relatively obscure beginnings as the son of a minor Leicestershire landowner.

By the time Charles I acceded to the thrones of England and Scotland in 1625, the Duke of Buckingham was unarguably the most important subject in the kingdom: not only the monarch's principal adviser but also his greatest friend. Three years later, however, he had become the most unpopular man in the country and the scapegoat for foreign and domestic crises. Having fallen victim to an assassin's knife – a murder greeted with universal rejoicing across the nation – he was buried in Westminster Abbey in a tomb bearing the entirely apt inscription 'The Enigma of the World'.

Villiers was not the only good-looking young man groomed for success at the court of the homosexually inclined James I (ruled 1603–25), but he was certainly the most successful. In August 1614 he was brought before the king, in the hope that James would take a fancy to him. The ruse paid off: Villiers rapidly supplanted the current royal pin-up, Robert Carr, Earl of Somerset, and the king was soon besotted with him. James called Villiers his 'sweet child and wife' and cast himself as his 'dear dad'; and Villiers sensibly reciprocated his protestations of love, assuring the king that 'I naturally so love your person, and adore all your other parts, which are more than ever one man had [that] I desire only to live in the world for your sake.' As a result, Villiers was showered with gifts and titles, rising swiftly from a knighthood in 1615 to a barony and a viscountcy in 1616, the Earldom of Buckingham barely a year later, a marquessate in 1618 and the dukedom five years later. By 1623 Buckingham was the highest-ranking subject in the land outside the royal family.

> 'Christ had his John, and he had his George'
>
> James I's reported explanation of his attachment to Buckingham

Unsurprisingly, the rapid escalation in his status went to the young duke's head. In 1623 he was charged with accompanying the Prince of Wales, Prince Charles, to Spain to conduct marriage negotiations for the hand of the Infanta, Maria. In Spain the cocky Buckingham, under whose spell the nervously stuttering prince had already fallen, proved a wholly inept diplomat, overplaying his hand so badly that the discussions soon collapsed. The Spanish Ambassador asked Parliament to have Buckingham executed for his behaviour on his return from Madrid, but Buckingham cannily forestalled any potential fallout from the diplomatic disaster by immediately calling for war with Spain – which had, until James I's accession, been England's traditional enemy.

A year later, however, Buckingham's unsure political touch was seen once again when Charles's betrothal to Princess Henrietta Maria of France was announced. France may have been temporarily better disposed to England than Spain, then heavily involved suppressing the Protestant citizens of the Netherlands, but the fact remained that Henrietta Maria was still a Catholic. Buckingham was also blamed, with less justification, for the abject failure of the English-backed expedition of 1625 to recover the Rhineland territory of the Palatinate for James I's son-in-law, Frederick V, from the occupying (Holy Roman) Imperial forces. More generally, Buckingham was held responsible for England's failure to commit to what was widely seen as the Protestant 'side' in the unfolding Thirty Years War.

On the death of James I in 1625, few of the late king's courtiers kept their posts. Buckingham, however, saw his influence increase. Indeed, his relationship with the new young king seemed little different to that with James. In 1627 Charles told Buckingham that 'no man ever longed so much for anything as I do to hear some good news from you,' and he later assured him that 'No distance of place nor length of time can make me slacken much less diminish my love to you.' Charles's difficult marriage to the petulant Henrietta Maria, allied to his natural unease with women, intensified his relationship with the duke. He confided his marital problems to Buckingham and, revealingly, disparagingly compared his wife's qualities with those of his confidant. And the king let it be known that, in defiance of accepted parliamentary convention, any criticisms of Buckingham in his role as king's minister would be interpreted as a slur on the monarch himself, since the two were inseparable.

Fortified with this royal veneration, Buckingham sought to reinvent himself as an Elizabethan sea-general. The choice of his first objective, however, simply invited disaster. The 1587 raid on Cadiz had been one of Sir Francis Drake's most famous exploits; Buckingham's desire to emulate this celebrated achievement was a foolish attempt to appropriate the legendary admiral's reputation. Inevitably, the result was a huge disappointment: his troops were ill-equipped, ill-disciplined and ill-trained, and, having discovered a warehouse filled with wine, they were soon incapacitated by drink.

Buckingham tried to snatch victory from the jaws of defeat by lying in wait for an anticipated silver fleet from the Americas. Once again, a combination of bad luck and poor judgement ruined his plans: his army's appalling security meant that the Spanish were soon aware of the English strategy, and they diverted their fleet. With scores of men dying from starvation and disease every day and his fleet racked with scurvy, Buckingham limped ignominiously home with nothing to show for his expensive expedition.

Buckingham's next foray into foreign policy was even more wrongheaded and disastrous. He ignored eighty years of continental Catholic threats against England's Protestant monarchy when he agreed with the French first minister, Cardinal Richelieu, to loan English forces to help subdue the French Protestants (Huguenots) of La Rochelle. In return he was supposed to secure French aid in a quixotic and wholly impractical scheme to attack the Spanish and Imperial armies then occupying the Palatinate. Once more, the naive Buckingham was comprehensively outmanoeuvred on the international stage: France never had any intention of involving herself at this stage of the war in the liberation of the Rhineland, while Parliament – and Englishmen in general – was horrified at the prospects of English Protestants fighting French Protestants. Buckingham's clumsy attempts to forge an anti-Spanish alliance to serve his own purposes, rather than serve the pan-European goals of the Thirty Years War, were invariably doomed to failure. His eagerness to deal with Catholic powers also intensified parliamentary suspicion that Charles's court, increasingly dominated by the 'popish' queen, was seeking to re-establish Catholicism in England by the back door.

The criminal justice system became more lenient, the death penalty was removed from many crimes, and torture was abolished. In 1774 the liberty of the press was proclaimed, within certain limits. The following year, free trade in grain was promoted and oppressive export tolls were abolished, laws governing the poor were amended, and in the officially Protestant country limited religious liberty was proclaimed for both Roman Catholics and Jews. Gustav even designed a new national dress, which was in general use among the upper classes from 1778 until his death. (It is, indeed, still worn by the ladies of the Swedish court on state occasions.)

In foreign policy, Gustav tied Sweden to his adored France. The result of his devoted adherence was a 300,000-*livre* subsidy from Louis XV, the Caribbean island of Saint-Barthélemy (bizarrely), and an invitation to visit Paris once again, which Gustav duly did in 1784.

To bolster his foreign ambitions, Gustav also increased the size of the navy, creating galley-based fleets – designed to cope with the treacherous shallows and inlets of the Baltic – at Stockholm and Sveaborg (near present-day Helsinki), and a British-style battle fleet based on sailing ships-of-the-line at Karlskrona.

Gustav also embarked on an ambitious building programme on land, using Franco-British neoclassicism as his model for a variety of eclectic royal structures. An 'English' park and palace were planned for Haga, complete with a Kew Gardens-style Chinese pagoda (in the manner of George II's favourite architect, the Swedish-born William Chambers) and fake-medieval stables; a neoclassical theatre was built at Gripsholm; and a homage to Versailles's Petit Trianon was erected to the north of Stockholm.

Increasing royal expenditure and the subsequent rising tax burden, however, caused rising disquiet by the middle of the 1780s. It was then that Gustav made his most critical mistake: he embarked on what he gambled would be a short and victorious war against Sweden's neighbouring arch-enemies, Denmark and Russia. In 1788 he took advantage of Catherine the Great's preoccupation with the Turkish War to invade Russian-administered Finland (using as his pretext an attack by Swedish soldiers dressed in 'Russian' uniforms). The campaign did not start propitiously. In failing to obtain the consent of the estates for war, Gustav had violated his own constitution of 1772: it was a clumsy mistake that led to a serious mutiny by the 'Anjala Confederation' among his aristocratic officers in Finland. Meanwhile, the hoped-for victories failed to materialize. The naval battle of Suursari in July 1788 was inconclusive, its only notable result being a grimly tragic one: the captured Russian ship Vladislav brought an epidemic of typhus to its new Swedish home, Karlskrona, where over 5000 seamen died before the disease spread inland.

In 1790 Gustav personally led his galley fleet to a crushing defeat of Russian naval forces at the Battle of Svenskund. Long regarded as Sweden's greatest-ever naval victory, Svenskund saw the loss of only 6 Swedish ships as compared to the Russians' 50 vessels sunk or captured. Charles XII's defeat by the Russians 70 years before was ostensibly avenged. But in the subsequent Treaty of Värälä with Russia of 1790 almost nothing was gained: no territory, no compensation.

Gustav in brief

1746 Born in Stockholm, heir to the Swedish throne.

1771 Becomes king on the death of his father.

1772 Effects a royal coup against the aristocratic Cap faction and imposes new Swedish constitution, increasing royal power but also civil and religious liberties. Thus he begins his rule as 'enlightened despot'.

1774 Introduces moderate press freedom.

1776 Institutes currency reform.

1788–90 War with Russia over possession of Norway arouses discontent and mutiny, but also sees a major Swedish naval victory at Svenskund (July 1790).

1789 With support of the lower estates in the Riksdag, increases royal power further against aristocratic interest.

1790 Attempts unsuccessfully to coordinate pan-European action against the French Revolution.

1792 Shot by aristocratic conspirators while attending a masked ball (16 March). Dies on 29 March.

'A MASKED BALL'

THE MELODRAMA OF GUSTAV III's life and death is naturally suited to the theatre that Gustav himself patronized so keenly. His story became the basis of an opera libretto by French playwright Eugène Scribe (1791–1861), which was set to music both by Daniel Auber in 1833 and, most famously, by Giuseppe Verdi in 1859. Verdi's opera *Un ballo in maschera* (*A Masked Ball*) features constantly in the international repertoire.

Verdi's task in adapting the tale to Italian audiences, however, was not a straightforward one. In 1859 the city-states of most of Italy were under the authoritarian rule of the Austrian Habsburgs, the Neapolitan Bourbons or the papacy. As he wrote the opera in Naples, Verdi was required by the local censors to make extensive changes to the plot. The liberal composer's patience eventually snapped: he broke his contract and was sued by the theatre. He then transferred the production to Rome's opera house, but here, too, papal-appointed government censors feared the political allegories that could be drawn from a tale featuring the assassination of an absolute monarch. Verdi, worn down by months of wrangling, finally agreed that the setting of the story would be moved from Europe, and that the rank of the leading character would be reduced from king to colonial governor. Thus the revised opera was unaccountably set in Boston during the British colonial period, with the leading character's identity ludicrously changed from King Gustav to one Richard ('Riccardo'), Earl ('Count') of Warwick – a title that belongs properly in the 15th century rather than the 18th.

Many modern stagings of the opera, however, have respected Scribe and Verdi's original intentions, and have restored the original Swedish setting and characters' names, once more making Gustav III the centrepiece of his own tragedy.

Gustav predictably viewed the burgeoning French Revolution and the subjugation of his adored Bourbon dynasty with horror. While other Baltic rulers distanced themselves from the events, Gustav and the Swedish aristocrat Count Axel von Fersen (the latter probably a former lover of France's queen, Marie Antoinette) plotted to liberate the French royal family. Fersen organized their escape by coach, while Gustav himself travelled to the Rhenish city of Aachen to greet them. However, once Fersen left Louis XVI at Bondy, their progress became increasingly lumbering. Recognized at Varennes, Louis and his family were taken back to Paris under arrest.

The downcast Gustav returned to a situation not unlike that faced by his Bourbon patrons. Stockholm was seething with unrest at Gustav's financial impositions – the national debt was now at massive proportions, while royal expenditure continued to rocket – and anti-monarchical plots abounded. Despite the obvious lessons emanating from Paris, Gustav appeared to believe he could remain immune from revolutionary intrigue. This was not, however, the case. On the evening of 16 March 1792 he attended a masked ball at Stockholm's opera house. A disaffected army officer, Captain Jacob Anckarström, sidled up to him and shot him in the back.

Gustav did not die immediately, and Anckarström was arrested before his co-conspirators could stage the coup they had planned. However, the king's wound turned gangrenous, and he died on 29 March. With him died Sweden's abortive enlightenment. Gustav III's successor, his young nephew Gustav IV Adolf, was not interested in social reform, and preferred to sit on the sidelines during the early years of the Revolutionary Wars that divided Europe. Sweden once more lapsed into relative international obscurity.

Gustav III, talented, visionary and energetic, was the right man at the wrong time. The man who was the patron of poets, who penned historical dramas and perceptive historical essays (which included the prescient prediction that the newborn United States would grow to be the world's greatest power), belonged to a bygone age of chivalry and romance. Instead, he became one of the many sovereigns who were to lose their lives as the French Revolution changed European politics beyond all recognition.

Jean-Paul MARAT

1743–1793, FRENCH REVOLUTIONARY LEADER

ASSASSIN Charlotte Corday
DATE 13 July 1793
PLACE Paris, France

If Jean-Paul Marat had died before 1788, he would have been known to the world as a Swiss-born French scientist and physician who, if not quite a Newton or a Descartes, certainly made a significant contribution to scientific advance. Indeed, he might have been better known in Britain than in France, since it was in England that he published most of his ground-breaking scientific papers. As it is, it was by his political activities during the last five years of his life that we now know him best. And perhaps more than any other assassin's victim, it was the manner of his death that has made him a household name the world over, the inspiration of artists and revolutionaries alike.

By the time Marat was 30, he had settled in London, where he became well known as a doctor specializing in the treatment of skin and eye conditions. His first published, work, however, was his *Philosophical Essay on Man*, published (originally in English) in 1773. It was an accomplished assault on the French philosopher Claude Helvetius, who had, in his *De l'Homme* (published posthumously in 1772) declared knowledge of science to be unnecessary for a philosopher. Marat riposted that physiology alone could solve the problems of the connection between the soul and the body. This argument in turn attracted the attention of the most celebrated of the French *philosophes*, the now aged Voltaire, who penned a swift attack on the *Essay* after reading the French-language translation of 1775. Marat was now a figure whose opinions were regularly debated in the enlightened salons of Paris.

'Unsparing with the blood of slaves'

From the Marquis de Sade's eulogy for the dead Marat, and intended as a compliment

In 1774 Marat extended his field of interest to the politics of his adopted country. His essay *The Chains of Slavery* urged British electors to reject the politicians favoured by George III – effectively, the illiberal Tory government of the weak and indecisive Lord North, whose punitive measures against the American colonists the king backed steadfastly – and to adopt radical candidates instead. Overnight Marat was a Whig Party hero, joining the ranks of John Wilkes and John Locke and earning honorary memberships in the patriotic societies of Carlisle, Berwick and Newcastle.

The polymath Marat followed up this success with a solid essay on one of the most unpleasant but common medical conditions of the day. His 1775 essay on the sexually transmitted disease 'gleets' (gonorrhea) led to his election as an MD of the University of St Andrews. His next paper, *An Enquiry into the Nature, Cause, and Cure of a Singular Disease of the Eyes*, secured his reputation in London as one of the greatest medical authorities of the age. It also got him noticed in France, where in 1777 he was appointed physician to the guards of the Count of Artois. With what, in hindsight, appears to be great irony, the future radical revolutionary joined the payroll of the prince who, as Charles X of France, was to prove one of France's most reactionary monarchs (and, indeed, the last of France's Bourbon sovereigns).

Marat was soon in great demand as a doctor among the French aristocracy at Versailles. He continued his scientific researches into heat, light and electricity, and was admired by figures as diverse as Johann Wolfgang von Goethe and Benjamin Franklin (who frequently visited him). However, he failed to be elected to the venerable Académie des Sciences, as he had hoped, owing to his over-confident attack on the great master Isaac Newton. As a result, he spread his interests even more widely, publishing in 1780 a novel, *Plan de législation criminelle*; he also took care to publicly reaffirm his support for Newton's theories with his 1787 translation of the great man's magisterial opus *Opticks*.

At the outbreak of the French Revolution in 1789, Marat threw himself into the political arena, placing his career as a scientist and philosopher behind him. When the Estates-General met in June 1789 – for the first time since 1614 – he published a number of papers calling for a liberal, written French constitution. In September he went further, starting up a radical newspaper, which, having initially appeared in the guise *Moniteur patriote* ('Patriotic Watch') and the *Publiciste parisien*, was finally named *L'Ami du peuple*. The acerbic and fearless 'Friend of the People' coined the immortal and ominous phrase 'enemies of the people' for all those whom Marat suspected of reactionary intentions. His academic arrogance was directed at some of the most influential and powerful groups in France, including the Municipal Corps, the Constituent Assembly, and Louis XVI's increasingly nervous ministers. The result was, in this early stage of the revolution, government prosecutions for libel, actions that encouraged the doctor to take refuge in London.

Safely back in England, he wrote the vicious *Denonciation contre Necker*, an attack on the international banker Jacques Necker, who was trying – in vain, as it turned out – to introduce some semblance of order and solvency to the government's chaotic finances. In May 1790 Marat returned to Paris to continue *L'Ami du peuple*, issuing a stream of increasingly vehement condemnations of the government, of the aristocracy and of the monarchy. He condemned the National Assembly's decision to sell church property to fund the state's debts, arguing that the land in question would be better used to meet the needs of the propertyless poor; but at the same time he opposed the proposed abolition of guilds, warning that unlimited competition would force down the quality of products. Scurrying into hiding in order to avoid arrest became second nature to Marat in the subsequent months.

The revolution took a sharp turn leftwards in 1792. Following their abortive attempt at flight the previous year, when they were recognized and recaptured at Varennes, the royal family was kept under house arrest at the old Tuileries Palace in Paris (which Louis XIV had originally vacated for the newly-created glories of Versailles). Their prospects worsened with the Duke of Brunswick's proclamation calling on the powers of continental Europe to crush the revolution, the declaration of the French Republic in September 1792, and the subsequent 'September massacres' of royalists and moderates. That same month, Marat was elected to the National Convention, and he changed the title of his *L'Ami du peuple* to the *Journal de la république française*. Few of his fellow-representatives escaped the barbs of his journalism, with the result that the good doctor swiftly became one of the most hated figures of the revolution.

Never one to sacrifice principles for pragmatism, Marat's attitude to the king's trial infuriated even his revolutionary colleagues. He declared that it was unfair to accuse Louis of anything before he had accepted the revolutionary constitution in 1791, and he would

Marat in brief

1743 Born in Boudry, Switzerland.

1770–7 Active in London as a doctor, and begins publishing medical and philosophical essays.

1777–86 In France as doctor to the Count of Artois, and continues to publish.

1789 Begins a radical political newspaper, *L'Ami du peuple*.

1790 With the French Revolution underway, goes into hiding after advocating violent political action in print.

1792 Elected to the revolution Convention as a Deputy for Paris: becomes a leading radical Montagnard vying with the more moderate Girondins for power.

1793 Called before a tribunal (9 April), but acquitted: the Girondins are outmanoeuvred. Assassinated (13 July) by Charlotte Corday, a Girondin sympathizer.

MARAT'S LEGACY

MARAT'S DEIFICATION FOLLOWED SWIFTLY. The talented painter Jacques-Louis David (1748–1825) was to record key moments of revolutionary and Napoleonic achievement, from Marat's death to Napoleon's coronation. Not only did he paint an immensely successful memorial of Marat's assassination (*see* p.51), but he was also given the task of organizing a grandiose funeral ceremony. The entire National Convention was present at the event, and his remains were ceremoniously transferred to the Panthéon on 25 November 1793.

Marat became almost a Christ-like figure: busts of Marat replaced crucifixes and religious statues in Parisian churches, while his funeral elegy declared that 'like Jesus, Marat loved ardently the people, and only them; like Jesus, Marat hated kings, nobles, priests, rogues; and, like Jesus, he never stopped fighting against these plagues of the people'. The port town of Le Hâvre de Grâce changed its name to Hâvre de Marat, and then Hâvre-Marat. When the radical Jacobins (the faction headed by Robespierre and St Just) began their de-Christianization campaigns, Marat was elevated to near-sainthood.

However, the wheel of fortune revolved all too swiftly for the Jacobins, who began imploding in 1794: having despatched Hébert (too radical) and Georges Danton (too soft), Robespierre and his acolyte St Just also faced the guillotine. By early 1795 the bloodletting of the Terror was over, and Marat's reputation had fallen from its Olympian heights. On 13 January 1795, Hâvre-Marat became simply Le Havre. The following month, Marat's coffin was removed from the Panthéon and reinterred in the cemetery of Saint-Étienne-du-Mont, and the various busts and sculptures installed in the capital's churches were destroyed.

In 1860 the French painter Baudry revisited the subject of David's great painting. But this time Charlotte Corday was both the centre of attention and, implicitly, the hero of the event.

A curious coda. After Marat's death, the bathtub in which he was assassinated disappeared. In 1885 a journalist finally tracked it down, and its owner – a modest *curé*, who hoped its sale could earn his parish a good deal of money – offered it to the Musée Carnavalet in Paris. The museum's director turned the offer down, due its dubious provenance and high price. However, after rejecting offers from Madame Tussaud's waxworks and the circus entrepreneur Phineas Barnum, the curé sold the tub for 5000 francs to the waxworks of the Musée Grevin. It is still there today.

not allow Louis XVI's counsel, the venerable Malesherbes, to be attacked in his paper. Notwithstanding Marat's stance, however, the king was found guilty and guillotined on 21 January 1793.

Following the king's death, Marat fought bitterly with the Girondins, the moderately revolutionary party who found themselves increasingly isolated by the shriller radicalism of Marat, Robespierre (1758–94) and Hébert (1755–94). Swayed by the Girondins, the Convention ordered that Marat should be tried before the Revolutionary Tribunal, but he was acquitted and returned to the Convention a popular hero. The Girondins' days were now numbered, and their leaders either fled or were sent to the guillotine during June.

The fall of the Girondins, however, proved a death sentence for Marat himself. One of the main reasons why, as a celebrated doctor, Marat had been so enthusiastic about curing diseases of the skin was that he suffered from one himself, a severe form of dermatitis, which also caused emaciation. By June 1793 the ailment was seriously affecting his ability to conduct official business; he was spending far more time soaking his wracked body in a cold bath than attending the debates of the Convention. He was lying in his bathtub on 13 July 1793 when a woman claiming to be a messenger from Caen, where fleeing Girondins were trying to establish a regional base, begged to be admitted to his quarters. He turned her away at first, but when she returned, later that evening, he ordered that she be admitted to his bathroom. On her arrival he asked her the names of the Convention deputies who were abetting the Gironde; having recorded their names, he solemnly proclaimed that 'They shall all be guillotined.' The young woman, Charlotte Corday, then drew a knife – bought minutes before at a nearby shop – and stabbed the recumbent Marat in the chest. He called out 'A moi, ma chère amie!' ('Help me, my dear friend!'), but died almost instantly.

Charlotte Corday has become almost as famous as her victim. Born into an impoverished aristocratic family – her proper title was Marie Anne Charlotte de Corday d'Armont – she had sworn to kill Marat following the violence of the September 1792 massacres. Her trial lawyer, Claude Chauveau-Lagarde, had previously represented Queen Marie Antoinette. While obliged by the Revolutionary Tribunal to agree to a plea of insanity, in order to remove any taint of political motivation from the assassination, he used his legal skills to ensure that no-one was left in any doubt as to the dubious legitimacy of the proceedings and the genuine reasons for Corday's actions. Corday herself testified that she had carried out the assassination alone, saying 'I killed one man to save 100,000' – a deliberate paraphrase of Robespierre's callous exclamation just before the execution of King Louis XVI.

Inevitably, Corday was found guilty. She was guillotined on 17 July. Immediately after her decapitation, one of the executioner's assistants — a man, hired for the day, named Legros — lifted her head from the basket and slapped it on the cheek. Amid the carnage and disruption of the revolution, there were still some uncrossable boundaries: this was considered an unacceptable breach of guillotine etiquette, and Legros was subsequently imprisoned for three months.

Corday's body was disposed of in a trench, along with other victims of the guillotine. It is uncertain whether the head was interred with her or retained as a curiosity: it has been suggested that her skull found its way into the possession of the Bonaparte family and their descendants. Her victim, meanwhile, was raised to the status of a revolutionary saint.

PAUL of Russia

1754–1801, TSAR OF RUSSIA

ASSASSINS General Nicholas Zubov and other army officers
DATE 23 March 1801
PLACE St Petersburg, Russia

On the night of 23 March 1801 (or 11 March, in the Old Style Russian calendar), a band of drunken aristocratic officers, recently dismissed because Russia was now allied to Napoleon's France and supposedly at peace, burst into the bedroom of the Tsar of Russia at the heart of St Petersburg's newly built St Michael's Castle. Tsar Paul had heard them coming and had hidden behind the curtains. Nevertheless, the assassins spied him there, dragged him out, forced him to sit at a table and tried to compel him to sign his abdication. Paul resisted and was, as a result, stabbed with a sword, strangled, and then trampled to death. One of the assassins, General Nicholas Zubov, promptly sought out Paul's eldest son, who was sleeping elsewhere in the castle, and acclaimed him Emperor Alexander I.

Paul's manner of death was, even for Russia, shockingly unusual. But then his upbringing had not been entirely conventional. His parents – Peter III and Catherine II – had both, in turn, ruled the vast Russian Empire. His mother's memoirs implied that he was not Peter's son but rather the offspring of her lover, Sergei Saltykov. (In fact, there is no evidence to support this claim. Paul's appearance certainly resembled that of his Romanov father.) Peter enjoyed only a few months as 'Ruler of all the Russias' before he was removed from the throne by his wife and shortly afterwards murdered – again, probably at the instigation of his wife, who succeeded him as Empress Catherine II, later titled 'the Great'.

Paul, meanwhile, knew little of his mother. He was born in 1754, but as a baby he was removed from his mother's household and brought up by his paternal grandmother, the Empress Elizabeth. Her spoiling of her impressionable and insecure grandchild helped create in him an abrupt, authoritarian manner and a nervous instability. These characteristics were to grow more pronounced as he grew older.

The manner of Peter III's death bore many ominous foreshadowings of his son Paul's own assassination, 39 years later. After Peter acceded to the throne in 1762, he immediately withdrew Russia's forces from what later became known as the Seven Years War and allied with Russia's former enemy Prussia, despite the fact that Russian troops now occupied the Prussian capital, Berlin. Instead of furthering Russian aims in this globally strategic conflict, Peter planned to involve his armies in a self-indulgent sideshow, a war with Denmark designed to win back the tsar's personal fiefdom of Schleswig. Disaffected soldiers of the Life Guard (including Grigory Orlov, another of Catherine's lovers), encouraged by Catherine, mutinied. They seized the tsar and forced him to abdicate.

By his mid-twenties, Paul was already showing signs of mental instability – or, as kinder historians have suggested, obsessive-compulsive disorder. He believed (with considerable justification) that he was about to be the target of assassins. He suspected his mother was behind the plotting, and once openly accused her of causing broken glass to be mixed into

> 'The least infraction of Paul's commands was punished with exile to Siberia'
>
> From the *Memoirs* of Elisabeth Vigée Lebrun (1755–1842), a painter and habituée of the Russian court

Paul in brief

his food. He lived in terror of becoming the victim of a palace coup staged by one of his mother's many aristocratic lovers.

The Pugachev rebellion of 1773–4 further undermined Paul's position, since the pretender Pugachev attempted to impersonate Paul's late father. Soon after the birth of Paul's eldest son Alexander, in 1777, the baby was – in an obvious echo of Paul's own treatment 20 years before – taken away from his parents and brought up by his grandmother. As a result, young Alexander grew to adore Catherine and to view his father, Paul, with great suspicion.

Catherine the Great finally died on 17 November (6 November, Old Style) 1796, and was peacefully succeeded – much to his surprise – by her 42-year-old son. Paul was extremely anxious lest Catherine's will bequeath the throne to her grandson, Alexander, as was widely rumoured, but no such testament existed. (And to make sure this situation never occurred again, Paul immediately issued a law establishing the principle of primogeniture.)

On assuming power, Paul carefully obliterated much of his hated mother's legacy: he clamped down on Francophile culture and the use of the French language; he readmitted his mother's critics into the country or liberated them from prison; he repealed Catherine's anti-serf laws and gave Russian peasants greater freedom of action. Additionally, still privately insecure about his paternity, Paul stressed his descent not from his egocentric mother but from his illustrious predecessor of a century earlier, Peter the Great. Most significantly of all, Paul reburied his father's body with great ceremony in the Peter and Paul Cathedral in St Petersburg. His homage to the father he barely knew did not end there: just as his father had done, Paul dramatically reversed Russia's system of international alliances and pulled the country out of a major war. He recalled the army, then poised to attack Persia on his mother's orders, and helped to create the Second Coalition against Napoleon in 1798–9.

Three years later, with no advance warning, Paul's foreign policy completely changed direction yet again. Paul made peace with Napoleon and now threatened his former ally, Britain, with armed neutrality. At the time of his death, Paul was even making plans for a joint Franco-Russian invasion of Britain and the raising of a Cossack expeditionary force to seize British India.

Paul's martial schizophrenia fused with his constant dissatisfaction with his noble officers, with tragic consequences. The tsar's excessively romantic vision of how military affairs should be conducted evolved into an obsession with recreating the Russian army as a modern-day equivalent of a medieval chivalric order. His unrealistic model was the Knights Hospitaller of Malta (or Order of St John, founded in 1080), to whom he gave shelter following their ejection by Napoleon in 1798. He promoted those sycophantic officers who appeared to concur with his unrealistic ambitions. The many that did not, however, were swiftly dropped: 7 field marshals and 33 generals were sacked during Paul's brief reign. This mass purging of the army's aristocratic officer caste, together with the tsar's bewildering policy U-turns, ultimately prompted some of his exasperated senior officers to mutiny and regicide in 1801.

Unusually, the aftermath of Paul's assassination did not involve a lurch towards governmental repression. Indeed, the young Alexander I even appeared to implicitly condone his father's murder. The officers responsible were never tried or disciplined. Instead, Alexander used his accession as an excuse to draw up an ambitious scheme of internal reform, proposing the prohibition of torture, the curtailing of the activities of the internal police and the institution of a constitutional monarchy on British lines. It was as if Tsar Paul had never lived.

While Tsar Paul's reign lasted only five years, in one sense he did manage to exercise lasting influence on the map of Europe. In 1776 he married his second wife, Sophia Dorothea of Württemberg, who was instantly rechristened Maria Feodorovna for her Russian subjects. Their ten children – his progeny a stark contrast with Paul's own status as an only child – were to marry into an astonishing variety of European aristocratic families, and two of them, Alexander I (1777–1825) and his younger brother Nicholas I (1796–1855), ruled Russia as tsars.

Some of Paul's children married into European royalty: Alexandra Pavlovna (1783–1801) married Archduke Joseph Anton of Austria, the son of the penultimate Holy Roman Emperor, Leopold II. Anna (1795–1865) married William II of the Netherlands, later a veteran of Waterloo and a monarch who successfully weathered the revolutions of 1848.

Constantine (1779–1831) was married twice: to Princess Juliane of Saxe-Coburg-Saalfeld (Russified as Anna Feodorovna) and, after their divorce, to Joanna Grudczińska of Łowicz, by which action he forfeited his status as Alexander I's heir and instead ruled Poland, then part of the Russian Empire. Elena (1784–1803) married Frederick of Mecklenburg-Schwerin; Maria (1786-1859) married Carol Friedrich, Grand Duke of Saxony-Weimar-Eisenach; and Catherine (1788–1819) married first Duke Peter of Oldenburg and then Wilhelm I of Württemberg. Michael (1798–1849) married Charlotte von Württemberg and had five children, two of whom married into the ducal families of Luxembourg and Mecklenburg-Strelitz. Thus did Paul's unstable genes end up populating the courts of Germany.

RUSSIA IN THE NAPOLEONIC WARS

FOLLOWING PAUL'S DEATH and the resumption of European war in 1804, Russia's record in combat was initially less than illustrious. In April 1805 Britain, Russia and Austria signed a treaty with the aim of removing the French from Holland and Switzerland. Yet the Austrians were crushed at the Battle of Ulm and, in December 1805, an Austro-Russian army nominally led by Alexander I was decimated at Austerlitz. Prussia entered the coalition in place of the exhausted Austrians, only to find its army outclassed, and, in October 1806, French troops entered Berlin. The French then chased Russian forces out of Poland and forced Alexander to conclude a humiliating peace at Tilsit in July 1807. Russia was now Napoleon's ally, and in return for Finland – stolen from neighbouring Sweden – entered the lists against Britain and Austria.

In 1810 the French Empire reached its greatest extent. However, Franco-Russian relations had deteriorated to the extent that Alexander was now a very unwilling ally in the fight to eliminate British maritime power. In April 1812 Britain, Russia and Sweden signed secret agreements directed against Napoleonic France. And later that same year Napoleon committed his greatest mistake – one that was to lead directly to his final downfall. His Grande Armée of 650,000 men invaded Russia. By November 1812, when its remnants crossed back into Poland and were peremptorily deserted by their emperor, only 27,000 fit soldiers remained. The great army of Ulm and Austerlitz was no more.

Spencer PERCEVAL

1762–1812, PRIME MINISTER OF GREAT BRITAIN

ASSASSIN John Bellingham
DATE 11 May 1812
PLACE London, England

Violence is something that has largely remained alien to the parliamentary tradition of British politics, which lends the assassinated Spencer Perceval (1762–1812) a unique distinction. He remains the only British prime minister – or politician of any kind – to have been attacked within the precincts of the ancient Palace of Westminster. (The assassination by car bomb of Conservative minister Airey Neave in 1979, by Irish Republicans, took place outside the palace, in the car park.) Although he is otherwise one of Britain's least-known premiers, Perceval could have been one of the great names of British politics, a Tory politician who had seemingly inherited the mantle of the late, great William Pitt the Younger.

Perceval became prime minister in 1809, at a time when Napoleon's triumph over the rest of Europe looked complete. The Austrians had been heavily defeated, the Russians were benevolently neutral, and the Prussians were actually allied with France. At the beginning of Perceval's short-lived premiership, Britain effectively stood alone against the might of Napoleonic Europe, with only her navy keeping her from invasion or starvation. The glorious victory of Trafalgar (1805) seemed a long time past, while in 1809 the likelihood of a Waterloo-style victory seemed unimaginable. Yet Perceval looked like the sort of inspired, moral figure that could restore Britain's tattered fortunes and rebuild the shattered alliance.

In many assassinations, a life of immense promise is cut short. In Perceval's case the timing was particularly tragic. In 1809 Napoleon was assembling his armies to march on Russia, while the Duke of Wellington's troops were finally making their presence felt in the Peninsula – developments that would lead ultimately to Napoleon's defeat and eventual fall only two years later.

> ## 'I have nothing to say to the nothing that has been said'
>
> Perceval's withering riposte during a parliamentary debate on electoral fraud

Spencer Perceval did not, like his great Tory rival George Canning, rise to prominence from humble beginnings. His was born on 1 November 1762 and his background was very much a privileged, aristocratic one. However, he was the second son from the 2nd Earl of Egmont's second marriage, which left him on a low rung of the inheritance ladder. In fact, when Egmont died Spencer was only ten, and there was no financial provision for him. Thus Perceval realized from an early age that he could rely on neither paternal influence nor family money to advance himself, and he would have to, therefore, rely on his own abilities. This background helped to forge the undisguised ambition and strength of conviction of his adult years.

Perceval took a conventionally upper-class educational route, processing from Harrow School to Trinity College, Cambridge. At university he was heavily influenced by the new evangelical Anglican movement; in later years he always demonstrated a strong streak of Christian morality and even wrote religious pamphlets on the subject of prophecy. (His one modern biographer even subtitled his book 'The Evangelical Prime Minister'.) Perceval's early career was relatively smooth. He trained as a barrister, and used his family's local connections to become 'deputy recorder' of Northampton and, subsequently, a 'commissioner of bankrupts' – ironically, a well-rewarded legal sinecure. So far, so predictable for a

PERCEVAL AND THE RADICALS

IN THE EARLY 1790s, PERCEVAL TOOK CENTRE stage in the prosecution of two of the government's most vociferous and eloquent critics. In 1792 he acted for the crown against the radical writer Thomas Paine and, two years later, against the polemicist John Horne Tooke.

Paine had finished his ground-breaking *Rights of Man* in 1791. It was written as a rebuttal of the neo-conservatism of Edmund Burke's *Reflections on the Revolution in France* (1790) and not only strongly supported the French Revolution but was also highly critical of the absolutist European monarchies that, from 1792, ranged themselves against the French revolutionary regime.

Pitt's government took fright at Paine's incendiary book, and put Paine on trial *in absentia* for seditious libel. Perceval helped secure his conviction, but Paine wisely decided to stay in France. Here he eventually found himself a victim of the Terror, being arrested and imprisoned in December 1793. He was released only after Robespierre's fall in 1794, and he fled not to Pitt's England but to the newly independent United States of America.

The government's attempt to demonize and stifle the radical academic and pampleteer Horne Tooke, however, ended in farce. Tooke had been arrested for treason and melodramatically commuted to the Tower of London. Despite Perceval's prosecutorial arguments, however, the jury took only eight minutes to order Tooke's acquittal.

younger son of a minor aristocrat. However, once established as a successful lawyer, Perceval's political sympathies became fully evident. In the wake of the French Revolution of 1789, and particularly after the radical turn of events in France following Louis XVI's abortive flight of 1791, Pitt's government passed a series of draconian acts designed to stamp out radical opposition groups and to ensure that the British did not follow the same precarious path as the French. Perceval made sure that he took a leading part in William Pitt's anti-radical crusade, a campaign that saw many frightened Whig Party moderates, such as the Duke of Portland, scurry across to the safety of Pitt's increasingly reactionary administration.

Perceval's prominent, enthusiastic role in Pitt's conservative clampdown was duly noted. In 1795 Perceval was considered as a possible chief secretary to the Lord Lieutenant of Ireland. Unsure about pursuing a political career, he ultimately rejected the offer, but he did accept nomination as MP for his local borough of Northampton in 1796. As a novice MP, he made several effective speeches fiercely attacking Charles James Fox and the radical rump of the Whig opposition – conservative eloquence that highly impressed Prime Minister Pitt. Already Perceval was being tagged as a future star, and by some as a possible successor to Pitt himself.

Perceval's fervent Anglicanism (a term which then was not viewed as an oxymoron), caused him to part with Pitt on the issue of civil rights for Catholics – 'Catholic Emancipation'. Pitt had clashed with George III over his passionate advocacy on the issue and, to general surprise, had actually resigned as prime minister over it in 1801. Perceval stayed with the government and was rewarded by Pitt's lacklustre successor, Henry Addington, with two of the most senior legal posts in the nation: the solicitor-generalship in 1801, and the post of attorney-general in 1802. Yet Perceval soon realized he had backed the wrong horse. Addington's inept government relied too much on the Peace of Amiens, negotiated with Napoleonic France in 1802 – a treaty that Napoleon regarded merely as a breathing space for his war effort. When the peace fell apart in 1803, so did Addington's administration. Perceval, who had sensibly taken care to confine his comments to legal issues while serving under Addington, retained his office when Pitt returned in 1804.

At Pitt's funeral in January 1806, Perceval was one of the chief mourners; and, as one of the most prominent of 'Pitt's Friends', it was expected that he would be a leading candidate to succeed him as prime minster. However, in the event the 1806 election returned a slim Whig majority, prompting the formation of an unwieldy, broad-bottomed Whig coalition satirically labelled 'the Ministry of All the Talents'. When this fell in 1807, the Duke of Portland, the former Whig grandee, put together a shaky coalition of senior Tories, with Perceval as chancellor of the exchequer and leader of the House of Commons. Portland was old and unwell, and so effectively it was Perceval's government. Perceval even lived at 10 Downing Street for much of the time. On 6 September 1809 the ailing duke, who had recently suffered a stroke, was forced to resign. George III was anxious to support Perceval's bitter rival Canning, whom he thought 'essential to his government', but ultimately chose Perceval as the new premier, reportedly regarding him as 'the most straightforward man he had almost ever known'.

In office, Perceval promoted his strongly Christian morality where he could. As chancellor, he had helped to pass William Wilberforce's bill abolishing the British slave trade in the Atlantic. Many of his measures as prime minister, however, were markedly less liberal. He continued to oppose any moves towards parliamentary reform, staunchly opposed Catholic Emancipation (which was not finally attained until 1829), and passed the severe but ostensibly necessary 'Orders in Council', which strictly regulated foreign trade in an effort to disrupt and dissolve Napoleon's effective, anti-British trade embargo (the 'Continental System'). In the event, of course, it was Wellington's armies rather than Perceval's policies that helped to unseat Napoleon, and the Orders' main contribution to history was to provoke the highly unnecessary War of 1812 with the United States.

By the spring of 1812, things were looking better for Britain and its embattled prime minister. With George III's growing incapacity now undeniable, Perceval's government had no choice in January 1811 but to confer regency powers on George, Prince of Wales. Prince George had made much of his affection for the Whigs in his youth, and it was widely assumed that, on assuming the regency, he would dismiss Perceval's Tories and bring in a Whig government in memory of his long-dead mentor, Charles James Fox. In the event, though, the indolent prince kept Perceval in office – his first measure as regent being to appoint himself as a field marshal! Thereafter, the prince gave Perceval his full support, even after being accorded full regency powers in February 1812, and the two worked together well. Perceval's political position had never looked so secure.

All this came tumbling down on the afternoon of 11 May 1812. Perceval had spent much of the day preparing for the forthcoming debate on the Orders in Council, and he was waylaid on his way to Parliament by William Wilberforce, who launched into an affectionate eulogy on the prime minister's 'worth and principles', so arrived late at the Palace of Westminster. As he stepped into the crowded lobby through its St Stephen's entrance, he was confronted by a deranged and unemployed bankrupt, John Bellingham, who had been prevented from presenting his petition (demanding compensation for business debts) to 10 Downing Street. Bellingham fired a pistol at point-blank range into Perceval's heart, then calmly sat down on one of the lobby benches. Perceval cried out

'I am murdered, murdered!' before falling to the ground. He was carried into a side room, gave 'two heavy groans and no more' and expired.

Bellingham put up no resistance, and he was committed to Newgate Prison for trial. He was found guilty at the Old Bailey and hanged at Newgate a week later. Perceval's body lay at 10 Downing Street for five days, attended by his wife and children, before burial at the Church of St Luke, Charlton – near the house where he was born. Although his government colleagues had pressed for a grand funeral in Westminster Abbey, Perceval's wife, Jane, had insisted on a small, private ceremony. The government did, however, grant generous pensions to Jane and her children, while the prince regent ordered Richard Westmacott to design a fine memorial in the abbey.

Many believed that Perceval's assassination was intended to be the signal for an English revolution rather than the work of one lone madman. (Even on the scaffold Bellingham was questioned about possible accomplices, but he denied having had any.) Posters demanding 'Rescue Bellingham or Die' went up all over London, and the prince regent ordered that all arms depots in London be immediately secured and that more troops be ordered to Newgate. Radical groups lit bonfires across Britain, and mob violence, originally inspired by the anti-industrial Luddites, broke out anew.

However, as with most British scares about public order issues, the disturbances came to nothing. The colourless Lord Liverpool was persuaded to take up the reins of government, and he inherited much of Perceval's administration. He would preside over fifteen years of Tory government, years that redefined the Pittite cause as a more liberal creed, laid the foundations for the modern-day Conservative Party, and saw the vanquishing of the Napoleonic order. In 1815 British armies led the final rout of Napoleon's forces. But Perceval was not there to earn the crowds' acclamations.

Abraham LINCOLN

1809–1865, 16TH PRESIDENT OF THE UNITED STATES

ASSASSIN	John Wilkes Booth
DATE	14 April 1865 (died 15 April)
PLACE	Washington, D.C., USA

The play being shown at Ford's Theater in downtown Washington, D.C., on the evening of 14 April 1865 was Tom Taylor's *Our American Cousin*. It was a highly successful farce, which had played to packed houses for seven years. Concerning the arrival of an awkward American relative at an aristocratic English family seat, it was just the sort of undemanding fare that President Abraham Lincoln needed. After all, it was just five days previously that Robert E. Lee had surrendered his Confederate armies at Appomattox Court House, so putting an end to four tumultuous years of civil war that had wracked the young nation.

Halfway through Act III, Scene 2, the character Asa Trenchard, played by actor Harry Hawk, uttered a line that, every night for seven years, had provoked an enormous laugh. A fellow actor and friend of the theatre's owner John T. Ford intended to use this laughter to mask the sound of gunfire. The ploy worked. He slipped into Lincoln's box and shot the president in the back of the head with a .44 Deringer pistol. Lincoln's friend Major Henry Rathbone, also in the box, immediately tackled him, but he was stabbed and slashed by a dagger that the assassin had brought with him for such an emergency, and was forced to let the murderer go.

'Now he belongs to the ages'

Edwin M. Stanton, US secretary of war, the day after Lincoln's death

The assassin then jumped from the box to the stage, reputedly breaking his leg after it was snagged by the patriotic bunting used as stage decoration. Some witnesses later claimed he shouted 'sic semper tyrannis!' ('Thus always to tyrants', the Virginia state motto); others insisted it was a more prosaic 'The South is avenged'. Whatever his comments, the assassin then staggered to his waiting horse and rode to the nearby house of a sympathetic doctor, to have his injured leg treated.

The assassin, John Wilkes Booth, was born in Maryland in 1838. From his earliest childhood he was steeped in the classics, and particularly in Shakespeare's plays. Small wonder, then, that he developed into a skilful Shakespearean actor. Strikingly handsome, a proficient athlete and an excellent swordsman, he was the Laurence Olivier of his day. A fervent supporter of the Confederate cause from the very beginning of the war, he lived in a state – Maryland – that, despite lying north of the national capital, was predominantly Southern in its allegiance. Nevertheless, he promised his pro-Union mother that he would not enlist in the Confederate army, and he lived out the war performing as an actor – and, behind the scenes, as a Confederate spy – in Washington, D.C.

President Lincoln was an avid theatre-goer. Indeed, in November 1863 he had actually seen Booth playing at Ford's Theater in Washington. On that occasion Lincoln had asked to meet the actor after the play, but Booth had huffily refused.

Soon after this event, Booth began planning to kidnap the president, allegedly in order to secure the release of 10,000 Southern soldiers held in Northern prisons. Approaches to the Confederate Secret Service came to nothing, however, and, fired by the Confederates' military collapse, Booth and a small band of co-conspirators began to plot an even more dramatic act of revenge. His final scheme involved not only the assassination of the president; his assistants were also supposed to murder Secretary of State William Seward and Vice-President Andrew Johnson, while Booth himself was to subsequently kill the that the Confederate government could reorganize and continue the war.

Booth did not evade capture for long. He was eventually cornered by Union troops in a barn near Bowling Green, Virginia, on 26 April. The barn was set on fire, and Booth was fatally wounded by gunfire. Dragged from the barn by soldiers, he expired on the farmhouse porch. His body was later buried in an unmarked location in the family plot at Greenmount Cemetery, Maryland.

Lincoln himself had not died immediately. Although doctors declared that the wound was fatal, he lay in a coma for nine hours before he was officially pronounced dead at 7.22 a.m. on 15 April 1865. Lincoln's legacy, though, as the 16th president of the United States, is immense. He is judged by many to have been the most skilled and, in hindsight, successful of all American premiers. His adherence, even in the darkest days of the civil war, to the cause of American nationhood, and his redefinition of exactly what that meant, have helped inspire succeeding generations.

Born in a one-room log cabin in Illinois in 1809, by 1846 Lincoln had become a Whig member of the US House of Representatives as well as a reasonably successful Illinois lawyer. He helped found the new Republican Party, anchoring its policies firmly to the abolition of slavery. Thus it was not surprising that, although he won the Republican nomination for the presidency in 1860, his support was garnered entirely from Northern, non-slave states. Yet the ensuing contest split the Southern, largely Democratic Party vote, enabling Lincoln's to come through.

The Confederate act of belligerence in attacking Fort Sumter, South Carolina, in April 1861 made civil war inevitable. But over the next four years, Lincoln constantly insisted that he was fighting primarily to preserve the Union, and not to abolish slavery. He saw his Emancipation Proclamation of 22 September 1862, freeing slaves in territories not under Union control from 1 January 1863, largely as a way of weakening the economic base of the South rather than as an anti-slavery measure. That came later, when the Thirteenth Amendment to the US Constitution permanently abolished slavery throughout the nation. Lincoln's leadership was vital in securing ultimate victory. He dismissed those senior generals who failed – beginning with Commander-in-Chief George B. McLellan, who was to stand against him in the 1864 election. But when he found a military leader who seemed to have the right answers, in the person of Ulysses S. Grant, he defended him from vicious internal criticism. Lincoln was an outstanding diplomat, successfully defusing a war scare with Britain in 1861. His Gettysburg Address of 19 November 1863, although little heeded at the time, brilliantly articulated the rationale behind the Union effort. At the same time, Lincoln managed his own landslide re-election in 1864, winning all but two states and capturing 212 of 233 electoral votes – an astonishing achievement at the time of a bitterly divisive civil conflict.

Lincoln in brief

1809 Born of humble origins in Hardin County, Kentucky.

1816–30 Family lives in Indiana.

1831–3 Now in Illinois, works as store clerk, shop owner (bringing him debts), postmaster, surveyor.

1834 Elected to the State of Illinois's House of Representatives (as a Whig), serving until 1842.

1836 Begins practising law, largely self-taught.

1854 Elected to Congress.

1856 Becomes a leading figure of the new Republican Party, which opposes any spread of slavery.

1860 Elected President of the United States, but 7 southern states secede to form the Confederacy.

1861 Confederate forces attack Fort Sumter, initiating the American Civil War.

1862–3 Issues two presidential proclamations freeing slaves in all territory currently controlled by the Confederacy.

1863 Delivers his 'Gettysburg Address', memorializing this Union victory.

1864 Wins second term as president.

1865 Shot (14 April) by John Wilkes Booth, a Southern sympathizer, and dies the next morning. In December, the US Constitution's 13th Amendment is ratified, abolishing slavery throughout the country.

THE GETTYSBURG ADDRESS

LINCOLN'S BRIEF GETTYSBURG ADDRESS, of 19 November 1863, was made at the height of the civil war. Ostensibly a memorial to the dead of the Battle of Gettysburg, Pennsylvania (1–3 July), it outlasted its immediate context to became a foundational text of American self-identity:

Four score and seven years ago our fathers brought forth on this continent a new nation, conceived in Liberty, and dedicated to the proposition that all men are created equal.

Now we are engaged in a great civil war, testing whether that nation, or any nation, so conceived and so dedicated, can long endure. We are met on a great battlefield of that war. We have come to dedicate a portion of that field, as a final resting place for those who here gave their lives that that nation might live. It is altogether fitting and proper that we should do this.

But, in a larger sense, we can not dedicate – we can not consecrate – we can not hallow – this ground. The brave men, living and dead, who struggled here, have consecrated it, far above our poor power to add or detract. The world will little note, nor long remember what we say here, but it can never forget what they did here. It is for us the living, rather, to be dedicated here to the unfinished work which they who fought here have thus far so nobly advanced. It is rather for us to be here dedicated to the great task remaining before us – that from these honored dead we take increased devotion to that cause for which they gave the last full measure of devotion – that we here highly resolve that these dead shall not have died in vain – that this nation, under God, shall have a new birth of freedom – and that government of the people, by the people, for the people, shall not perish from the earth.

Lincoln was always keen to get involved, spending hours reading dispatches from his generals. He frequently visited battle sites, and seemed fascinated by scenes of war. Nor was he afraid of decisive action: he used his war powers to proclaim a blockade, to suspend legal limitations of *habeas corpus* and to imprison 18,000 suspected Confederate sympathizers.

Lincoln's assassination was immediately recognized as an irreparable loss. He became the first president to lie in state, and thousands lined the route as his body was carried by train in a grand funeral procession through several US states on its way back to Illinois, where he was buried in Oak Ridge Cemetery, Springfield. In 1874 his 177-foot long granite tomb, surmounted by large bronze statues, was finally completed. Yet in the face of repeated attempts to steal Lincoln's body and hold it for ransom, in 1901 his son Robert Todd Lincoln had the late president reinterred at the site encased in thick concrete.

Lincoln would have doubtless made an excellent peacetime president. Unfortunately, his successor was not cast in the same mould. Andrew Johnson (1808–75) had been selected as Lincoln's running mate largely because he was that rare animal, a pro-war and anti-secession Southern Democrat. In 1861 he had been the only Southern Senator (representing Tennessee) who had not joined the Confederate cause. After 1865, his former Democrat allies in the South never let him forget it. Nor did he cut an impressive figure at the time of his election: blind drunk at Lincoln's presidential inauguration, his speech to the assembled Senate was rambling and incoherent. Lincoln warned his aides 'Do not let Johnson speak outside', and next day the Senate voted the chamber as an alcohol-free zone.

Johnson was saved from assassination on 14 April only by the cowardice of his nominated assassin, George Atzerodt. Johnson never escaped from accusations that he, as a Southerner, had been complicit in Lincoln's murder, and Congress forbade him to sack any of his Cabinet. The first of two attempts to impeach him occurred in 1867, making him the first US president to be humiliated in this fashion, and the second attempt failed to enact impeachment by only one vote. Finally, his party brusquely discarded Johnson for the 1868 presidential election, and he lived the rest of his life in ignominy in Tennessee.

Had Abraham Lincoln survived to serve his complete second term ... that remains one of the great 'what-ifs' of history.

ALEXANDER II

1818–1881, TSAR OF RUSSIA

ASSASSIN	Ignacy Hryniewiecki
DATE	13 March 1881
PLACE	St Petersburg, Russia

The history of the Romanov tsars of Russia did not have to end in a dank cellar in Ekaterinburg in July 1918. In the second half of the 19th century, one ruler seized the chance to inaugurate genuine reforms of Russia's ossified institutions. On the eve of the American Civil War – and two years before Abraham Lincoln's own Emancipation Act – Tsar Alexander II freed all of Russia's millions of serfs at the stroke of his pen. Other profound reforms followed. Russia seemed as if it could finally liberate itself from its medieval shackles, and truly embrace the modern era.

Inevitably, for many the pace of change was frustratingly slow. At the same time, the agent of change – however promising the reforms he proposed – was still an autocratic sovereign. In the event, lifting the lid on Russia's long-suppressed freedoms merely prompted the contents to boil over. On 13 March 1881 (1 March, Old Style Russian calendar), Alexander II was assassinated by a revolutionary suicide bomber – a savage means of execution that is by no means a peculiarly 21st-century phenomenon. Russia was plunged back into reaction, and the foundations were soon laid for the tragic events of 1917–18.

'I did more for the Russian serf ... than America did for the negro slave'

Alexander, in 1879, comparing himself favourably to Abraham Lincoln

Any reform of Russia seemed an impossibility in 1855, the year in which Alexander came to the throne. His father and predecessor, the repressive Nicholas I, had turned Russia into the policeman of Europe, and his own territories into little more than a police state. Personal and official censorship was rife, and criticism of the authorities was regarded as a serious offence. Any semblance of protest was crushed with extreme vigour.

Young Alexander soon showed he was very different from his stolid, reactionary father. To the horror of the martial Nicholas, his eldest son showed no love of soldiering. Instead, Alexander preferred parties and patronizing the arts – a far cry from the frigid reception given to artistic innovation and achievement by his father's philistine regime.

Alexander's first actions on ascending the throne in 1855 demonstrated his distaste for military adventures. Russia was still mired in the Crimean War, which had reached a stalemate outside the fortress-city of Sebastopol. Alexander soon extricated his country from this meaningless conflict, achieving peace with honour and ensuring that his exhausted opponents, Britain, France and Turkey, gained little of worth.

With the war successfully ended, Alexander embarked on what was, for Russia, an astonishing sequence of political and social reforms. His first goal was to apply Western standards of commercial development to the nation's backward approach to business. The Russian economy was liberalized, and – for the first time in Russia's long history – privately financed companies and initiatives were actively encouraged. Twenty years after Western Europe and North America had begun to build their railway networks, Alexander commenced his own vast programme of railway construction. (His model was, admittedly, more that of Second Empire France or Hohenzollern Prussia than Victorian Britain or Post-bellum America: a large and efficient railway system would, he reasoned, be able to move troops around his vast country with relative ease.)

SERFDOM

THE ORIGINS OF SERFDOM IN RUSSIA stretch back to the 11th century, but the dependent status of peasants was legally defined only in 1497, in a law that restricted their mobility and emphasized that they were merely the chattels of their landowner. In the 17th century some serfs were given their own lands, but once again they were forbidden to travel. In 1723 Peter the Great transmuted household slaves into house serfs, but the status of serfs themselves remained unchanged.

From the end of the 17th century, areas of Russia were periodically paralysed by serf rebellions. All were savagely quashed, although some serfs did manage to escape to Poland (before its dismemberment in 1795) or to the Cossack lands in the south of the country.

By the mid-19th century, serfs composed roughly a third of the population of the Russian Empire. (According to the census of 1857, the number of private serfs stood at 23.1 million, out of a Russian population of 62.5 million.) The institution was abolished in the Russian Baltic provinces, but not in the rest of the empire. Yet serfdom was actually harming Russian agriculture: yields remained low throughout most of the 19th century. Thus Alexander II's decree of 1861 had an eminently practical result. Former serfs now had a genuine stake in their own land, and an incentive to improve their lot.

Alexander was happy to borrow from any international source. The administration of the army and navy was modernized in 1874, using Edward Cardwell's British Army reforms of 1870 as its starting-point. The judiciary was reformed in 1864, on the Napoleonic model. Local government was dramatically overhauled in the manner of Western European nations in the 1860s, with locally elected assemblies gaining restricted rights of taxation. Police activity was curbed and centrally controlled, and capital punishment abolished.

Alexander's greatest achievement was the ending of the institution that, to the rest of the world, symbolized Russia's endemic conservatism: serfdom. The first sign of a thaw came with Alexander's encouraging response to his Lithuanian nobles, who had authorized the formation of committees 'for ameliorating the condition of the peasants'. The tsar then distributed a circular to the provincial governors of European Russia, holding up the Lithuanian landowners as a model and suggesting that others might like to follow their lead. As a result, emancipation committees were formed all over Western Russia and its satellites. Finally, on 3 March 1861, on the sixth anniversary of his accession, Alexander signed the emancipation law freeing the serfs.

Alexander's ground-breaking reforms inevitably met with protests from both Left and Right. What is particularly impressive about his character is that repeated assassination attempts throughout his reign – the first came as early as 1866 – did not deter him from his reformist programme. Nor did the tsar shrink from military intervention where it was politically advantageous. The 'Monument to the Tsar Liberator' in Sofia commemorates Alexander II's decisive role in the part-liberation of Bulgaria from Ottoman rule during the brief, one-sided Russo-Turkish War of 1877–8.

Alexander's liberalism did not, however, extend to all the territories in the Russian Empire. Poland and Lithuania were expressly excluded from his reforms, and Alexander made it clear that autonomous rule in these states would remain a pipe-dream. The Polish 'January Uprising' of 1863–4 was savagely suppressed: thousands of Poles were executed, and tens of thousands deported to Siberia. Martial law was imposed in Lithuania, lasting from 1863 until the First World War, while native languages were banned in all the western lands. (The Polish language was banned, in both oral and written form, from everywhere except the notional Congress, where it was allowed in private conversations only.)

While dissent in Poland, Lithuania, Belarus and the Ukraine was ruthlessly expunged, however, Alexander became strangely sympathetic to the nationalist cause in what was then known as the Grand Duchy of Finland. In 1863 he re-established the Diet of Finland,

Alexander in brief

1818 Born the son of Tsar Nicholas I.

1855 Accedes to Russian throne and begins his Western-influenced 'Great Reforms'. Also permits greater freedom of conscience, political expression and worship.

1856 Ends serfdom via the Act of Emancipation, and negotiates end to the Crimean War.

1863–4 Puts down a rebellion in Poland.

1864 Adopts a French-based legal system and overhauls local government and education.

1866 Escapes (narrowly) the first of several assassination attempts, encouraging a clampdown on revolutionary politics and nationalist aspirations within the western empire.

1874 Supports British-style military reforms.

1877–8 Takes Russia to war with the Ottoman Empire, resulting in limited gains at the international Congress of Berlin (but including the liberation of Slavic Bulgaria).

1880 Prepares to announce modest constitutional reforms.

1881 Assassinated (13 March) by 'The People's Will' plotters, who have tried before.

encouraged the use of Finnish as a national language for all classes (it had previously been regarded largely as a peasant tongue) and permitted the reintroduction of Finland's own currency, the *markka*. In 1864, while Poles were denouncing Alexander's ruthless attempts to eradicate expressions of Polish nationhood, the Finns were erecting a monument to Alexander 'The Liberator' in Helsinki.

The Finns' adulation was not, however, matched by the reactions to the reign of many of the tsar's more disenchanted subjects. As his rule progressed, Alexander grew used to assassination attempts. On 4 April 1866 one Dmitry Karakzov attempted to shoot him in St Petersburg. On the morning of 20 April 1879, Alexander Soloviev shot at the fleeing tsar five times, but missed. In December 1879, a radical group calling themselves 'Narodnaya Volya' ('The People's Will') blew up the railway line between Livadia and Moscow – but missed the tsar's train. On the evening of 5 February 1880 the same revolutionaries set off a charge under the dining room of the Winter Palace. The resultant explosion killed or injured 67 people, mainly guards, but Alexander himself was safe: late for dinner, he had not yet arrived.

The last of Alexander's nine lives expired on 13 March 1881. Even then, it seemed at first as if the tsar had survived yet another attack. A bomb was thrown at his bullet-proof carriage while it was travelling in the centre of St Petersburg, but, while several bystanders were injured, the tsar emerged unharmed. This time, though, the revolutionaries had a backup plan: a suicide bomber carrying hand-made grenades immediately assaulted the shaken tsar. The assassin was, predictably, a Pole: Ignacy Hryniewiecki, from Bobrujsk (now Babryusk in Belarus). Hryniewiecki died instantly; Alexander lingered for a few hours.

Hryniewiecki's fellow-plotters were soon rounded up, tried and hanged. More seriously, the reaction to the assassination dissolved any prospect of reform. The Russian grip on Poland was tightened, and thousands of Jews were expelled from Russia – for no good reason, other than the pronounced anti-semitism of the new tsar, Alexander III. (Many of the Russian Jews, together with Russian and Polish radicals, settled happily in East London.) Almost all of Alexander II's reforms, except his abolition of serfdom, were reversed by this boorish, brusque and innately conservative second son. Alexander II's plans for a genuinely representative assembly – completed the day before he was assassinated – were thrown away. Such an assembly would not be convened until 1917; and by then, it was already too late.

James GARFIELD

1831–1881, 20TH PRESIDENT OF THE UNITED STATES

ASSASSIN Charles Guiteau
DATE 2 July 1881 (died 19 September)
PLACE Elberon, New Jersey, USA

James Abram Garfield has a feeble claim to history: his presidential term, at six months and fifteen days, was the second shortest in US history. (The shortest was that of William Henry Harrison, who died in 1841 after standing in the freezing rain for two hours to deliver his inaugural address.) Garfield was also the second American president to be assassinated, after Lincoln. However, he was unsurpassed at one thing: the canny ability to forge political advancement in even the most unlikely of circumstances.

Garfield was born in Orange Township (now Moreland Hills) in Ohio, in the proverbial log cabin – a testimony to his modest beginnings, and now open to the public. His father died in 1833, when he was only 18 months old, and he grew up in poverty, cared for by his mother and an uncle. Yet from an early age he showed great intellectual promise. In 1856 he graduated from Williams College in Massachusetts, and then taught classics at the Eclectic Institute (later Hiram College) in Hiram, Ohio, where he subsequently became its president. Here he indulged in the traditional academic pastime of marrying one of his former students, one Lucretia Randolph, in 1858. However, the fiscal rewards of academia were not sufficient for a man of Garfield's ambitions and, looking to enter politics, he took the tried-and-trusted route of training as a lawyer before seeking election as a State Senator (for Ohio) in 1859.

Garfield later portrayed himself as a civil-war hero, but in truth his wartime service was somewhat inglorious. He was a protégé of the powerful secretary of the treasury, Salmon P. Chase, and he certainly rose to eminent military positions of responsibility. Having enlisted in the Union Army, he was made Colonel of the 42nd Ohio Volunteer Infantry in 1861;

'From the tow path to the White House'

Garfield's autobiographical campaign slogan in 1880

but his one minor victory, at Middle Creek, Kentucky, in January 1862, was marked by his failure to exploit his undoubted advantage as the Confederates withdrew. Later he was promoted to brigadier-general, in which capacity he served General William Rosecrans's Army of the Cumberland as chief of staff. However, Rosecrans found Garfield's performance indecisive and lacklustre, and, faced with defeat on the Chickamauga by General James Longstreet's Confederates, he was happy for Garfield to act as glorified messenger to the neighbouring Union forces rather than to direct the withdrawal as he should have done.

After Chickamauga, Garfield sensibly re-entered politics, and got himself elected to the US House of Representatives – and, thanks to his contacts in Washington, simultaneously but inexplicably promoted to the rank of major-general. In the immediate postwar period he posed as one of the most hawkish Republicans. He survived the financial scandal of 1872, whereby Congressmen were offered cheap shares by the Crédit Mobilier company in return for federal subsidies: at one point it threatened to engulf President Grant's vastly corrupt administration. Garfield then went on to become Leader of the House in 1876. In this capacity he was instrumental in awarding the disputed presidential election of 1876 to the Republican candidate, Rutherford Hayes. As a key member of the special electoral commission, he transferred a crucial 22 electoral votes to a grateful Hayes.

In 1880 Garfield was chosen as a replacement Senator for the empty Ohio seat, and he used this as a platform to challenge for the presidential nomination. Few took his ambition seriously at the start of the Republican Convention; indeed, Garfield himself declared that

THE BATTLE OF CHICKAMAUGA

JAMES GARFIELD'S ALLEGED MOMENT of military glory came at one of the lowest points in the fortunes of the Union during the American Civil War. The Battle of Chickamauga (18–20 September 1863) was a costly defeat for Abraham Lincoln's forces – the most significant Union defeat so far – and it seemed to mark the end of the Union campaigns in the west.

General Rosecrans aimed to force the Confederates, led by Braxton Bragg, out of Chattanooga by threatening their supply lines to the south. However, after he was reinforced with troops arriving from Virginia under James Longstreet, Bragg unexpectedly advanced on the disorganized Union Corps from their supply base at Chattanooga.

The Union forces began to retreat, carrying the hapless Rosecrans along with them. Only General Thomas stood firm – a resolution that earned him the soubriquet 'The Rock of Chickamauga', and which saved the Union army from complete disaster. Bragg's army, however, was in no condition to pursue the fleeing Union forces. Bragg had won, but he had lost 18,454 men to the Union's 16,170.

Rosecrans, who had already dismissed Garfield, was himself relieved of command after the battle. His replacement was one Ulysses S. Grant, a leader of an entirely different calibre.

he had come there to support John Sherman's nomination. However, his wily machinations and studied patience as the unexpected 'dark horse' candidate proved ultimately successful, and he was finally nominated on the Convention's 36th ballot.

After this astonishing victory, the subsequent election proved comparatively easy. Garfield defeated the Democratic Party candidate Winfield Scott Hancock – a genuinely distinguished former Union Army general, the hero of the Battle of Gettysburg, whose civil-war exploits deserve to be better known – by 214 electoral votes to 155. It was a margin that belied the closeness of the popular vote, but it was a result that testified to Garfield's manipulatory political skills.

Garfield now seemed to have the world at his feet. He appeared to be the consummate politician. A man of moderate ability and undistinguished, even ugly, appearance, he had given his mediocre war record the lustre of martial valour and had barnstormed his way from State Senate to the House of Representatives, and from the US Senate to the White House in a mere 22 years. But no amount of clever political posturing could stop an assassin's bullet.

Charles Guiteau was a disappointed office-seeker and a religious extremist, who declared his philosophy to be 'Bible Communism' and his employer as 'Jesus Christ & Co'. During the 1880 election campaign, he made a nuisance of himself at New York's Republican headquarters. He sought the post of US Consul in France, a position for which he had no qualifications whatsoever. Garfield had no time for him at all, but Guiteau was befriended by Garfield's vapid, gluttonous running mate, Chester A. Arthur. Eventually Guiteau reasoned that the best way to gain advancement was to kill Garfield and thereby make Arthur president.

Guiteau was obsessively thorough. He bought a gun with a pearl handle, since he reasoned this would look nicer in the museum display that would inevitably house it. He visited the principal jail in Washington, D.C., to check it was sufficiently comfortable. And he practised marksmanship constantly, in woods not far from the White House.

In those days of lax security – and with the authorities seemingly unmindful of Lincoln's assassination 16 years before – Guiteau had many chances to shoot the president. On one occasion he held his fire because Mrs Garfield was also present, and he didn't want to shock her. Finally, at 9.30 a.m. on 2 July 1881, he encountered the president on his way to a Williams College reunion, at Washington's Sixth Street Station (a site that is now occupied by the National Gallery of Art). Guiteau shot Garfield in the back, announcing that 'I am a Stalwart of the Stalwarts!' (the conservative 'Stalwart' faction was bitterly opposed to

Garfield in brief

1831 Born on a poor farm in Cuyahoga county, Ohio.

1840s Works as farm labourer and drives canal boats. Attends Western Reserve Eclectic Institute (Hiram College), at which he later teaches Classics.

1856 Graduates from Williams College, Massachusetts.

1857 Appointed President of Hiram College.

1859 Elected to the Ohio State Senate as a Republican.

1861–3 Civil war military experience as an officer, but resigns command for politics.

1862–80 Serves as an Ohio Congressman in the US House of Representatives for 9 terms, where he opposes free trade but supports Reconstruction in the defeated South.

1880 Elected to the US Senate. Emerges to win the Republican nomination and then, narrowly, the US presidency.

1881 Shot in the back (2 July) and dies 2 months later (19 Sept.).

Garfield's more moderate 'Half Breed' followers) and that 'I did it and I want to be arrested!' His subsequent claim that 'Arthur is president now' encouraged many to believe that Vice-President Arthur had indeed been behind the crime, a claim that appears to have upset Arthur but which has never been entirely disproved.

Garfield was still conscious as he left the station. One bullet had gone through his shoulder and had exited from his back, just missing an artery; the second bullet had lodged in his chest and could not be found. Alexander Graham Bell subsequently devised a metal detector in an attempt to find the bullet, but the metal bedframe Garfield was lying on made the instrument malfunction. Meanwhile, the doctors attending the president probed clumsily with unwashed fingers for the missing bullet. One physician actually managed to puncture Garfield's liver. As a result of these unhelpful ministrations the president developed a serious wound infection, which weakened his heart and immune system, causing bronchial pneumonia and his eventual death.

In his last days Garfield's doctors moved him, unnecessarily, to the seaside town of Elberon, New Jersey, in the hope that the sea air would aid his recuperation. In the event, however, their unsterilized interventions ensured that the president died of a massive heart attack at 10.35 p.m. on 19 September 1881. It is highly likely that he would have survived but for the appallingly amateur fumblings of his physicians.

Guiteau was found guilty of assassinating Garfield, despite his lawyers claiming he was insane and despite Guiteau's own (wholly justifiable) insistence that incompetent medical care had really killed the president. The assassin was executed by hanging on 30 June 1882, in Washington, D.C.

Chester Arthur, nervous lest the blame for the assassination be heaped on his head, took care to be sworn in as president only after Garfield's death. His subsequent administration was one of the most corrupt and directionless in US history, with the party-loving president preferring to indulge in vast dinners and the company of young women rather than to direct policy. As he defiantly declared, 'I am President of the United States, but my private life is nobody's damned business.'

Garfield, meanwhile, had been buried in a vast, neo-Norman mausoleum in Lakeview Cemetery in Cleveland, Ohio, and in 1887 was commemorated in Washington by the unveiling of the striking James A. Garfield Monument. (His former home in Menton, Ohio, is also now maintained by the National Park Service.) Shortly before the monument's completion, President Arthur's potentially incriminating personal papers were posthumously burned, at Arthur's express request. We will never know what damning evidence went up in smoke.

Lord Frederick
CAVENDISH

1836–1882, CHIEF SECRETARY OF IRELAND

ASSASSINS Joe Brady, Tim Kelly and other 'Invincibles'
DATE 6 May 1882
PLACE Dublin, Ireland

On 6 May 1882, the British Viceroy of Ireland, Earl Spencer, was expecting two guests for dinner at his handsome, late-Georgian vice-regal lodge in Phoenix Park, Dublin: his new chief secretary, Lord Frederick Cavendish, and the under-secretary, Thomas Burke. It was Cavendish's first day in office, but he had already met Spencer to discuss his governmental brief and the problems besetting Prime Minister Gladstone's liberal Irish policy. Gladstone had yet to declare for Irish Home Rule and he was still uncertain how to deal with the rising, and increasingly articulate, tide of Irish nationalism. When he did announce his support for this most divisive of issues, it was to split the Liberal Party irrevocably in 1886.

Cavendish was a typical second son of an English aristocratic family. He was constantly in the shadow of his elder brother, who would inherit the family title, and little was expected of Frederick except a sober and industrious career in public service. This he had duly delivered; only in the dramatic manner of his death did he briefly eclipse his elder brother's far brighter star.

Cavendish's father was the 8th Duke of Devonshire; his elder brother was the Marquess of Hartington, who was not only the brilliant heir to the dukedom but also widely tipped as Gladstone's successor at the helm of the Liberal Party. Frederick Cavendish, though, had none of his brother's brilliance and dash, being regarded as unexceptional and plodding.

'Nihilism has invaded Ireland'

The pro-Irish *Boston Globe*'s verdict on the Phoenix Park murders, 7 May 1882

However, thanks to his brother's pre-eminence and his own, artful marriage to Gladstone's niece, Lucy, he found a moderately senior government position far away from Westminster, where he could perhaps do some good and would likely come to little harm.

As he looked out of the lodge window that summer evening in 1882, Earl Spencer saw a park full of early-evening activity, with strollers, young couples and cyclists criss-crossing over the lawns and a polo match taking place beyond. He also glimpsed what (he later declared) he took to be a group of scuffling drunks. Even the passing cyclists in the park did not pay the disturbance much attention. Yet the kerfuffle was in fact Spencer's dinner guests being brutally murdered by a gang of seven men.

The assassins were members of an extreme Irish nationalist sect calling themselves 'The Invincibles'. Their target was not actually Cavendish – he had arrived in Ireland only two days previously, and the Invincibles had no idea who he was – but his assistant, Permanent Under-Secretary Thomas Henry Burke. The scion of an old, Catholic Irish family, Burke, though only a civil servant, was considered a traitor to his country by the radical nationalists. Their anger at his alleged betrayal of Ireland was demonstrated by the savage way in which they performed their assassination: the two government officials were not merely stabbed to death, but were also slashed across their bodies, their throats cut with surgical knives in a final, horrifying *coup de grâce*.

Spencer was, naturally, deeply shocked by the Phoenix Park murders. Gladstone, too, was extremely upset when he learned of the affair: he had regarded the genial and unthreatening Cavendish almost as a son and had often stayed with him and his wife when he was in London. Indeed, the whole nation seemed devastated, with every national and regional newspaper demanding instant retribution.

Five of the assassins – Thomas Caffrey, Daniel Curley, Joe Brady, Tim Kelly and Michael Fagan – were hanged a year later, and other Invincibles were imprisoned. This was largely thanks to the evidence of two conspirators: James Carey, who had come under suspicion as early as July 1882, and Michael Kavanagh, who helped some of the assassins flee the park. A pariah in the more extreme Irish nationalist circles for turning queen's evidence, Carey was later smuggled under the name 'Power' to South Africa by the grateful British authorities. However, he was not particularly circumspect about his real identity, and while sailing from Cape Town to Durban on board the *Melrose* he was murdered by one Patrick O'Donnell – who had himself been an Invincible – and unceremoniously tossed overboard. The luckless O'Donnell was shipped back to England, tried, and hanged, becoming in the eyes of some nationalists a martyr to the cause. A memorial was erected to him in Glaslevin Cemetery, Dublin, paid for by sympathizers in New York.

The brutal double assassination of Cavendish and Burke had the effect, though, of uniting British and much of Irish (and Irish American) opinion against the more extreme forms of Irish nationalism. For a while it seemed that the cause of Irish independence, even of Irish Home Rule, would be irredeemably lost. But Gladstone was adamant that his liberal policy towards Ireland would not be stopped in its tracks. He assured Cavendish's widow that her husband's death 'will not be in vain'. She subsequently wrote in her diary that 'there fell a bright ray of hope, and I saw in a vision Ireland at peace, and my darling's life blood accepted as a sacrifice for Christ's sake, to help bring this to pass.'

Cavendish was buried at the family home of Chatsworth, Derbyshire, on 11 May 1883. Over 30,000 attended the funeral, including almost half of the House of Commons. His 'martyrdom' became something of a cult in later years, before the two tragic deaths of Cavendish and Burke (the latter tended to be forgotten in all the memorializing and commemoration) were eclipsed by the carnage of the First World War.

The Phoenix Park tragedy, though, had serious ramifications. For one thing, it spurred Cavendish's brother, the Marquess of Hartington, into leadership of the breakaway 'Liberal Unionists', opposed to Home Rule. And the events particularly threatened the position and future career of the shining hope of the parliamentary Irish Nationalists, Charles Stewart Parnell. He immediately offered to resign from Parliament in protest at what he called 'these vile murders', an offer turned down (probably as he expected) by Gladstone. The affair, however, returned to haunt Parnell. In the same month (April 1886) as Gladstone introduced his Irish Home Rule Bill into Parliament, the London *Times*, already steadfastly opposed to Home Rule, was offered what purported to be a letter from Parnell regretting 'the accident of Lord F. Cavendish's death' but stating that 'Burke got no more than his desserts'. After issuing a series of veiled references, the *Times* launched what it believed to be its devastating scoop on 18 April 1887, accusing Parnell of condoning the murder of Burke if not of Cavendish. Parliament instantly set up a Special Commission of Enquiry to investigate the evidence. After interviewing 445 witnesses and asking 150,000 questions,

Cavendish in brief

1836 Born at Compton House, Eastbourne, the second son of the 7th Duke of Devonshire.

1855–8 Attends Trinity College, Cambridge, graduating with BA.

1859–64 Works as Lord Granville's private secretary.

1864 Marries Lucy Caroline Lyttleton, a niece of Liberal Party leader W.E. Gladstone.

1865–82 Serves as a Liberal MP for the West Riding of Yorkshire.

1872–3 Private secretary to Gladstone.

1880–2 Financial secretary to the treasury.

1882 Accepts the position of chief secretary for Ireland and travels to Dublin. Two days later, he and Under-Secretary Thomas Burke are assassinated by republican extremists.

THE FENIANS

THE TERM 'FENIAN' HAS BEEN USED loosely since the mid-19th century to denote Irish nationalists. Originally, though, the Fenians were a secret republican organization, founded by James Stephens in 1858 and dedicated to fomenting armed revolt against the British.

From its early years, the Irish-American community provided valuable funds for the Fenians across the Atlantic. The American chapter of the Fenian movement, powerful until the middle of the 20th century, was alternatively called the Irish Republican Brotherhood, or IRB. The British goverment managed to arrest several leading Fenians in the 1860s, and the movement was further damaged by divisions over tactics.

Internecine squabbles in Ireland meant that by 1865 there were two Fenian Brotherhoods. And, after 1916, the Irish use of the term 'Fenian' became less precise, as the IRA (Irish Republican Army) won increasing support.

the commission discovered that the letter had been forged by an embittered Irish journalist named Richard Piggott. Parnell was cleared unconditionally; Piggott fled to Paris and committed suicide.

Parnell was now a national hero in both Britain and Ireland. The Liberal MPs rose to applaud him when he next appeared in the House of Commons; Earl Spencer publicly shook hands with him in Dublin; he was made a lifelong member of the Liberal Club; and ladies of all ages feted the handsome, 42-year-old Irish champion. The auguries seemed excellent for Irish Home Rule, with Parnell, the acceptable face of moderate Irish reform, likely to be installed as the island's first premier.

Yet the following year Parnell's career, and all hopes of Irish Home Rule, came crashing down in ruins. In December 1889 the MP for Galway, the bankrupt adventurer Captain William O'Shea, sued for divorce, naming Parnell as his correspondent. Parnell and O'Shea's wife Kitty had effectively lived as man and wife for years – all with the connivance of O'Shea, whom Parnell had bought off by using his personal prestige to help the hellraising captain win his parliamentary seat. In this hypocritical age, Parnell was ruined. Gladstone had no choice but to ask him to resign from the leadership of the Irish Nationalists. (Gladstone also gave credence to rumours that the anti-Home Rule Liberals, led by Joseph Chamberlain, had originally persuaded O'Shea to launch his divorce petition.) Parnell then rounded on Gladstone, denouncing his conception of Home Rule as a tepid half-measure, and thereby sunk the Home Rule lobby entirely.

Gladstone persevered with another Home Rule Bill in 1893, but it was summarily rejected by the House of Lords. Parnell died, aged only 45, worn out and crushed (though now finally married to Kitty) at Kitty's side in their Brighton home in October 1891.

Lord Frederick Cavendish is barely remembered today, especially in an age in which Victorian history is as remote to most school children as the Assyrian Empire. He is not even remembered in Phoenix Park. Only his monument at Chatsworth survives to tell us of his family's great loss.

ELISABETH
of Austria

1837–1898, EMPRESS OF AUSTRIA-HUNGARY

ASSASSIN	Luigi Lucheni
DATE	10 September 1898
PLACE	Geneva, Switzerland

Somehow, the bizarre and violent end of Elisabeth, Empress of Austria-Hungary, was almost predictable. Walking along the placid promenade of Lake Geneva on a sunny autumn day in 1898, about to board a steamship for Montreux with her Hungarian lady-in-waiting, the empress was suddenly stabbed to death by a deranged anarchist armed only with a small file. Elisabeth of Austria's last words were 'What happened to me?' – a fitting epitaph for a life that seemed constantly trapped in an alien world, a world she had always refused to accept.

The subsequent international cult that grew around Empress 'Sisi' is comparable to the immense outpouring of public grief and the posthumous reputations sustained by two British Princesses of Wales of which much had been hoped: Charlotte, the only legitimate child of George IV, in 1817, and Diana, in 1997. Indeed, the similarities between Sisi's character and behaviour and the life of Diana, Princess of Wales, are telling.

Elisabeth Amalie Eugenie, daughter of the Duke of Bavaria, was born in Munich on Christmas Eve, 1837. From an early age she was called 'Sisi' by family and friends – a nickname that has since been re-used by her legions of admirers. Aged only 16, she caught the eye of her 23-year-old cousin, Franz Josef, who had already been emperor of Austria for five years. Her parents had deliberately journeyed to the Austrian resort of Bad Ischl in order to thrust their eldest daughter, Helene, at the unmarried young emperor. In the event, it was the stunningly beautiful Elisabeth to whom Franz Josef was drawn. Persuaded by her ambitious parents that the marriage would be in her (and Bavaria's) best interests – it would, after all, link the South German dukedom closely with its Catholic neighbour, rather than with the aggressive, martial Prussians to the north – she wed the emperor on 24 April 1854.

'What happened to me?'

Elisabeth's incredulous question on being fatally attacked, 1898

The marriage had a clear political agenda. The Austrian Empire now seemed firmly anchored to Bavaria, setting the stage for Austria to extend her influence – already established by the German Confederation of 1815 – over the rest of German-speaking Europe, and at the expense of Protestant Prussia. To Elisabeth, however, the political gains of the wedding were far outweighed by her personal discomfort. She later wrote that, from the time of her marriage, her life had been one of misery and boredom.

Elisabeth was a spoilt child, immensely vain and self-absorbed. As such, she found little in common with her diligent husband, to whom the honour of serving his country was paramount. She made little effort to accommodate herself to the imperial court she had willingly married into, and began to display wilful, almost unbalanced behaviour. She soon tired of her dutiful but dull emperor. Having (she thought) secured the succession by rapidly giving birth to three children, including an imperial heir – Sophie in 1855, Gisela in 1856 and Crown Prince Rudolf in 1858 – she rarely visited the marital bed thereafter. (Ten years later she gave birth to another daughter, Marie Valerie, but rumours quickly spread that this was not the emperor's child.) Nor did she take any interest in bringing up her children, happily leaving them to be raised by her mother-in-law.

Mental instability had been a prominent characteristic in the Wittelsbach family, the ruling house of Bavaria, and by 1860 Elisabeth was showing signs of having inherited this most distressing of family traits. It is instructive that the Wittelsbach relative who was closest to her was her cousin, Ludwig II, the 'Mad King' of Bavaria. She nicknamed him her 'eagle'; to him, Empress Elizabeth was his 'seagull'.

Restless and petulant, Elisabeth stayed in Vienna as seldom as possible. She was constantly abroad, visiting places as varied as Madeira, Britain and Corfu, where she built her own castle. She never travelled with her children but was usually in the company of her Hungarian ladies-in-waiting, and occasionally a lover. (Her many lovers included George Middleton, a Scottish officer who was probably the father of Clementine, later the wife of Winston Churchill.)

Considered one of the most beautiful women in the world, Elisabeth was obsessive about maintaining her looks and her hourglass figure. In this context she more resembles a modern celebrity than a 19th-century queen. At 5 feet 8 inches, she was unusually tall for women of the time and, even after giving birth to three children, she went to extreme lengths to preserve her legendary 20-inch waist. Accordingly, she spent hours a day exercising, preferably in the gym or on horseback: an extremely skilled horsewoman, she was back in the saddle a few weeks after the birth of each of her children. She also ate very carefully; indeed, medical historians now speculate that she suffered from that most modern of conditions, *anorexia nervosa*.

Like a temperamental diva of today, Elisabeth was particularly obsessed about her long, lustrous black hair. Arranging her coiffure took three hours each day; and woe betide the hairdresser who accidentally removed even one hair from her royal head – an occurrence that would prompt fits of anguished rage. If her hairdresser fell sick, Elisabeth simply refused to appear in public.

Elisabeth continued to see relatively little of her children. She was, though, understandably shocked by the sudden death of her only son, Rudolf, in 1889. The 31-year-old crown prince and his young, morganatic partner, Baroness Vetsera, both committed suicide at the secluded royal hunting lodge of Mayerling. This dramatic lovers' pact not only horrified Europe (and deeply shocked Rudolf's father, whose closest male heirs were now his brother, Karl Ludwig, and Karl's son, Franz Ferdinand), but also provided writers and composers with a suitably tragic theme for decades to come. However, even Rudolf's death was reinterpreted by his mother as a fashion statement: the stunning black creations that Elisabeth continued to wear from 1889 – stark contrasts to the homely mourning garb worn by Britain's Queen-Empress – fascinated all of fashionable Europe.

Elisabeth's interests embraced the cultural sphere, too. She wrote romantic poetry in the vein of Heinrich Heine, and studied ancient and modern Greek. She became an enthusiastic devotee of Homer's works, and she often quoted from Shakespeare, often referring to herself as the fairy queen Titania.

To her many admirers inside and outside the Austrian Empire, Elisabeth was indeed Titania reborn. Her subjects saw a glittering, gorgeous figure that added lustre and glamour to the dull Habsburg monarchy, a dynasty that in 1848 had seemed in danger of ignominious extinction. In this sense, Elisabeth was an enormous asset to the imperial family. What her adoring public did not see, however, were her capricious whims, her self-absorption and her carelessness.

Elisabeth's limited value as an expression of Teutonic amity was exposed in 1866. Austria's ambition to win control over the whole of Germany clashed directly with Prussia's

Elizabeth in brief

1837 Born the daughter of Duke Maximilian Joseph of Bavaria.

1853 Meets her cousin, Emperor Franz Josef of Austria.

1854 Marries Franz Josef, becoming Empress Consort of Austria, but later spends much time away from Vienna and the emperor.

1855–8 Gives birth to three children, including the imperial heir, Rudolf.

1867 Uses influence to help the passage of the Compromise creating the Dual Kingdom of Austria-Hungary, so becoming Queen of Hungary too.

1889 Crown Prince Rudolf commits suicide.

1898 Assassinated (10 Sept.) in Geneva by an opportunist anarchist.

long-cherished aim of establishing economic and political hegemony over Teutonic Europe. The two powers inevitably came to blows, and in the one-sided war of 1866 Austria's alliance with Catholic Bavaria, which Elisabeth's marriage had cemented, was shown to be of little military use. Austrian troops were annihilated by the numerically inferior Prussians at Sadowa (also known as the Battle of Königgrätz) on 3 July, and their Bavarian allies were similarly swept aside. After only seven weeks of fighting, the Peace of Prague saw Austria's German Confederation dissolved and many of its former allies forcibly annexed by Prussia. Four years later Bavaria was reluctantly incorporated into the new German Reich, which the Prussian Chancellor Bismarck and his new emperor, William (Wilhelm) I, declared in the Hall of Mirrors at Versailles.

Austria now stood humiliated and dangerously isolated, outside a Prussian-dominated Germany. Its response was to run eastwards, to its traditional Habsburg territories. Franz Josef's first postwar gesture was thus to the perennially restive Hungarians. In order to head off an incipient Hungarian revolt against the seriously weakened Austrian armies, the 'Dual Monarchy' of Austria-Hungary was declared in the *Ausgleich* ('Compromise') of 1867, a move intended to bolster support for the Habsburgs in this most crucial of their polyglot lands. Elisabeth was thus now not only Empress of Austria but also Queen of Hungary.

Typically, Elisabeth used her new position to undermine her husband's Viennese court and government. She promoted Hungarian courtiers and insisted that her attendants speak Hungarian. One of her principal lovers was the Hungarian noble Count Andrassy, who later became Franz Josef's foreign minister. However, her adoption of the Hungarian language did not extend to the championing of Hungarian liberties. As always, Elisabeth remained generally uninterested in politics. Nevertheless, Hungarians took her death particularly badly, and named several sites in her memory – notably the renowned Erzsébet híd (Elisabeth Bridge) in Budapest.

On 10 September 1898, while passing through Geneva on one of her many aimless tours, Elisabeth was stabbed to death by a young anarchist named Luigi Lucheni. It was a grim irony that she had not been Lucheni's intended victim: the anarchist had been targeting a French, Orléanist prince, but failing to find him, and encountering the Empress of Austria, he despatched her instead. Demonstrating his impeccably individualistic credentials as a lone anarchist, he later declared that 'I wanted to kill a royal. It did not matter which one.'

Elisabeth was buried in the Habsburgs' Kaisergruft (Imperial Crypt) in Vienna, a dark and grim location she would surely not have chosen herself. Her burial, though, merely signalled the start of the cult of 'Sisi', a phenomenon that, with its torrent of books, articles and mementoes, shows no signs of abating.

ANARCHISM

ELISABETH OF AUSTRIA WAS NOT the only monarch or politician to die at the hands of anarchists in the 19th and 20th centuries. However, these individual assassins were working outside the (admittedly very vague) boundaries of mainstream anarchism.

Anarchism is a philosophy that rejects any form of compulsory government and promotes its elimination. The word is derived from a Greek word meaning 'without rulers'. Nevertheless, while the first anarchist leaders, Pierre-Joseph Proudhon

(1809–65) and Mikhail Bakunin (1814–76), believed in the formation of 'spontaneous order' in society, from which organization would emerge without any central political or religious authority, they denounced the use of assassination to spark an anarchistic revolution. In their view assassination was counter-productive, or even, in Bakunin's view, counter-revolutionary. Both Proudhon and Bakunin were also strongly opposed to Marxism, which they saw simply as substituting one system of state control with another.

William McKINLEY

1843–1901, 25th PRESIDENT OF THE UNITED STATES

ASSASSIN Leo Czolgosz
DATE 6 September 1901 (died 14 September)
PLACE Buffalo, New York, USA

William McKinley had served as a Congressman and as governor of his home state, Ohio, before he became the 25th President of the United States in 1897. He did well in the civil war, rising from the humble rank of private in 1861 to 'brevet' (i.e. temporary) major by 1865. Thereafter he became a protégé of his former commanding officer, fellow-Ohioan (and 19th US president) Rutherford B. Hayes, who encouraged him to leave his law firm and run for Congress.

In the 1880s the rookie Congressman swiftly made his name as a vehement defender of protectionism, championing high tariffs against the Democrats' quixotic advocacy of free trade. The legislative result was the notorious McKinley Tariff of 1890, a statute that embodied the commercial xenophobia and international isolationism of an increasingly confident nation.

As governor and as resident, McKinley was celebrated for his manners. He took care to remember the names of everyone who came to see him, and he turned down disappointed office-seekers with a cheery phrase and a carnation for their lapel. In the words of his secretary of war, Elihu Root, 'He had a way of handling men so they thought his ideas were their own.' In contrast to his predecessors, he encouraged press coverage of his administration, building the first White House press room and feeding journalists a carefully chosen stream of favourable information. This warm relationship with the media in turn helped him to anticipate public opinion and emerging trends. (Congressman Joe Cannon, later Speaker of the House, declared that McKinley kept his ear so close to the ground 'it was full of grasshoppers'.)

'The mission of the United States is one of benevolent assimilation'

McKinley's subtle interpretation as the USA acquired former Spanish colonies, 1898

Ohio's rising star was always a friend to business. At the 1896 Republican Convention his primary benefactor, the Cleveland tycoon Marcus Alonzo Hanna, lauded McKinley as 'the advance agent of prosperity'. McKinley subsequently had the good fortune to become president just as the US economy was recovering from the depression that had followed the 1893 'Panic', which saw financial turmoil and hundreds of banks closing. Like most presidents before and since, McKinley was quick to claim credit for turning things around.

McKinley was also famously devoted to his epileptic wife, Ida. When she had one of her seizures – which was often, and frequently at state dinners and public speeches – he simply covered her face with his handkerchief, claiming that the darkness soothed her and eased her distress. Indeed, his first words after being shot were in recognition of his wife's delicate condition: 'My wife – oh … be careful how you tell her!'

McKinley's belligerent foreign policies as president, however, belied this nice-guy image. In 1898 he was largely responsible for manufacturing the Spanish–American War. He began by sending the battleship *Maine* to Havana, supposedly to protect American interests during the three-year-old Cuban Revolution. McKinley alleged that the Spanish colonial government's treatment of the rebels had 'shocked and offended the humane sensibilities of our people'; more significant, however, was his revealing admission that the revolution had 'caused enormous losses to American trade and commerce'. Having publicly emphasized America's neutrality in the dispute, McKinley then declared war on Spain when the *Maine* blew up while at anchor in Havana harbour, but he took care to pose merely as the executor of Congressional will. (The battleship was, in truth, most likely lost due to an accidental internal explosion; McKinley's administration, though, ultimately blamed a fictitious Spanish mine.) Three months later the United States had trounced the feeble Spanish forces on sea and land, a hundred-day turkey shoot that culminated in Admiral George Dewey's annihilation of the decrepit Spanish fleet at Manila Bay on 1 May. Spain's rapid capitulation brought the United States massive territorial gains: the former Spanish colonies of Puerto Rico, the Philippines and Guam. Even Cuba itself, now nominally independent, was effectively tied to Washington as a vassal state. And in the ensuing imperialist euphoria, McKinley even persuaded Congress to annex independent Hawaii and the strategically important Pacific outpost of Wake Island.

McKinley's imperial America thus took its place alongside the colonial powers of Western Europe. Two years later US troops underlined their newly won international status when the president sent a force of over 3000 troops to help quash the anti-Western 'Boxer Rebellion' in China. (The 9th and 14th US Infantry regiments are still nicknamed, respectively, the 'Manchus' and the 'Golden Dragons' in memory of this intervention.) In the aftermath of the brief action, McKinley audaciously and somewhat cynically reversed his stance on international free trade, and declared that China should henceforth have an open-door trade policy with the West. This did not, though, lead him to demolish tariff barriers in the United States.

Rapturous public endorsement of McKinley's aggressively expansionist foreign policy ensured that the president crushed his Democratic Party opponent, William Jennings Bryan, at the 1900 election. The luckless Bryan – who raised only $50,000 to spend on his election, as opposed to McKinley's war chest of $3 million – had also been the loser to McKinley four years earlier. In 1896 he had lost by the largest margin for a presidential election in 24 years; but in 1900 the gap was even wider. It seemed nothing could stop the onward progress of the man who was popularly seen as the embodiment of the brawny, nationalistic America that had just erupted into the 20th century. One brooding, immigrant anarchist, however, did just that.

On 6 September 1901 the president visited the Pan-American Exposition in Buffalo, New York. Great international exhibitions were then all the rage. Following the success of the grandfather of them all, the 1851 Great Exhibition at the purpose-built Crystal Palace in London, similar international showcases were staged in all the major cities of the West. In 1900 the Paris Exposition had helped to launch the Art Nouveau style, while the vast 'Columbian Exposition' in Chicago in 1893 established the grandiose and overbearing Beaux Arts style of classical revivalism as the preferred architectural idiom of McKinley's America.

The Buffalo Exposition was remembered, however, not for the diversity or quality of its architecture or its exhibits, but for the unnecessary manner of the president's death. On 6 September 1901, Leo Czolgosz, a friendless and deranged anarchist, shot McKinley twice

McKinley in brief

1843 Born in Niles, Ohio, the son of an industrial manager.

1861–5 Fights in US Civil War and rises to rank of 'brevet' major.

1865–77 Enters US House of Representatives as Republican Congressman for Ohio's 17th district and a strong advocate of import tariffs.

1890 The 'McKinley Tariff' is introduced. Loses House seat because of Democratic boundary changes.

1890–6 Serves two terms as governor of Ohio.

1896 Comfortably wins the Republican nomination and then the US presidency, backed by the powerful businessman M.A. Hanna.

1897 Increases US trade tariffs to their highest levels.

1898 Commits USA to war against Spain, ostensibly over Cuban independence, resulting in controversial US acquisition of Puerto Rico, Guam and the Philippines.

1900 Wins second term as president, again beating William Jennings Bryan.

1901 Shot (6 Sept.) by an anarchist in Buffalo, New York, and dies on 14 Sept.

THE SPANISH–AMERICAN WAR

THE SPANISH–AMERICAN WAR of 1898, viewed with horror by Spaniards and embarrassment by Americans ever since, was very much a one-sided affair. At the US naval victory of Manila Bay, Commodore George Dewey defeated the Spanish in a few hours for the loss of only one seaman, who died of a heart attack. On 13 August US commanders, unaware that a peace treaty had been signed between Spain and the United States the previous day, captured the city of Manila. Elsewhere in the Pacific, the Spanish island of Guam was captured without a shot: the Spanish commander was unaware that war had been declared, and came out to the Americans' ship to ask if he could borrow supplies.

In the Caribbean, the Spanish fleet was annihilated at the Battle of Santiago de Cuba on 3 July, from which only one Spanish vessel survived, by being scuttled. Two days earlier, US ground forces in Cuba had made their most famous assault of the war: 15,000 American troops, including Theodore ('Teddy') Roosevelt and his self-styled 'Rough Riders', attacked entrenched Spaniards in frontal assaults at the battles of El Caney and San Juan Hill. Thereafter, however, the US advance was halted, and America turned instead to the negotiating table. The resulting Treaty of Paris confirmed the loss to Spain of Cuba, Puerto Rico, Guam and the Philippines.

at 4.07 p.m. at point-blank range while he was viewing the exhibition. One bullet was quickly found, but the second remained hidden deep in his body. As chance would have it, a recently developed 'x-ray' machine was being exhibited at the fair; yet no-one dared to try it out on the wounded president. Had they done so, his life might have been saved. Similarly, while the Exposition's stands demonstrated countless examples of the newly developed electric light bulb, electricity had not yet been incorporated into the exhibition's temporary hospital. As a result, doctors had to use a pan to reflect sunlight onto McKinley's wounds, and they never located the second bullet.

The assassin Czolgosz was one of seven children of Russo-Polish immigrants. Brought up, ironically, in the same state as McKinley, his life was hugely different from his victim's. At the age of ten he was working at the American Steel and Wire Company in Cleveland under appalling conditions. It was an environment that not only caused much industrial unrest, but also, in Czolgosz's own case, both radicalized and unhinged him. By 1900 he had cast himself as an avenging anarchist, although regional anarchist groups (if that is not an oxymoron) disowned this strange and violent individual. Czolgosz was hugely impressed with the Italian anarchist leader, Gaetano Bresci, who on 29 July 1900 assassinated Umberto I of Italy. Such was Czolgosz's hero-worship that the gun he bought, an Iver Johnson revolver (now on public display in Buffalo), was identical to that used by Bresci, while a newspaper clipping of Bresci's act was found in Czolgosz's pocket when he was caught.

McKinley died eight days after he was shot, at 2.15 a.m. on 14 September 1901. He had eventually died from the results of physical shock, the second bullet still lodged in his body, and was buried in Canton, Ohio. Czolgosz, meanwhile, was subsequently tried and executed in the electric chair. Just to make sure fellow-travellers were not able to make use of his martyred corpse, sulphuric acid was thrown into his coffin so that the body would dissolve in a few hours.

McKinley had already been enthusiastically memorialized. In 1897 America's highest peak, 20,320 feet tall and sited in one of the most remote areas of Alaska, was named Mount McKinley. In the aftermath of his assassination, however, monuments to the fallen president sprang up all over America, from Philadelphia to California. While subsequent generations have found McKinley's unabashed imperialism somewhat uncomfortable, today he has recaptured his stature as the quintessentially bullish American president.

José CANALEJAS

1854–1912, PRIME MINISTER OF SPAIN

ASSASSIN Manuel Pardiñas
DATE 12 November 1912
PLACE Madrid, Spain

For much of the 19th century Spain was the sick man of Western Europe. The days of colonial riches and formidable, all-conquering armies were long past. Instead, the country was riven with internal divisions, which all through the 19th century threatened to erupt into coruscating, full-scale civil war. The century ended disastrously for Spain, with the United States exploiting Cuba's three-year-long struggle to shake off the Spanish yoke in order to help itself to what remained of the Spanish Empire. The result was utter, humiliating defeat for Spain in 1898, and the loss of most of her remaining colonies: Puerto Rico, Guam, the Philippines and, of course, Cuba itself.

Spain entered the 20th century looking for a new role. Early signs were encouraging: for the first time in decades, the birth rate began to overtake the death rate; industrialization (and electricity) reached the furthest parts of the country; and the cities of Barcelona and Madrid recast themselves in the exuberant architectural and design idiom of Art Nouveau style. In 1899 there was a national budget surplus for the first time in decades. Revolutionary sentiment prospered, too – particularly in the anarchist strongholds of Andalucia and the socialist-dominated province of Catalonia. A peasant army tried to take Jerez in 1892, while Córdoba was paralysed by a general strike in 1903. Industrial and nationalistic unrest appeared to be endemic.

To moderate reformers, the way to staunch revolution was to liberalize, not to repress. And few were more ardent in their championing of egalitarian interventionism than the Ferrol-born politician José Canalejas y Méndez, who in 1910 became Liberal Prime Minister of Spain.

Canalejas boasted an impeccably intellectual pedigree. Born into a wealthy railway-owner's family, he had graduated in 1871 from the University of Madrid, taken a doctorate only one year later, and by 1873 was lecturing in literature at his alma mater. His subsequent volumes embraced works on Spanish railways and a two-part history of Latin literature.

This ambitious polymath was also intrigued by politics, and, once he devoted his formidable energies to the Spanish Liberal Party, he rose quickly in its ranks. Elected deputy for Soria in 1881, he became under-secretary for the prime minister's department in 1883, minister of justice in 1888 and minister of finance in 1894. He was 'President of the Chamber' in the government of Segismundo Moret, and ultimately prime minister and leader of the Liberal Party in 1910.

Canalejas's heroes were Britain's Liberal ministers of 1906 and the programme of state-run welfare that they had introduced after their landslide election victory. He sought to rebuild Spain after the disasters of 1898 by using Prime Minister Herbert Asquith's government programme – in particular, David Lloyd George's 'People's Budget' of 1909 – as a template. State intervention was, he believed, necessary to realize social justice. Thus, state-run arbitration machinery was introduced for industrial disputes; hours and conditions were properly regulated for the first time; and workers' insurance and accident compensation were

'We are simply defending the sovereignty of the state'

Canalejas's justification of his stand on Spanish–Vatican relations, as reported by the *New York Times*, 26 June 1910

brought in. Canalejas also sought to reform the conditions of the rural poor, and he was one of the few national politicians who dared to express such humanitarian desires. At the same time, he was no pacific appeaser: he wanted a strong army, allied to a muscular foreign policy, to ensure that disasters on the scale of 1898 never happened again.

Canalejas's prime-ministerial term was to be tragically short; but he achieved much within it. He replaced the pernicious food tax, which hit the peasantry hardest, with measures that guaranteed him the lasting enmity of the wealthy: an equitable income tax, which cut deeply into the pockets of the rich, and a 'progressive' tax on urban rents. He ended the practice by which wealthier citizens could buy themselves out of military service. He overhauled local government and made it more accountable to the electorate. He was even prepared to negotiate with the Catalan nationalists, something his predecessors had never dared to do.

Canalejas's energy and boldness inevitably won him many enemies. To Spanish conservatives he was a dangerous social radical; to the anarchists he was just another vacillating politician. He was accused of substi-tuting personality for policies; certainly, his American-style national speech tours, communicating with the electorate over the heads of their elected representatives, introduced something never before seen in Spain.

The pro-military king, Alfonso XIII, welcomed Canalejas eagerly, seeing his pragmatic liberalism as a means of achieving moderate reform in Spain while protecting the monarchy's position. But Canalejas did not endear himself to the Far Right. One of his first measures in a country where the Vatican and church hierarchy held considerable power was to announce the right for non-Catholics to worship in public and to insist on enforcing laws by which all religious orders had to be state authorized. In the subsequent dispute he suspended diplomatic relations with the Vatican – a development that attracted the vitriol of conservative Catholics and the aristocratic lobby. Nevertheless, Canalejas was right: calmer conservative politicians, and the Vatican itself, came to recognize that if Canalejas's moderate reform of the relationship between church and state was not supported, far more radical figures could supplant him and sweep everything away.

Canalejas was unfortunate in having to deal with a wave of strikes, whose origins lay in the bitter industrial disputes of previous years. In 1910 he successfully negotiated an end to the Bilbao city strike. However, faced with a national general strike in 1911, he abandoned diplomacy, suspending constitutional guarantees and censoring the press. In 1912 he went even further, declaring that the threatened railway strike was illegal, and summoning the army to intervene. His patience seemingly exhausted, he was gradually moving towards more authoritarian solutions to Spain's almost intractable industrial problems.

By the middle of 1912 Canalejas was under attack from all sides. Socialists saw him as an instrument of repression and depicted him as a murderer of strikers. Right-wing Catholics viewed him with alarm as an anticlerical revolutionary. The rich loathed him for his punitive taxation system; the liberal republican reformists disowned his heavy-handed

Canalejas in brief

1854 Born in El Ferrol, Galicia, Spain, son of a railway owner.

1871 Graduates from the University of Madrid, where he later gains a doctorate and teaches literature.

1881 Elected to the Cortes General, the Spanish parliament, initially representing Soria.

1883 Appointed under-secretary to the president.

1888 Further ministerial appointments, in departments of justice and public works.

1894 Appointed finance minister under Liberal Party Prime Minister Sagasta.

1902 Becomes joint minister for agriculture and industry, again under Sagasta.

1910 Appointed prime minister on fall of Moret administration, and attempts fiscal and social reforms as well as some autonomy for Catalonia. Religious reforms cause a breach with the Vatican.

1912 Assassinated by an anarchist in Madrid (12 Nov.).

PRIMO DE RIVERA

JOSÉ CANALEJAS'S DEATH was a signal to many that only strong, authoritarian government would succeed in Spain. On 23 September 1923, a group of military officers, headed by Captain General Miguel Primo de Rivera in Barcelona, overthrew the parliamentary government and established Primo de Rivera as dictator. In an attempt to legitimize the coup, King Alfonso responded by naming him prime minister.

Primo de Rivera and the king dismissed the Spanish parliament (the Cortes Generales), censored the media, repressed separatists from the Basque provinces and Catalonia, and created a new political party – the Patriotic Union – centred on the dictator. Primo de Rivera went to Morocco, where he led a Franco-Spanish army to victory over their rebellious colonial subjects. At home, he built a modern network of roads, initiated an ambitious hydroelectric programme, improved the backward Spanish railway system, and unveiled protectionist legislation aimed at reducing foreign imports. Imitating Benito Mussolini in Italy, he forced management and labour into an uneasy partnership by replacing existing unions by a series of industrial corporations.

However, Primo de Rivera failed to address the complex minefield of desperately needed agricultural reform, and he failed to invest his personalized political party with a recognizable identity. The economy faltered in the wake of the 1929 worldwide economic crash and, with student protestors on the streets, he lost the support of the army. When the generals failed to confirm their support for his regime, he resigned on 28 January 1930 and fled to Paris, where he died from diabetes barely three months later.

intervention in industrial disputes; and even the monarchists began to believe that he would soon be unable to control the radical Left.

We will never know for certain whether Canalejas would have been able to weather this storm. On 12 November 1912 an anarchist, Manuel Pardiñas, shot Canalejas several times outside a Madrid bookshop, before turning the gun fatally on himself.

After Canalejas's death, the Liberal party split into warring factions, and Spain staggered from crisis to crisis. In 1917 the country stood on the brink of revolution as the army, the growing anti-monarchical movement and proletarian socialists all simultaneously assaulted the government. Order finally prevailed, but Spain was still a bitterly divided nation. Short, feeble administrations lasted until 1923, when Primo de Rivera took advantage of the governmental chaos to make himself dictator. Even he, however, was unable to shake Spain out of its fatalism. In 1936 the country collapsed into its horrifically bitter and violent civil war, from which it emerged as a shadow of its former self and on the periphery of European politics.

Would Canalejas have prevented the drift to civil war if he had lived? Spanish historians have speculated that he would have moved further to the Right after 1914, jettisoning constitutional barriers to becoming an enlightened *caudillo* or dictator. He might even have involved Spain in the First World War, enabling the country to benefit materially from the terms of the Treaty of Versailles (or, alternatively, bankrupting it). Salvador de Madariaga, the liberal historian, has argued that the disasters Spain experienced during the 1930s can be directly traced to Canalejas's murder, which deprived Spain of one of its few genuine statesmen and a figure who could, with the monarchy's support, have ultimately united Left and Right.

Such virtual history must ultimately remain conjecture. However, most will agree that Canalejas's senseless assassination undoubtedly hastened the coming of the Spanish Civil War.

Archduke Franz
FERDINAND

1863–1914, HEIR TO THE THRONE OF AUSTRO-HUNGARY

ASSASSIN	Gavrilo Princip
DATE	28 June 1914
PLACE	Sarajevo, Bosnia-Herzegovina

Herzegovina. The aim of the visit was a goodwill tour of a dangerously restive province, which would begin with a motorized cavalcade through the streets of the city. Franz Ferdinand and his wife, Sophie, were placed in the second car of the public procession, behind that of the commissioner of police and the Mayor of Sarajevo. And the top of the royal vehicle was rolled back in order to allow the crowds a good view of its occupants.

Bosnia-Herzegovina was then the Austro-Hungarian Empire's most southeasterly outpost. Serbian nationalists, who wished to unite the Serbian parts of Bosnia with an independent Serbia, had taken advantage of the turbulent state of Balkan politics – with two local wars in the past three years – to form a nationalistic group, the Black Hand, devoted to attaining Serbian independence by violent means. They had already attempted – unsuccessfully – to assassinate Emperor Franz Josef himself in 1911. Now, in Franz Ferdinand's state visit to Bosnia, they saw their chance to rid the world of his heir, and thereby throw the tottering Austrian Empire into disarray. What they could not predict was that their actions would unleash the most bloody war seen to that date.

The target of the conspiracy had begun life as the classic Poor Little Rich Boy. The eldest son of Archduke Karl Ludwig of Austria, who was the younger brother of Emperor Franz Josef, Franz Ferdinand became heir to the dukedom of Modena when he was aged only 12 and thereby one of the richest individuals in Europe. Typically for a wealthy young aristocrat of the time – one who at that time seemed far removed from the imperial throne – he indulged his passions for hunting and travel. However, his life suddenly lost its levity in 1889, when his cousin, Crown Prince Rudolf, committed suicide together with his mistress at his hunting lodge in Mayerling. Franz Ferdinand's father, Archduke Karl Ludwig, was now first in line to the throne of Austria-Hungary. But he was old, and all eyes were thus now on Franz Ferdinand, his eldest son, to reinvigorate the hardening arteries of Austria's shaky, polyglot empire.

> 'Don't die, don't die! Stay alive for our children!'
>
> Reputedly Franz Ferdinand's last words to his wife Sophie, according to eye-witness Count von Harrach

In his treatment of his newly important nephew, Emperor Franz Josef showed that he had learned nothing by the tragic suicide of his son Rudolf, whose morganatic marriage (i.e. to someone of a lesser rank, affecting inheritance) he had consistently opposed. History appeared to be repeating itself when, in 1895, Franz Ferdinand met minor aristocrat Countess Sophie von Chotek, lady-in-waiting to the Duchess of Teschen, at a ball in Prague. They quickly fell in love, keeping their affair secret for two years. However, Habsburg marriages were traditionally conducted with the reigning families of Europe. The Choteks were emphatically not one of these, and when the affair was discovered in 1898, not only was Sophie immediately dismissed from her position, but the emperor forbade them to wed.

While Franz Josef appeared oblivious of recent history, other European sovereigns – among them such illustrious names as Tsar Nicholas II of Russia and Kaiser Wilhelm II of Germany – were not, and they begged the ageing Austrian Emperor to reconsider. In 1899

Franz Joseph finally relented, but only on the basis that Sophie should not share the rank or precedence of her husband (effectively consigning her to the shadows whenever they appeared in public together) and that the descendants of the marriage would not succeed to the throne. As it happened, the empire itself had only 19 years of life left.

Neither the emperor nor any member of the Austrian royal family attended the couple's wedding on 1 July 1900. Sophie was fobbed off with the courtesy title of Princess of Hohenberg; although upgraded to a duchess nine years later, she still remained physically distant from her husband at public functions involving other members of the royal family. By 1918 such distinctions seemed absurd and ludicrous; yet in the innocent world that existed before the senseless events of 1914, many of Europe's most distinguished families thrived on such artificial and wounding social stratifications.

It is one of history's cruellest ironies that the First World War, with its millions of dead, was precipitated by an amateurish, almost pantomime event. In a double irony, Franz Ferdinand was actually one of the most liberal of the senior Habsburgs, and had been toying for some time with the notion of restructuring the empire as a looser confederation of autonomous nationalities. This distinction, though, escaped the plotters. Seven members of the Black Hand were accordingly charged with the archduke's assassination. On the day, though, their plan – with each of the seven being given a chance to take a shot at the passing car – dissolved into a series of bungled fiascos.

The first conspirator on the route to see the royal car was one Muhamed Mehmedbašić. Yet, standing by the Austro-Hungarian Bank, he lost his nerve and allowed the car to pass and did nothing. Mehmedbašić later said that a policeman was standing behind him and he feared he would be arrested before he had a chance to throw his bomb.

A few minutes later, as the six-car procession passed the central police station, a 19-year-old plotter named Čabrinović hurled a grenade at the archduke's car. In an impressive display of reactive driving, chauffeur Franz Urban accelerated and the bomb exploded under the wheel of the next car. Two of this car's occupants, Eric von Merizzi and Count Boos-Waldeck, were seriously wounded, while a dozen spectators were hit by bomb splinters. But the archduke and archduchess were, for the time being, both unharmed.

By now, the five other conspirators were left trapped in the crowds as the cars sped away. Čabrinović himself swallowed a cyanide pill and jumped into the nearby river, but he was hauled out and arrested.

GAVRILO PRINCIP

GAVRILO PRINCIP (1894–1918) WAS BORN into a very different world from his victims, the son of an impoverished Bosnian postman. His early life was marked by penury and the tuberculosis that would eventually kill him. As a young man he not only joined 'Young Bosnia', the pan-Slavic and ecumenical political movement aimed at securing the region's independence from Austria-Hungary, but also its shadowy terrorist counterpart, the Black Hand. Expelled from school in February 1912 for taking part in anti-government demonstrations in Sarajevo, he fled to the Serbian capital Belgrade. Here, however, he was deemed too young and too small to win promotion within the Black Hand, which fought its shadowy war against both the Turks (who still ruled the Balkan territories to the east) and the Austrians. Stung by this rejection, he returned to Sarajevo determined to do his bit to loosen Austrian rule and to prove his worth to the leaders of the Black Hand.

After the assassination of Archduke Franz Ferdinand, Princip, like Čabrinović, tried to kill himself by ingesting cyanide. The poison, though, was past its sell-by date and did not work, while his pistol was wrestled from his hand before he had a chance to shoot himself. Astonishingly, though, Princip was not executed. The Austrian authorities admirably stood by the letter of the law and, since Princip was under 20 at the time of the offence and thus too young to merit the death penalty, he was sentenced to 20 years in prison. He died in his cell, of tuberculosis, on 28 April 1918.

Franz Ferdinand in brief

1863 Born in Graz, Austria, son of Archduke Karl Ludwig of Austria-Este.

1875 Inherits dukedom of Modena and great wealth.

1889 His elderly father becomes heir to the Austro-Hungarian throne on the suicide of Crown Prince Rudolf.

1895 Meets Sophie von Chotek, a minor countess, at a reception: their romance is deplored by the ageing emperor Franz Josef on account of their difference in rank.

1896 His father dies, making him the new Austrian heir apparent.

1900 Marries Sophie, but their future children must give up any rights of royal succession.

1908–9 Austria annexes Bosnia-Herzegovina from the Ottoman Empire.

1912–13 The two Balkan Wars reconfigure the fragile balance of power in the region, with Serbia now seen as a threat by Austria and an asset by Russia. Franz Ferdinand becomes inspector general of the Austrian army, but attempts to improve Austro-Russian relations.

1914 Franz Ferdinand and Sophie are assassinated (28 June) in Sarajevo by Serb nationalist Gavrilo Princip. A resulting Austrian declaration of war on Serbia activates the European alliances, and by August the First World War has begun.

Franz Ferdinand nobly decided to go to the hospital and visit the victims of Čabrinović's failed bombing attempt. In order to avoid the city centre, General Potiorek, the Governor of Bosnia-Herzegovina, sensibly decreed that the royal car should travel straight along the Appel Quay to the Sarajevo Hospital. However, Potiorek forgot to inform the driver, Urban, about this decision. On the way to the hospital, Urban thus took a wrong turn into Gebet Street. Realizing the mistake, he began to back up. As he was doing so, however, he stalled the engine.

By an astonishing coincidence, one of the Black Hand conspirators, Gavrilo Princip, had retired, disconsolate, to a café in Gebet Street to reflect on yet another failed assassination attempt. While eating, he saw, to his astonishment, the archduke's car reverse and stall directly in front of him. Such an opportunity seemed God-given: Princip leaped forward, drew his pistol, and shot several times into the car from about five feet away. Franz Ferdinand was hit in the neck, and Sophie in the stomach. Sophie died instantly; Franz Ferdinand lasted a few minutes more. So ended a life that would set in motion a war.

Serbia was delighted with the assassination, while Austria held the Serbian nation directly responsible for the tragic event. An Austrian ultimatum, which effectively demanded control of the newly independent country's affairs, was presented to the Serbian government on 23 July, once Austria had assured itself of the support of Germany. Supported by their fellow-Slavs in Russia, Serbia resisted, and on 28 July Austria declared war on the embattled Balkan state. This prompted Russia to mobilize its armed forces, which in turn encouraged Germany to do likewise. The First World War had begun.

Meanwhile, with war looming and his succession in jeopardy, the ancient emperor could still not bring himself to endorse Franz Ferdinand's marriage even posthumously – an issue that seemed increasingly irrelevant as the stormclouds gathered over Europe. The assassinated couple were buried not in the Imperial Vault (the Kaisergruft) in Vienna – as was traditional for Austrian emperors, their consorts and heirs – but in the Archduke's personal retreat of Artstetten Castle, deep in the Austrian Wachau. Two years later, in 1916, Franz Josef himself finally died, while in 1918 the Austro-Hungarian Empire, now ruled by Franz Josef's great-nephew Karl, was itself dissolved. By then many could barely remember how, or why, the War To End All Wars had actually started.

In Bosnia and Serbia, Princip (whose arrest is shown on p.93) is still revered as a national hero. He is commemorated in Sarajevo by street names, a bridge, and a museum, the last of which was refurbished as recently as 2003. Yet little is remembered of Franz Ferdinand (except the name of the contemporary British rock group) save the fact that it was his death that sparked the carnage of the 1914–18 war. Reassuringly, an exhibition devoted to the ill-fated Habsburg couple does survive at Artstetten Castle.

ASPUTIN

Os–1916, RUSSIAN ROYAL FAVOURITE AND MYS

ASSASSIN	Prince Felix Yusupov and othe
DATE	29/30 December 1916
PLACE	St Petersburg, Russia

Grigory Yefimovich Novykh – 'Rasputin' (a nickname meaning 'dissolute') – may not have been single-handedly responsible for the 1917 Russian Revolution, but his assassination in 1916 did nothing to stem the tide of nationwide protest. However, his appalling reputation as a fake, as an indiscriminate womanizer, and as an malign influence who held the tsar and, particularly, the tsarina under his spell – some said in sexual thrall – eroded any lingering respect that the Russian intelligentsia held for the royal family. To some extent, a direct correlation can be made between the ascendancy of the mystical Siberian monk in the years immediately preceding the 1917 Revolution and the execution of the Romanovs in a damp Siberian cellar, barely 18 months after Rasputin's own untimely and excessively violent death.

We don't know for certain when Rasputin was born; it could have been any time in the decade after 1863. What we do know is that in 1903 rumours surfaced in the Russian court at St Petersburg that a mystical monk in Siberia had healed the sick and accurately predicted drought. In December of that year Rasputin appeared at the religious academy in St Petersburg: a dirty, stocky man with bedraggled hair and strong body odour, who already boasted a chequered reputation based on intense religious devotion alternating with complete sexual abandon. But he already enjoyed powerful patrons, including the Grand Duke Nicholas, whose dog he allegedly healed. Another royal admirer, the Grand Duchess Militsa, introduced the reprobate monk into the royal palace to see if he could help cure the tsar's son and heir Alexis, a chronic haemophiliac for whom even the slightest accident could prove fatal.

'We all drown in blood'

Rasputin, in a letter to Nicholas II at the beginning of the First World War

To the incredulity of the royal doctors, Rasputin did appear to have some healing effect on Alexis. Every time the boy had an injury that caused him internal or external bleeding, the tsarina called on Rasputin and the young tsarevich subsequently got better. Rasputin later admitted to a friend that his 'cures' were based on a combination of hypnosis, obscure Siberian drugs, placebos and mere willpower. Often just the soothing effect of his voice seemed to be enough to calm the boy.

Rasputin used his resulting position in the royal household, and especially the adoration of the tsarina, to great effect (as the satirical drawing, p.97, suggests). He addressed the imperial couple as fellow-peasants – a fantasy in which the easily led Nicholas II was happy to indulge – and cleverly appealed to their moral outrage at the excesses of the Russian nobles.

As Rasputin grew more sure of his position, his excesses proliferated. He frequently entered the princesses' bedroom at night, and when their governess complained, it was she who was sacked. He seduced the tsarevich's nurse, and slept with dozens of compliant aristocratic women. And he preached the blasphemous doctrine of attaining divine grace through sin – a handy if somewhat un-Christian dogma, which had been repeatedly denounced by Christian leaders since the time of Christ himself.

Government ministers complained, but the tsarina would hear no ill of her pet prophet. In 1911 even the Metropolitan of Russia, the country's leading churchman, complained to the tsar about Rasputin's antics but was flatly told that the imperial family's private affairs did not concern him. And from 1913 Rasputin began to use his seemingly boundless influence to control the tsar's political appointments. Accordingly, in the years before the 1917 Revolution the Russian government grew increasingly reactionary, deaf to the voices of the mounting opposition.

The outbreak of the First World War in 1914 only increased Rasputin's ascendancy. He was deeply opposed to war, both from a moral point of view and as something likely to lead to political catastrophe. But he used the tumultuous events of 1914–16 as a cover for increasingly reckless behaviour. His public drunkenness, barely concealed sexual promiscuity and notorious willingness to accept bribes did nothing to improve his reputation. By 1915 church affairs had effectively been abandoned to Rasputin's discretion, and almost all new ministers had first to win the monk's approval. The monk regularly shouted orders at the prime minister, insisting he 'do what he was told by mother' – the tsarina, who was of course herself wholly dependent on Rasputin. By 1916 Rasputin seemed, to all intents and purposes, the arbiter of Russia's destiny.

Rasputin clearly saw himself as the embodiment of peasant Russia – and, as such, more representative of the Russian people than Nicholas II himself. He held *levées*, elaborate morning social rituals, in the manner of the French *Ancien Régime*: to would-be post-holders, these events were far more accessible and useful than the tsar's own restricted audiences. But when Rasputin expressed an interest in going to the Front to bless the troops early in the war, the commander-in-chief (and his one-time supporter), Grand Duke Nicholas, promised to hang him if he dared to show up.

Rasputin responded by feeding the tsar's ambition to personally command his armies. Nicholas loved the simple, open-air life of the army, and yearned to escape the complex politics of St Petersburg. When Rasputin claimed that he had had a vision that the Russian armies would not be successful until the tsar personally took field command, Nicholas seized on this as an excuse to transfer himself to the Front. The consequences for Russia were to be dire.

With Nicholas away, Rasputin's influence over Tsarina Alexandra increased yet further. Already established as her confidant and personal adviser, he now convinced her to fill governmental and military offices with his own handpicked candidates. Thus, in March 1916 Alexandra, egged on by Rasputin, bullied her vacillating husband into dismissing the last effective war minister, General Polivanov.

By the autumn of 1916 Russia's war effort, as well as her economy, were in ruins. The talented General Brusilov had won victories against the weak Austrian armies in the south, but elsewhere Russian forces were retreating in the face of the more efficient German divisions. Supply of the armies – and indeed of the civilian population – was disintegrating, and mutinies and desertion were common.

In this chaotic atmosphere, with government ministers finally daring to denounce Rasputin in the sessions of the Duma, scions of Russia's cowed nobility at last summoned

Rasputin in brief

c.1863–73 Born Grigory Yefimovich Novykh into a peasant family in Pokrovskoye, Siberia, and receives some education as a boy.

1890s Absorbs various mystical and monastic traditions, evolving a personalized credo that justifies sexual excess as the basis for ultimate godliness. Acquires reputation for healing and prophecy.

1903 Enters aristocratic and religious circles at St Petersburg, despite (or because of) his extraordinary appearance and reputation as a 'holy man'.

1905 Meets the Romanov royal family.

1908 Appears to 'cure' one of young Prince Alexis's haemophiliac episodes, and soon becomes integral to Romanovs, especially the tsarina. His ill-concealed licentiousness outside court earns him the nickname 'Rasputin' ('Dissolute').

1911 Expelled from court for several months by the tsar, on Prime Minister Stolypin's insistence, but soon returns to administer to Alexis.

1915 With the tsar away from court supervising the army, Rasputin reaches the apex of his political influence, including the powers to appoint and dismiss ministers and interfere militarily.

1916 Poisoned, shot and eventually drowned (night of 29/30 Dec.) by a group of conservative aristocrats and Romanov relatives.

A BRITISH PLOT?

RESEARCH CONDUCTED ON RASPUTIN'S assassination since 1945 has suggested that, of those bullets fired at Rasputin in Yusupov's courtyard, at least one, a Webley .455-inch bullet, was fired from a British revolver. Witnesses to the murder stated that the only man present at the scene in possession of a Webley revolver was a British officer attached to the British Secret Service, Lieutenant Oswald Rayner, who had been an old school friend of Yusupov's. Rayner's chauffeur later wrote that 'it is a little known fact that Rasputin was shot not by a Russian but by an Englishman', and he implied that his former boss was centrally involved.

On his return to England, Oswald Rayner not only confided to his cousin that he had been present at Rasputin's murder, but also showed family members a bullet which he claimed to have acquired at the murder scene. Sadly, Rayner burnt all his papers before he died in 1961. It is thus difficult to conclude whether Rasputin's death was indeed the result of the machinations of the British government.

up the courage to move against the universally hated monk. The leader of the plot was Prince Felix Yusupov, a highborn noble who had attended University College, Oxford, and who had returned to marry the tsar's niece. His associates included a member of the Duma and Grand Duke Dmitry Pavlovich, cousin of Nicholas II. On the night of 29/30 December 1916 (17/18 December, Old Style Russian calendar), Yusupov invited Rasputin to his house, ostensibly to meet his wife, who was, in fact, not there. In his cellar, while his co-conspirators sat upstairs, Yusupov fed Rasputin poisoned wine and poisoned cakes – but to no apparent effect. (It has since been suggested that Rasputin's hyperacidity negated the effect of the cyanide.) Yusupov ran upstairs to consult the others, and then came back down with a hidden revolver. While showing the monk a crystal crucifix, he shot Rasputin at point-blank range in the chest. The rest of the company rushed downstairs and, examining the body, pronounced Rasputin dead. Some then left, while Yusupov and a few others discussed what they should do next in the upper room. After a short while, Yusupov went to check up on the body. To the prince's astonishment, Rasputin opened his eyes, grabbed Yusupov by the throat and ripped off his epaulette before falling back. Yusupov ran out in terror, and the conspirators then heard the monk clambering up the stairs on all fours. Rasputin erupted into the courtyard, roaring with fury; the assassins shot at him and missed, but finally gained the courage to aim properly, hitting him twice.

The assassination was not over. Yusupov, having been violently sick, examined the 'corpse' to find that Rasputin was still breathing and had one eye open. The prince then grabbed a metal press and began to beat it against Rasputin's head until he was dragged away. Soldiers were called (who promised silence), and they wrapped the body in a blanket, fastened it with a rope, and drove to the ice-bound River Neva. There they threw Rasputin's body – followed by the weights, which they had forgotten to attach – into its icy depths.

Three days later, the body of Rasputin was recovered and given an autopsy. The cause of death was deemed to be hypothermia. Rasputin's arms were found in an upright position, as if he had tried to claw his way out from under the ice. Water in his lungs also suggested that he had still been alive when he entered the river.

On 3 January 1917 the royal family buried Rasputin's body in the grounds of the royal palace at St Petersburg, accompanied by an icon signed by the tsar, the tsarina and all their children. The following month revolution erupted in Russia; as a consequence, his body was exhumed and burnt on a bonfire.

Yusupov was never arrested or tried; as a White Russian exile in the 1920s, he published an unlikely account of the plot, which he later varied when asked to give evidence to libel juries in 1934 and 1965. The royal family were ultimately captured by revolutionary forces, denied asylum in Britain, and then brutally shot at Ekaterinburg, in Siberia, on 16 July 1918.

Engelbert DOLLFUSS

1892–1934, CHANCELLOR OF AUSTRIA

ASSASSINS	A group of Austrian Nazis
DATE	25 July 1934
PLACE	Vienna, Austria

The Austro-Prussian War of 1866 had dissolved Austrian ambitions to dominate German-speaking Europe. The Peace of Versailles that ended the First World War saw Austria shorn completely of her empire and reduced to a size far smaller than her intensely competitive neighbour to the north, Germany. Austria was now a land of a mere 6 million inhabitants, with a vast, overstaffed imperial civil service charged with looking after one capital city and a series of thinly populated Alpine valleys.

In the endemic political and economic unrest in Central Europe between the world wars, it was perhaps inevitable that Austria would be dragged into the territorial embrace of its former ally. Austria's economic base was too weak to enable it to stand up to the far larger German state; the choice was thus alliance with either Germany to the north or with Italy to the south. In the event, when Hitler's armies crossed the Austrian border in March 1938 to cement the forced marriage of the two countries, they were enthusiastically welcomed by most of the Austrian population. But a few years earlier, there were concerted attempts to preserve Austrian independence in the face of German provocation. Through means of assassination, Hitler's Nazis extinguished them in a typically brutal manner.

> 'It is quite misleading to call it a dictatorship. It is merely a ... corporative state under authoritarian leadership.'
>
> Dollfuss's fine distinction concerning his regime, quoted in *Time* magazine, 2 October 1933

The hero of the struggle for Austrian self-government was an unlikely figure. The deeply religious Engelbert Dollfuss was a short, squat man of 4 feet 11 inches, who was quickly nicknamed 'the Jockey' or (punning on 'Metternich', the renowned 19th-century Austrian chancellor) 'Millimetternich'. Since black was the party colour adopted by Dollfuss's right-wing Catholic allies, the locals in Viennese cafés began to order a 'Dollfuss' coffee rather than the accustomed 'short black'. He was even initially rejected from the Austro-Hungarian army in 1914 because of his short stature. However, he did eventually serve on the bitter Italian Front and was taken prisoner there in 1918. Ironically, 14 years later his policy as chancellor was to be grounded on Italian support.

Dollfuss's postwar career was unconventional for an embryonic dictator. After the war he worked for the ministry of agriculture as secretary of the Peasants' Association, and from there rose to become director of the Lower Austrian Chamber of Agriculture in 1927, president of the federal railways in 1930, and minister of agriculture and forests in 1931.

Austria suffered worst of all European nations from the Great Depression. Its fragile economy, bereft of much of the industrial base and raw materials that had sustained it before 1918, quickly buckled. Plagued by enormously high unemployment and by political opinions rapidly polarizing to left and right, the Depression lasted longer in Austria than anywhere else. By 1936 a third of the adult population was still unemployed.

To solve the seemingly intractable economic crisis, Austrians looked for a new figure untainted by the political turbulence of the previous decade. Eyes settled on the ambiguous but seemingly harmless Christian Social Party's agriculture minister. Thus did Dollfuss become Austria's chancellor on 20 May 1932, at the head of a broad coalition. However, his parliamentary majority was almost non-existent, any deflationary policies would inevitably prove highly unpopular, and the extremist Right, particularly in the shape of the Heimwehr (Home Guard) and the Austrian Nazis of the DNSAP, were gaining votes.

Much to Austria's surprise, Dollfuss quickly showed that he was no liberal Captain von Trapp. His methods of dealing with political threats were unambiguously authoritarian. As Hitler (made chancellor in January 1933) was squeezing out multiparty politics across the border, Dollfuss aimed to create a one-party state with himself as effective dictator. In March 1933 he suspended parliament indefinitely and proceeded to govern by decree. He absorbed the Heimwehr into the Christian Socials, calling the resultant party the Vaterländische Front ('Fatherland Front') and banned both the Social Democrats and the Nazis. Protests in the 'Red' suburbs of Vienna were dealt with by troops firing howitzers, prompting the ever-opportunistic Hitler to claim to the world's press that Dollfuss was being unduly aggressive and should try persuasion instead.

Dollfuss recognized that Hitler's Germany posed the principal threat to Austrian autonomy. His solution was to pose as the client of Mussolini's Italy. His realigned Austrian politics on Italian Fascist lines, creating a hybrid political creed, since labelled 'Austrofascism'. This he did in return for Mussolini's guarantee of Austrian sovereignty, backed up by Italian divisions camped in the Brenner Pass. At the same time, Dollfuss purged the public sector of Nazis at home, interning them or deporting them to Germany.

Hitler's initial response to Dollfuss's subjugation of the Austrian Nazis was cleverly calculated. The cost of a tourist visa for Austria was raised massively, with the result that only 8000 Germans holidayed in Austria in 1933, compared to the 98,000 who had done so in 1932. The Luftwaffe dropped anti-government leaflets on the Austrian population; the German army sent candlelit swastikas floating down the Danube; and loudspeakers broadcast pro-Nazi propaganda across the border.

Such measures did not, though, encourage Dollfuss to alter his position. So, only three weeks after his SS Praetorian Guard had bloodily liquidated their SA paramilitary rivals in the Nazi Party (the notorious 'Night of the Long Knives'), Hitler supported the disorganized rump of the Austrian Nazis in their wildly over-optimistic plot to stage a *coup d'état*. With his explicit encouragement, some Austrian Nazis burst into the chancellery building on 25 July 1934 and assassinated the diminutive Dollfuss.

In the event, this crude action failed to achieve Hitler's desired outcome. Austrian Nazis were far too weak and divided to effect a union with Germany in 1934. The assassins were caught and executed, and Mussolini moved four more divisions to the Brenner Pass. Dollfuss's successor as chancellor, Kurt Schuschnigg, continued his predecessor's fascist policies, giving the Fatherland Front a swastika badge and an SS-style 'Sturmkorps' with blue uniforms, and dissolving the Heimwehr. Hitler backed down – for the moment.

The years 1935–6 gave Germany just the opportunity it needed. Mussolini's invasion of Abyssinia (Ethiopia) and his thinly disguised intervention in the Spanish Civil War earned him widespread condemnation from the world community. By 1936 he desperately needed German support, and was willing to abandon Austria to achieve it. Schuschnigg had no alternative but to agree that Austria would not enter into any 'anti-German combinations',

Dollfuss in brief

1892 Born in Texing, Austria. Later studies law and economics in Vienna and Berlin.

1914 Initially rejected by Austro-Hungarian army because of his short stature, but eventually serves on the Italian Front.

1927 Appointed head of the chamber of commerce for Lower Austria. Becomes active in the conservative Christian Social Party.

1930 Placed in charge of the federal railway system.

1931 Appointed minister of agriculture.

1932 Becomes Chancellor of Austria as head of a coalition government.

1933 Having gained Italian guarantees of Austrian territorial security, suspends parliament and establishes authoritarian regime based on Italian Fascist lines.

1934 Dissolves all political parties apart from his own, the Fatherland Front, following riots. Assassinated (25 July) by Austrian Nazis.

AUSTRIA IN 1945

THE *SOUND OF MUSIC* has a lot to answer for. The image of Austria as an unwilling victim of Nazi aggression has, thanks to the evergreen musical, become a popular and enduring one.

In reality, many Austrians not only welcomed the *Anschluss* of 1938, but also prospered as enthusiastic partners of the new Nazi order. Many of the more unsavoury Nazi figures of the war were Austrian, including Amon Göth, the notorious commandant of Auschwitz, and Seyss-Inquart, who became the hated Reichs Commissioner of the Netherlands and was hanged at Nuremberg for war crimes. Hitler himself, of course, was Austrian by birth.

However, many Austrians stayed true to Austrian nationhood, in the admirable manner of Herr Kapitän von Trapp. This was graphically demonstrated in the dark days of 1945, as Hitler's forces retreated in the face of the unstoppable Soviet armies. Since 1944 resistance groups had been operating all over Austria, and were unified into a shadow army, called '0-5' after the first two letters of the country's German name, Oesterreich. They acted under the energetic and inspiring leadership of Major Carl Szokoll. On Easter Day 1945, 0-5's forces rose against the occupying SS divisions in Vienna in a move aimed at helping the approaching Russians and saving the Austrian capital from becoming a devastated battlefield. Having finally convinced the suspicious Russians of their good intentions, 0-5 took to the streets, a rising that provoked Hitler to advise his SS troops to 'proceed against the rebels in Vienna with the most brutal means'. Thanks to 0-5's intervention, the fighting in Vienna lasted only a few days and was over by 14 April. Szokoll was proclaimed civil commander of Vienna by the Russians, but in a development typical of Stalin's treacherous rule was arrested two days later and sent to a PoW camp. He escaped, was recaptured, and was finally released after three months.

to release imprisoned Nazis, and even to admit leading Nazis to government. Schuschnigg believed that these would be the last concessions he would have to make, but for Hitler – encouraged by British and French indifference to the fate of Austria – they were just the start. At a meeting with the Austrian chancellor on 12 February 1938, Hitler shrieked at Schuschnigg and threatened that, unless he admitted Austrian Nazi leader Arthur Seyss-Inquart into the government as interior minister, German troops would cross the frontier. A terrified Schuschnigg capitulated, but once back in Vienna made plans for a national plebiscite on the issue of unification with Germany. Hitler made much of the Austrians' right to self-determination – which, he strongly implied, would see Austria bed down with her neighbour 'in the interests of the German race as a whole' – but he did not want to take the risk of a popular vote. As a result, he claimed Schuschnigg had betrayed him and that Austrian Nazis were being persecuted and even murdered. To 'protect' his fellow-Aryans, Hitler sent in the German army on 12 March 1938 and annexed Austria. Shortly afterwards, he arranged a rigged plebiscite, which appeared to show that an astonishing 99.7 per cent of Austrians supported the annexation (*Anschluss*).

Military intervention by other European powers to stop the *Anschluss* in March 1938 would have been relatively simple. The roads into Austria from Germany were strewn with failed German armour, as the exercise graphically demonstrated to the Wehrmacht that their equipment could still do with substantial improvement. Fortunately for Hitler and his generals, the fragile German army was not put to the test, and the German divisions were met not with bullets but by cheering crowds. Meanwhile, the appeasing governments of Britain and France readily believed Hitler's arguments, while Mussolini had long been bought off by the promise of German support for his unrealistic imperial ambitions.

In 1934 Dollfuss had been buried in the Hietzing cemetery in Vienna, alongside his wife Alvine. In 1938 his successor, Schuschnigg, was hustled off to a concentration camp. Had he survived assassination, it is likely that Dollfuss would have suffered the same fate. In the event, despite years of torture and privation, Schuschnigg actually survived the war, and in 1946 emigrated to start a new life as an academic in America. He lived until 1977.

ALEXANDER
of Yugoslavia

1888–1934, KING OF YUGOSLAVIA

ASSASSIN Vlado Chernozemski
DATE 9 October 1934
PLACE Marseilles, France

Marseilles, France's second city and its principal window on the Mediterranean, has always been known as a centre of violence, intrigue and corruption. In the 1930s murders were commonplace and gun crime endemic. Even hardened residents, however, were shocked when the visiting King Alexander of Yugoslavia and France's own foreign minister, Louis Barthou, were assassinated in their midst, on 9 October 1934. The Bulgarian assassin was cut down by a nearby mounted policeman and then beaten to death by the crowd. The citizens of Marseilles were slightly mollified by the news that the deceased assassin was not a local. But the perennial problems of Europe's fragile southeastern underbelly had, it seemed, now emigrated to the most cosmopolitan and multiracial of French ports.

The Balkans had been the tinderbox that had set the First World War alight. Even after 1918, things were little better. The Treaty of Versailles confirmed the establishment of an independent Balkan state, carved out of the ruins of the Austro-Hungarian Empire. Properly speaking, this was the 'Kingdom of Serbs, Croat and Slovenes', but it is rather better known colloquially (and formally after 1929) as Yugoslavia. However, unrest seethed just below the surface, and assassination became a way of life. Bulgaria – which had allied with Germany during the war – felt cheated of its share of Macedonia and supported the terrorist gangs of IMRO (the Internal Macedonian Revolutionary Organization), which infiltrated Greek and Yugoslav Macedonia to assassinate local officials. (In 1923 IMRO even bit the hand that fed it: its agents assassinated the Bulgarian prime minister because he favoured a détente with Greece and Yugoslavia so that Bulgaria could concentrate on its internal problems.) And within the new Yugoslav kingdom itself, Croats were deeply suspicious – with good justification – that the Serbs sought to dominate the infant federation. The result was the formation of the Croats' own terrorist organization, the Ustashe, which soon formed close links with IMRO.

> '**Dictatorship outwardly resembles a splendid palace, but once you're in you can't find a way out**'
>
> Alexander's rueful reflection, as quoted by Kosta Todorov in his 1943 book *Balkan* Firebrand

The young sovereign of the new kingdom was himself a Serb. Alexander Karađorđević, the second son of Peter I of Serbia, was born in Montenegro in December 1888. A sickly child, he was promoted in the line of succession after his elder brother, George, displayed irrefutable evidence of his own mental instability by kicking a servant to death in a fit of rage. Alexander won fame as a successful military commander in the Balkan Wars of 1912–13; this reputation was to serve him well when he was asked to act as regent for his incapacitated father in June 1914. Plunged into the First World War a month later, Alexander acquitted himself well in the field against the invading Austro-Hungarian forces, before German intervention prompted the retreat of the Serbian army. In the autumn of 1918 his Serbian victories routed German and Austrian opponents and encouraged the German government to sue for an armistice. In the wake of these victories, Alexander was formally offered the regency of the newly independent Kingdom of the Serbs, Croats and Slovenes on 1 December 1918. Three years later, on the death of his father, he became king.

Alexander posed as a keen federalist, but inevitably became a magnet for Serbian nationalism. On 20 June 1928 Puniša Račić, a member of the Serbian Radical Party, assassinated Croat leader Stjepan Radić and his nephew, Paul, on the floor of the nation's parliament. Six months later, celebrations to mark the tenth anniversary of the kingdom deteriorated into street battles between Serbian troops and Croat mobs. The prime minister resigned, and on 6 January 1929 Alexander decided to seize the reins of government himself. With the reluctant support of most of the leading politicians of Croatia, Serbia, Slovenia and Bosnia, the king dissolved parliament, tightened internal policing and started to assemble a personal dictatorship. He also changed the name of the country to 'Kingdom of Yugoslavia' and appointed his old army crony (and reputed lover) Petar Živković as prime minister.

Many Croat leaders greeted Alexander's assumption of power with cynicism, and they fled to Italy or Bulgaria. With the financial assistance of Mussolini's government, which had designs on Yugoslav territory on the Adriatic, Croat émigré Ante Pavelić built up the Ustashe into a formidable paramilitary force. That year Mussolini told a French diplomat in Rome that 'Yugoslavia doesn't exist. It is a heterogeneous conglomerate, which you cobbled together in Paris.'

In March 1929 the Ustashe unleashed a vicious campaign of bombing and assassinations across Yugoslavia. Alexander's reaction was equally savage: the torture and murder of suspects became commonplace, and in 1931 the king announced a new constitution, which transferred all executive power to himself. The secret ballot was abandoned, and half the parliamentary upper house was subject to direct appointment by the king. Dictatorship had arrived.

The Ustashe in Italy and IMRO in Bulgaria, however, remained out of the range of Alexander's secret police. An Italian-backed Ustashe plot to assassinate the king on his birthday in December 1933 was uncovered only at the last moment. In response, Alexander encouraged his neighbours Czechoslovakia and Romania to join with him in strengthening the 'Little Entente' of 1920, which had been intended – with French help – to guarantee the sovereignty of the member nations against aggression by Germany, Italy or Russia. Unsettled by this display of independence, Hitler decided to use diplomacy to wean Yugoslavia away from its Entente partners. Alexander was given preferential trading status and offered German diplomatic support.

Yet Alexander did not live long enough to be able to enjoy the fruits of this new diplomacy. On Tuesday 9 October 1934 he arrived in Marseilles for a state visit aimed at emphasizing the vitality of the French-backed Little Entente. As the king was travelling by car through the city, a lone gunman took aim at the vehicle, killing the king, the French foreign minister (apparently) and even the chauffeur and some bystanders.

Alexander in brief

1888 Born in Cetinje, Montenegro, the second son of Prince Peter Karadordević. Spends his childhood in Swiss and Russian exile.

1903 His father accedes to the Serbian throne after King Alexander I Obrenović is assassinated.

1912–13 Achieves notable success as a commander in the Balkan Wars.

1914 Already heir to the throne, becomes regent because of his father's illness. Serves as Serbian commander-in-chief during the First World War.

1918 Becomes regent of the newly formed Kingdom of Serbs, Croats and Slovenes, which also absorbs some former Bulgarian territories.

1921 Becomes king on the death of his father, and survives an assassination attempt.

1929 Dissolves the parliament and begins autocratic rule, after assassinations, riots and political resignations threaten anarchy. He renames the country Yugoslavia and attempts to solve ethnic–national divisions through a centralized state.

1931 A new constitution formalizes the regal dictatorship, but opposition mounts.

1934 Assassinated (9 Oct.) in Marseilles, France, by a Bulgarian terrorist.

LOUIS BARTHOU AND CONSPIRACY THEORIES

THE FORGOTTEN MAN of 9 October 1934 was the French foreign minister, Jean Louis Barthou. Born in the Basses-Pyrénées region in 1862, Barthou was an experienced survivor of the politics of France's Third Republic and briefly prime minister for less than nine months in 1913.

More recently, he had been behind the ground-breaking Franco-Soviet Mutual Assistance Pact, which he had painstakingly negotiated with Stalin's Russia but which was ultimately signed by his successor at the foreign ministry, Pierre Laval.

In 1957, the German newspaper *Neues Deutschland* published alleged correspondence from 1934 between Hans Speidel, then an assistant to the German military attaché in Paris (and in 1957 a top NATO general), and Hermann Goering. The newspaper's allegation was that the assassination of Alexander and Barthou had been planned and prepared by Berlin. However, little additional evidence was produced to support this claim. In fact, Hitler would have been careful to retain and cultivate his new ally.

It was not until a further investigation, in 1974, that it was revealed that Barthou was not actually the victim of the assassin's bullet. The arm wound he received, severing his humeral artery so that he bled to death, came from a gun fired by a French policeman and not by Chernozemski. Barthou (and possibly the other victims on that day, apart from the king) had thus been caught in the panicked crossfire. Or perhaps the officers simply had a grudge against the Third Republic.

The assassin at first appeared to be a Croat, until the papers he carried with him were found to be false. In fact, he was a Bulgarian by the name of Vlado Chernozemski. With grim irony he was, himself, a chauffeur – as well as a trained marksman – though neither skill helped him survive the wrath of the crowd on that day. He had spent years as a dedicated fighter for the Macedonian cause, and his employer was Vanche Mihailov, the head of IMRO, who had organized the assassination in conjunction with Paveliç's Ustashe.

Alexander's death was one of the first assassinations captured on film. The shooting occurred straight in front of a cameraman, who happened to be standing only feet away. He captured not merely the assassination but also the immediate aftermath: the body of the dead chauffeur was jammed against the brakes of the car, allowing the cameraman to continue filming within inches of the dying king (*see* p.105).

King Alexander was buried in the Church of St George in Belgrade, which had been built by his father. As his son and heir Peter II was still a minor, Alexander's cousin Paul assumed the regency. Staunchly pro-German, Paul continued Alexander's policy of wooing Nazi Germany, and on the outbreak of war in 1939 Paul adopted a policy of benevolent neutrality towards the Axis powers. British diplomacy, conversely, concentrated on the young heir: thus on 27 March 1941 Peter, though only 17 years old, was proclaimed of age to rule, and Paul was deposed from his regency in a British-supported coup.

The initial euphoria soon turned to dismay as German troops overran not only Yugoslavia but also neighbouring Greece. The Ustashe sided with the Germans, and was rewarded with a puppet Croat state. The rest of the Kingdom of Yugoslavia was cynically divided among the Axis powers. Peter II himself finally found refuge in Britain, where he joined the RAF. He would be deposed by Marshal Tito's communist government in November 1945, and he later settled in the United States.

In the longer term, however, Peter II's pro-British declaration proved invaluable to the Allied cause. The Nazi conquest of the Balkans had caused the Germans to postpone the planned invasion of Russia, Operation Barbarossa. When Germany did attack Russia, it was late in the campaigning season. Early Nazi gains soon turned sour as the German advance became bogged down in the atrocious mud and snow of the Russian winter. The eventual Soviet victory at Stalingrad and the subsequent Russian advance thus owes much to King Peter II's quixotic but undoubtedly brave assertion of Yugoslav sovereignty. Would his father, Alexander, have shown such independence of spirit?

Huey LONG
1893–1935, GOVERNOR OF LOUISIANA

ASSASSIN Probably Carl Weiss
DATE 8 September 1935 (died 10 September)
PLACE Baton Rouge, Louisiana, USA

One of the most notorious US political figures of the 20th century, Huey Pierce Long Jr was indisputably a larger-than-life character. The so-called 'Kingfish' was a classic populist politician, a radical authoritarian who, as the self-appointed voice of the 'Little Man' and the originator of the utopian 'Share Our Wealth' programme, combined the brutal instincts of the contemporary European dictators with quasi-socialist egalitarianism. Initially an enthusiastic supporter of President Franklin D. Roosevelt, he began to harbour his own presidential ambitions. And he died as he had lived: dramatically. The flamboyant Long was gunned down at the zenith of his power, on the steps of the State Capitol. He died two days later, aged only 42.

Long was born on 30 August 1893 in a rural community deep in the heart of the state of Louisiana. The seventh of nine children, he showed great promise at school, but was expelled for agitation. Despite that temporary setback, he won a debating scholarship to Louisiana State University (LSU), and in order to afford the textbooks required he spent the next four years as a travelling salesman and auctioneer. In 1915 he passed the bar exam after only a year at Tulane University in New Orleans, and during the next decade he practised law in Shreveport. Most of his cases involved representing small plaintiffs against large businesses, including workers' compensation cases (he later boasted that he had never accepted a case against a poor man). He attracted national media attention by taking on the powerful Standard Oil Company, which he sued for unfair business practices. Thus began a lifelong obsession – to weaken Standard Oil's iron grip on the economic and political life of Louisiana, and to distribute the profits from the state's vast oil and gas resources more fairly.

'Don't let me die! I've got so much to do'

Reputedly Long's last words, as reported by his sister

Long's heartfelt enmity against Standard Oil won him a place on the Louisiana Railroad Commission in 1918, when he was still only 25. Here he perfected the techniques that subsequently marked his political career: the distribution of printed circulars and posters; the use of radio and sound trucks; an exhausting schedule of personal campaign stops throughout rural areas; and vehement, often personal attacks on his opponents. His work for the commission came to the attention of the US Supreme Court, prompting Chief Justice William Howard Taft to describe Long as one of the best legal minds he had ever encountered.

Having come a distant third in the race for Governor of Louisiana in 1924, Long spent the next four years building his reputation and his political organization, particularly in the Catholic south of the state. In 1928 he stood again, under with the slogan 'every man a king, but no-one wears a crown' – a phrase adopted from the populist presidential candidate William Jennings Bryan (1860–1925). His campaign sought to exploit the class resentment of rural Louisianians against the corrupt politicians of New Orleans and Baton Rouge. And this time he won, by the largest margin in Louisiana's history.

Installed as governor, Long began a massive clearout of those officials who had opposed him. Hundreds were fired from state and local government, their positions filled by Long's own supporters – every one of which was expected to pay a portion of his or her salary directly into Long's political war-chest.

His subsequent legislation fulfilled many of the promises he had made to the state's poor. He passed bills championing free textbooks for schoolchildren and night courses to combat adult illiteracy, and he began to build roads, bridges, hospitals and schools on a scale not seen before. His bills were forced through the state legislature by browbeatings, threats and blackmail, but this heavy-handed approach worked. He bought off the political machine in New Orleans and Baton Rouge by offering the former city a comprehensive programme of public works and the latter modern highways, an enlarged campus for LSU and a new State Capitol.

In 1929 Long addressed his favourite vested interest, proposing an 'occupational license tax' of five cents on each barrel of state-produced oil. Oil-funded opponents in the Louisiana Senate won support for Long's impeachment, which proceeded despite a brawl on the floor of the legislature. Long responded by appealing directly to the voters, and in a speaking tour he lashed out against the impeachment proceedings as an attempt by Standard Oil and other business interests to undermine his campaigns for ordinary men and women. Meanwhile, Long persuaded (generally armed with a bribe of money or offices) over one-third of the state senators to confirm in writing their support for Long, no matter what the evidence. The impeachment proceedings collapsed.

The failure of impeachment prompted Long to yet another clear-out of state officials. Given that the opposition now financed all of the state's newspapers, in March 1930 he founded his own title, the *Louisiana Progress*. In order to receive lucrative state contracts, companies were first expected to buy advertisements in Long's paper – a move that earned Long the first of many death threats, and which led him to appoint armed bodyguards. He also treated LSU as his personal fiefdom, choosing its president, interfering in academic affairs and even trying to coach the university football team. He did, though, increase its student numbers by 150 per cent and introduced numerous scholarships for the poor.

Long's opponents now alleged that the governor had become a virtual dictator. He relished his nickname of 'the Kingfish' – a reference to George 'Kingfish' Stevens, a character in the immensely popular radio show *Amos 'n' Andy*. But opposition to his control of state affairs erupted in 1931. Long was elected as a US Senator for the state in 1931, and one of his many powerful enemies, Louisiana Lieutenant Governor Paul Cyr, argued that Long could now no longer remain governor, declaring himself as Long's replacement. Long's response was swift and brutal: he surrounding the State Capitol with National Guard troops, declared Cyr sacked and appointed his crony Alvin King in Cyr's place. For the governorship, Long chose his childhood friend Oscar Allen as his candidate, campaigning under the slogan 'Complete the Work'. Allen strolled to victory, and Long finally resigned as governor.

Long in brief

1893 Born into a poor family near Winnfield, Louisiana, the seventh of nine children.

1915–25 Passes his bar examinations, and works as lawyer in Shreveport: his litigation against corporate interests and large utilities, in particular Standard Oil, attracts widespread popularity.

1918 Elected to the state Railroad Commission, which evolves into the more powerful Public Service Commission.

1924 Comes third in election for state governor.

1928 Finally elected state governor on a populist ticket and pursues an ambitious programme of public works, corporate tax increases, welfare legislation and educational reform. He also ruthlessly stifles or buys off opposition.

1929 Uses deft political manoeuvres and bribes to escape impeachment.

1930 Founds the *Louisiana Progress* newspaper to further his agenda.

1932 Elected a US Senator for Louisiana, resigning the governorship, but retains immense informal control personally and via successors loyal to him.

1932–5 As a Senator, pursues his anti-business and social welfare agendas, but falls out with President Roosevelt. Develops his 'Share Our Wealth' programme and adopts an isolationist stance in foreign affairs.

1935 Shot (8 Sept.) in the State Capitol, Baton Rouge, and dies two days later.

CASTING A LONG SHADOW

Long made a vivid impression in Washington, with his fiery speeches denouncing the concentration of wealth in the hands of the few. He became a vocal supporter of the presidential candidacy of Franklin D. Roosevelt, but after the latter's election in 1932 he realized that Roosevelt was not the radical he had hoped him to be and he began to act entirely independently. Roosevelt considered Long 'one of the … most dangerous men in America', and later compared him to Hitler and Mussolini. As Roosevelt restricted Long's access to federal funds destined for Louisiana, Long's radical rhetoric and his bullying manner did little to endear him to his fellow Senators: not one of his proposed bills, resolutions or motions was passed during his three years in the Senate.

In 1934, Long proposed the radical 'Share Our Wealth' scheme. By this, draconian taxes on corporations would be used to guarantee every family a basic household grant of $5000, free primary and college education, old-age pensions, veterans' benefits, federal assistance to farmers, public works projects and the establishment of a 30-hour working week. A national network of local Share Our Wealth Clubs was launched with the slogan 'Every man a King'. (There was even a campaign song, recently re-recorded by Randy Newman as part of an album largely devoted to Long's life and reputation.)

By 1934 Long had all but abolished independent local government in New Orleans, Baton Rouge and Alexandria, and abrogated to himself the power to appoint all state employees. He even boasted that he had 'taken over every board and commission in New Orleans except the Community Chest and the Red Cross'. His more ominous state initiatives included a 'tax on lying', a tax on newspaper adverts and the creation of a special force of plainclothes police answerable only to the governor. The following year he admitted that he intended to stand for president, and he wrote a book confidently entitled *My First Days in the White House*.

That book, though, would appear posthumously, for on 8 September 1935, Long was assassinated in the Capitol building at Baton Rouge. The official version has one Dr Carl Weiss – a medic whose father-in-law had been ousted by Long's supporters from his judge's office – shooting Long once. Weiss was himself immediately shot over 30 times by Long's bodyguards and nearby police. However, alternative accounts suggest that Weiss was merely about to punch Long, and the over-reacting bodyguards, firing wildly, hit not only Weiss but also Long himself. The debate still continues.

Long died two days later, from internal bleeding. Popular among ordinary voters to the last, his burial in the grounds of his new State Capitol in Baton Rouge attracted an estimated 100,000 Louisianians. The presiding minister notoriously blamed his death on 'the Roosevelt gang, supported by the New York Jew machine'.

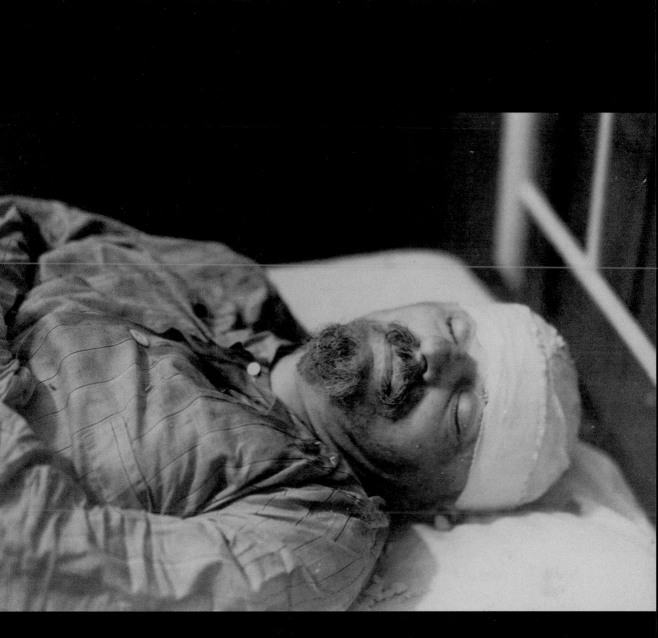

Leon TROTSKY

1879–1940, RUSSIAN REVOLUTIONARY

ASSASSIN Ramón Mercader
DATE 20 August 1940 (died 21 August)
PLACE Coyoacán, Mexico City, Mexico

'Leon Trotsky' was actually Lev Davidovich Bronstein, born on 7 November 1879 (or 26 October, in the Old Style Russian calendar). One of the key figures in the 1917 Russian Revolution, and instrumental in Russia's post-revolutionary struggle against opponents at home and abroad, he was purged by Stalin after Lenin's death and deported from Russia. By 1940, in exile in far-off Mexico, he seemed to have escaped the fate of countless fellow-Bolsheviks at home, hundreds of thousands of whom had been shot by Stalin's secret police, the NKVD. On 20 August 1940, however, Trotsky's luck ran out. A Soviet agent masquerading as a supporter drove an ice pick into his skull.

The fifth child of a wealthy but illiterate Jewish farmer, the young Trotsky had become a committed Marxist by the late 1890s. In January 1898 he was arrested, and spent the next two years in prison awaiting trial. (While in prison, he married a fellow Marxist, Alexandra Sokolovskaya.) In 1900 he was finally sentenced to four years in exile in Siberia; two years later he escaped, having forged a passport in the name of Leon Trotsky – possibly the name of a prison jailer, and a title which became his revolutionary identity. Once abroad, he moved to London to join Vladimir Lenin and other editors of the revolutionary newspaper *Iskra* ('Spark').

Shortly before the unsuccessful revolution of 1905, Trotsky returned secretly to Russia. By this time he had not only married again, but he was more closely aligned with the more democratically tinged 'Menshivik' grouping of Marxists than Lenin's Bolsheviks. In Russia, he wrote leaflets for an underground printing press in Kiev, but he soon moved to the capital, St Petersburg. Following the abortive rising, Trotsky and other revolutionaries were put on trial in 1906 on charges of supporting an armed rebellion. Trotsky was once more sentenced to deportation, but again escaped – this time from the train taking him east. Returning to London, he soon left for Vienna, where for several years he involved himself in Austrian left-wing politics and journalism. On the outbreak of war between Austria and Russia in 1914, he made himself *persona non grata* by condemning all the belligerents and, along with many other left-wing intellectuals, moved to neutral Switzerland. From there he went to France, was deported to Spain, and deported again to the United States, arriving in January 1917.

> ## 'Grave-digger of the revolution'
> Trotsky's verdict on Stalin in 1926, though the latter now wielded the power

Trotsky was living in New York City when the February Revolution of 1917 overthrew Tsar Nicholas II. He left New York on 27 March, but the British intercepted his ship and he spent a month detained in Nova Scotia. The new Russian foreign minister demanded that Trotsky be released, and Trotsky finally arrived back in Russia on 4 May 1917. But the Marxists were not yet in the ascendant, and Trotsky was again in prison, and now abandoned the Menshivik tendency for the Bolsheviks. Out of jail, Trotsky was elected chairman of the Petrograd (as St Petersburg was now renamed) 'Soviet of Workers' and Soldiers' Deputies' in the second revolution of the summer, the one that swept away the shaky liberal administration. More importantly for the future of the new regime, Trotsky soon revealed himself to be a superlative military manager, leading the efforts to repel a Cossack counter-revolution. Together with Lenin, he resisted attempts by other leading

TROTSKYISM

TROSTKY CAME TO BELIEVE THAT HE, rather than Stalin or even Lenin, was the ideological heir of Karl Marx and the idealistic revolutionaries of 1917. The label 'Trotskyite', however, began as a pejorative term used by Stalin and his supporters, and by 1936 it became shorthand in the Soviet Union to denote any state traitor or supposed counter-revolutionary. It was only during Trotsky's exile that the term became widely used by Trotsky's own followers, coming to represent the creed defined by Trotsky and his polyglot supporters at the grandly named 'Fourth International' of 1938. After the Allied victory of 1945 and the burgeoning Soviet influence that came with it, however, Trotskyite movements in places as far afield as Bolivia and Vietnam were brutally crushed on Stalin's orders. Today it survives in the form of marginal parties across the world.

Trotskyism's most celebrated tenet was a belief in the necessity of a worldwide 'permanent revolution' of the proletariat, which came to be seen as directly contradictory to the Stalinist credo of 'socialism in one country'. Otherwise, Trotsky believed, capitalist states, whether led by bourgeois governments or dictators, would combine to throttle any new socialist economy. Post-revolutionary Russia, Trotsky held, had degenerated into a state run by bureaucrats, whose interests were hostile to those of the working class. He argued that if the working class did not take power away from the Stalinist bureaucracy, the bureaucracy would restore capitalism in order to protect its own status and to make itself still wealthier.

By 1951, Trotsky's heirs concluded that Russia's communist empire comprised merely 'deformed workers' states', and that the Soviet leadership itself was counter-revolutionary. However, the movement's influence on Russian politics was, and remains, negligible.

Bolsheviks such as Zinoviev and Kamenev to share power with other socialist parties, and by the end of 1917 Trotsky was unquestionably the second man in the Bolshevik Party after Lenin.

In the new Bolshevik government, Trotsky was appointed 'People's Commissar for Foreign Affairs'. In that capacity he headed the Soviet delegation during the peace negotiations with Germany in Brest-Litovsk. Trotsky, like Lenin, hoped that the negotiations would be overtaken by a revolution in Germany. That did not transpire, however, and the resumption of the offensive by the Central Powers in February 1918 showed that the Russian army was in no shape to resist. On 18 February Trotsky accepted Germany's extremely harsh peace terms (far crueller than those meted out to a defeated Germany by the Allies in 1919).

On 13 March 1918 Trotsky metamorphosed into the People's commissar of Army and Navy Affairs, giving him full control of the Red Army. With Russia now deeply divided in its post-revolutionary civil war, he began transforming the Red Army from a ragtag network of small and fiercely independent detachments into a large and disciplined military machine. In this role he had his first clash with Stalin, then a commissar in the south of Russia who believed that the new army should be reorganized along strictly revolutionary lines. The more pragmatic Trotsky firmly believed that the armed forces should utilize the pre-revolutionary experience of former tsarist officers wherever possible. This argument laid the foundations for a bitter feud that was to result in Trotsky's disgrace, expulsion and eventual murder.

Trostky's military leadership successfully beat off military threats from the Czechs, the Ukrainians, the White Russians, the Cossacks, the Poles and their Western allies. He successfully defended Petrograd against the Whites in October 1919, and guided the Red Army through a series of hard-won victories of the like no impartial observers could have expected in 1918. However, his military successes did not improve his standing with his Bolshevik colleagues.

From 1921 Lenin's health deteriorated fast: he suffered three strokes after May 1922. By spring 1923 he was virtually paralysed and speechless, and he died on 21 January 1924.

1879 Born Lev Davidovich Bronstein, son of a Jewish farmer, in Yanovka, Ukraine.

1887–95 Educated in Odessa, living with relatives.

1896–8 Having absorbed Marxist theories, joins an underground workers' group.

1898–1902 Arrested for political activity and imprisoned for two years awaiting trial, but escapes from internal exile in Siberia. Travels to London to join Lenin and the 'Social Democrats'.

1905–7 Returns secretly to Russia, taking part in unsuccessful 1905 Revolution: put on trial, he escapes abroad again.

1907–17 Lives in Vienna, working as journalist and continuing political activity; then moves around Europe on outbreak of First World War (which he opposes), ending up in USA.

1917 Following the February Revolution, returns to Russia, but is imprisoned briefly. Joins the Bolsheviks and plays major role in the October Revolution.

1918–20 Negotiates Russia's withdrawal from the First World War, and organizes the new Red Army in its successful civil war with counter-revolutionary forces. Effectively becomes No. 2 to Lenin.

1924–8 Outflanked by Stalin for the leadership after Lenin's death, and becomes increasingly marginalized as Stalin establishes himself, leading to internal exile.

1929–40 Expelled from the Soviet Union, he lives in Europe before settling in Mexico, attempting to promulgate his views by writing and by establishing the 'Fourth International'.

1940 Attacked at home (20 Aug.) by a Soviet agent, and dies the following day.

The stage was now set for an epic power struggle for the mastery of the Soviet Union – a conflict that many assumed Trotsky, with the Red Army behind him, would win. However, Trotsky could not contend with one of the most devious and manipulative political minds of the century. Stalin isolated his former comrade by allying with two well-known opponents of Trotsky's, Zinoviev and Lev Kamenev. Together, this *troika* sidelined Trotsky as a man whose undoubted skills at military management were not suited to the politics of peacetime. Using a classic strategy, Stalin offered Trotsky demeaning, second-rank ministerial jobs he would be bound to refuse, and then claimed that this reluctance to play a part in government simply emphasized that Trotsky was yesterday's man. A year before his death, Lenin had attempted to oust Stalin from power and to ensure that Trotsky was confirmed as his successor; however, his last stroke swiftly terminated such a move, since Trotsky – who always seemed to lack Stalin's killer instinct – was reluctant to lead the charge.

The first victory of Stalin's campaign came in January 1924, when the party conference denounced Trotskyism as a 'petty bourgeois deviation'. However, Trotsky was still a popular figure in the country at large, and the *troika* was careful to keep him in all of his posts. Unfortunately for Trotsky, though, he was recovering from a serious bout of illness in the Caucasus when Lenin died later that month. He was about to come back when a telegram from Stalin arrived, giving an incorrect date of the scheduled funeral, a date on which Trotsky could not attend. Trotsky was thus absent from Moscow during the crucial days of interregnum, enabling Stalin and his allies to strengthen their grip on government.

Secure in power, in 1925 Stalin encouraged Zinoviev to demanded Trotsky's expulsion from the Communist Party. The move failed – Stalin himself skilfully playing the ostensible role of mediator. But Trotsky found he had less and less to do. At the party conference in October 1926 Trotsky could barely speak because of interruptions and catcalls. At the end of the conference he finally lost his Politburo seat. In October 1927 both Trotsky and Zinoviev (whom Stalin saw as almost as much of a threat to his position as Trotsky) were expelled from the party's central committee; the following month they were expelled from the Communist Party. While Zinoviev capitulated, Trotsky refused to admit he had made any mistakes or that he was fomenting counter-revolution. Accordingly, in January 1928 he was exiled to Alma Ata (now in Kazakhstan), and in February 1929 was ejected from the Soviet Union, accompanied by his wife, Natalia Sedova, and his son, Lev.

The next few years saw Trotsky return to his days as a wanderer. The family's first refuge was Turkey, staying for four years on a small island off the coast near Istanbul. In

1933 Trotsky was offered asylum in France by Premier Edouard Daladier, on condition that he did not visit Paris. By 1935, however, his welcome was all used up, and he moved to Norway. In 1937, allegedly because of Soviet pressure on the Norwegian government, he was placed under house arrest, but sympathetic Norwegian officials booked his passage to Mexico on a freighter before the NKVD could send its assassins. Arriving in Mexico, he was warmly welcomed by the progressive president himself, Lázaro Cárdenas, who had arranged a special train to bring him to Mexico City.

In Mexico, Trotsky lived at one point at the homes of the painter Diego Rivera and Rivera's wife and fellow-artist, Frida Kahlo. He became a prolific writer while in exile, penning his *History of the Russian Revolution* in 1930 and *The Revolution Betrayed*, a damning account of Stalin's dictatorship, in 1936.

'Do not kill him! This man has a story to tell.'

Trotsky's remarkably rational injunction regarding the attacker who had just buried an ice-pick in his skull.

Trotsky eventually quarrelled with Rivera, and in 1939 he moved into his own residence in Coyoacán, a suburb of Mexico City. On 24 May 1940 he survived a raid on his home by NKVD assassins, complete with machine guns. Three months later, however, he was not so lucky. On 20 August 1940 Trotsky was attacked in his home by a Spanish NKVD agent, Ramón Mercader, who had visited him several times. As Trotsky read an article his visitor had brought, Mercader seized an ice pick, a somewhat un-Mexican weapon he had imaginatively hidden under his coat, and drove it into Trotsky's skull.

Surprisingly, the blow failed to kill Trotsky outright, and the two struggled. This alerted Trotsky's bodyguards, who burst into the room and nearly killed Mercader. Bizarrely, Trotsky stopped them, allegedly shouting: 'Do not kill him! This man has a story to tell.' Trotsky was taken to hospital but, despite an emergency operation, died the next day.

Trotsky's grave lies in the garden of his house in Coyoacán, which is now preserved as a museum. Even in the age of post-communist freedom, however, Trotsky has never been officially rehabilitated by the Russian state. In contrast, his assassin, after spending 14 years in a Mexican jail (the death penalty having been abolished), earned Russia's highest accolade as 'A Hero of the Soviet Union'.

Reinhard
HEYDRICH

1904–1942, SENIOR NAZI OFFICIAL

ASSASSINS	Jan Kubiš and Jozef Gabčík
DATE	27 May 1942 (died 4 June)
PLACE	Prague, Czech Republic

I t may at first glance seem obtuse and even grotesque to document an assassination of one individual within the context of a worldwide maelstrom in which millions lost their lives. However, the killing of Nazi SS *Obergruppenführer* Reinhard Heydrich, the 'Hangman', was a momentous event in the history of the Second World War. It encapsulated one nation's resistance to brutal and seemingly unending repression and symbolized the world's protest against genocide.

The victim was no ordinary Nazi. Heydrich was not only a senior SS officer, but also chief of the hush-hush *Reichssicherheitshauptamt* (RHSA), the Reich Security Head Office where his responsibilities included running the Gestapo, and additionally the Reich's Governor of the Czech territories of Bohemia and Moravia. He was also regarded by many as a possible successor to Hitler. Most importantly, Heydrich was one of the principal architects of the Holocaust, having chaired the Wannsee Conference of 1942 where leading Nazis agreed plans for the extermination of European Jews.

Heydrich's evolution into an agent of mass murder cannot be put down to a deficient or brutalized upbringing. Far from it: born the son of a composer (Reinhard's second name was 'Tristan', after Wagner's opera *Tristan and Isolde*), he was a talented child who became a skilled violinist as well as an accomplished athlete. However, his glittering prospects took a turn for the worse when, in 1931, he was dismissed from the German Navy on the orders of Great Admiral Erich Raeder. The reason for Heydrich's fall from grace is still unclear. His own version – that he had refused to marry a woman with whom he had been sleeping, and whose father was a close friend of Raeder's – has now been discredited. Raeder himself survived the war, and always refused to disclose his reasons for sacking Heydrich. Perhaps the most presentable theory is that Heydrich was cashiered for spying on naval personnel for the Nazis. The fact that soon afterwards SS leader Heinrich Himmler appointed him to expand the SD (*Sicherheitsdienst*), the SS's new 'Security Service', gives this thesis considerable credence.

'The authority for directing the final solution of the Jewish question rests with the ... Head of the Security Police and the SD'

Heydrich's genocidal job description, from the Protocol of the Wannsee Conference, 20 January 1942

Heydrich's rise within the Nazi hierarchy after 1932 was rapid. Having taken care to build an elaborate card-file record of all potential 'threats' to the regime (which included many members of the Nazi Party itself), Heydrich recruited a large number of SD personnel from a wide variety of backgrounds. He also demonstrated a talent for dispassionate cruelty, which was singularly lacking in his superior, Himmler. (Himmler, who nicknamed Heydrich 'Genghis Khan', actually appears to have been afraid of his steely subordinate.) Heydrich's first reward came in 1934, when he also gained control of the Gestapo – the *Geheime Staatspolizei*, the civil secret police. Two years later the Gestapo was merged with the criminal-investigative police into the *Sicherheitspolizei* (SiPo, or Security Police) under Heydrich. On becoming head of the RHSA in 1939, he effectively ran both the SD and SiPo.

1904 Born 'Reinhardt', son of the head of the Halle Conservatory of Music. As teenager, becomes involved in anti-semitic nationalist politics.

1922–31 Signals officer in the German navy, but is dismissed, ostensibly for dishonourable conduct. Joins the Nazi Party and its SS paramilitary.

1933 With Hitler now German chancellor, helps achieve Nazi control of country's security and police apparatus.

1934 Becomes SS chief for Berlin. Helps coordinate the anti-SA purge of the 'Night of the Long Knives'.

1936 By now, has become head of the SD (the SS's security service), the Gestapo (the civil secret police) and the criminal police.

1938 Appointed head of the Central Office for Jewish Emigration. Helps purge senior military officers.

1939 Leads the new Reich Security Head Office (RHSA). With Eichmann, begins deporting Jews from Germany and Austria.

1940–I Oversees the corralling of Polish Jews into ghettos, and organizes the *Einsatzgruppen* mobile units to murder Jews and others.

1941 With Germany now at war with the Soviet Union (June), is charged by Goering with developing a new plan for the 'Jewish question'. Appointed *Reichsprotektor* (governor) of 'Protectorate of Bohemia and Moravia' (most of Czechoslovakia).

1942 Chairs the Wannsee Conference, which smoothes the way for the 'Final Solution' of the Jews: mass extermination.

1942 Wounded in his car by British-trained assassins (27 May), and dies (4 June) from septicaemia. The Nazi authorities enact revenge against Czech civilians.

Himmler soon found Heydrich indispensable, though exasperating. While Heydrich's ability was undoubted, the young Nazi was also extremely competitive and aggressive. (In 1940, for example, he told Hitler's deputy, Hermann Goering, and his council of ministers that the SD and Gestapo would exercise limitless powers whether they were officially granted them or not.) However, his scrupulous records detailing the activities of suspicious individuals within the Reich, together with his talent for muckraking espionage, made him invaluable to both Himmler and Hitler. It was his carefully planned (though, in the event, clumsily executed) ruse of a Polish attack on German forces at Gleiwitz that provided the pretext for the Nazi invasion of Poland in 1939.

In November 1938, Goering made Heydrich head of the euphemistically named Central Office for Jewish Emigration. Heydrich used this position to assert SS dominance over Jewish policy, a campaign that culminated in the Wannsee Conference of 20 January 1942, which Heydrich chaired. The fate of the Jews in Nazi-occupied Europe was thereby sealed. The 'Final Solution' of complete extermination was officially recommended by Heydrich on behalf of the conference delegates, and it was rubber-stamped by both Goering and Hitler.

In September 1941 Heydrich was appointed *Reichsprotektor* (governor) of the Czech puppet state, a region of the Reich defined by the Nazis (in deliberately anachronistic language) as the 'Protectorate of Bohemia and Moravia'. Heydrich's post was a vital one for Germany's war effort: many of Germany's guns and tanks now emanated from Prague's Škoda works, whose output was essential to maintaining the Nazi invasion of Russia. Accordingly, Heydrich instituted a strict regime of obedience. Czech workers who did not produce the required quotas were punished, and anyone associated with the resistance movement was tortured and executed. No-one was left in any doubt that it was Heydrich, and not the nominal Czech president and prime minister, who ruled the Czech homeland.

Heydrich's success encouraged Hitler to consider making him the Governor of Paris. News of this proposal reached London, and prompted British intelligence to concoct a plan to protect their painstakingly assembled French Resistance networks from Heydrich's ruthless but effective ministrations. (The plan was probably also fomented by the Czech government in exile.) They recruited two Czechs, Jan Kubiš and Jozef Gabčík, who had fled their country in 1941. After receiving appropriate training from Britain's newly formed Special Operations Executive (SOE), these two were parachuted back into Czechoslovakia in December 1941. And on 27 May 1942 they staged their assassination.

After the Conservatives' election defeat at the hands of Ramsey McDonald's growing Labour Party in 1929, Guinness retired from office. In 1932 McDonald's National Government coalition – a supposedly temporary expedient dictated by the economic crisis of the Great Depression – created him Baron Moyne of Bury St Edmunds. Throughout the 1930s, however, Moyne remained close to Churchill in the latter's 'wilderness years', often entertaining him at his homes or on his yachts. He was also a member of Churchill's 'Other Club', that gathering of politicians and journalists opposed to appeasement with Nazi Germany. And, like Churchill, Moyne spent much of the decade travelling the world (and writing about it), converting a 700-ton ferry for his personal use in this cause.

Churchill's dramatic wartime rise to the prime ministership in 1940, brought inevitable ministerial rewards for Moyne. In February 1941 Moyne was appointed colonial secretary and leader of the House of Lords.

On 9 June 1942 Moyne made a speech in the House of Lords attacking the Zionist proposal to bring 3 million Jews to Palestine after the war. Since the final death throes of the Ottoman Empire in 1918, much of the Middle East had been administered by the victorious European powers under League of Nations' mandates, and like many politicians Moyne saw the future mainly in a federation of Arab states. Moyne claimed that (British-mandated) Palestine was far too small and overcrowded, and he suggested instead that (French-run) Lebanon and Syria and (British-run) Transjordan could absorb a large number of Jews without threatening them as political entities. Partly as a result of his interest in the affairs of the Middle East, Moyne was appointed deputy resident minister in Cairo in August 1942 and promoted as full 'Resident Minister in Egypt and the British Middle East' two years later. As the man on the ground, he was effectively Egypt's ruler.

Having helped engineer the defeat of the German Afrika Korps in North Africa by 1943, thus relieving the pressure on Cairo and eliminating the German threat to the oil reserves of Persia (Iran), Moyne then received a strange proposal from the heart of Germany. Joel Brand, a member of the Jewish–Hungarian Aid and Rescue Committee, approached the British in April 1944 with a proposal from Adolf Eichmann, the senior SS officer in charge of deporting Hungary's Jews. Eichmann – part of a German occupying force that was under increasing threat from the advancing Russians – suggested that the Nazis could release up to 1 million Jews in exchange for 10,000 trucks and other goods from the Western Allies. Brand was arrested, taken to Cairo and questioned. (He later made an unauthenticated allegation that Moyne – who in reality Brand probably never met – exclaimed 'What can I do with a million Jews? Where can I put them?') In the event, the British dismissed the proposal as deliberately divisive, intended to divide the Allies rather than save Jews. Moyne and his officials also recommended that the offer could be safely ignored on the grounds that all the concentration camps would be liberated within weeks. As it turned out, this confident assertion was a disastrously over optimistic prediction. Between mid-May and early July 1944 approximately 437,000 Hungarian Jews boarded the

Moyne in brief

1880 Born Walter Guinness in Dublin, Ireland, third son of the 1st Earl of Iveagh. Educated at Eton and Oxford.

1899 Volunteers to fight in the Second Anglo-Boer War.

1907 Elected to the London County Council and House of Commons as Conservative MP for Bury St Edmunds (which he represents until 1931).

1914–18 Serves with the Suffolk Yeomanry in Egypt and at Gallipoli, and at Passchendaele in 1917.

1922–9 Holds various ministerial posts (under-secretary of state for war, financial secretary to the treasury and minister of agriculture).

1932 Created 1st Baron Moyne of Bury St Edmunds.

1934–8 Travels widely and writes.

1941–2 Returns to politics under Churchill; appointed colonial secretary and leader of the House of Lords.

1942 Appointed deputy resident minister of state in Cairo.

1944 Appointed resident minister in Egypt and the British Middle East (Jan.). Assassinated by Zionist extremists outside his Cairo home (6 Nov.).

PARTITIONING PALESTINE

IN NOVEMBER 1943, THE BRITISH CABINET proposed a partition of Palestine based loosely on the 1937 Peel Commission plan: this included a Jewish state, a small residual mandatory area under British control, and an Arab state, designed to be absorbed in a large Arab Federation of Greater Syria. The Cabinet approved the plan in principle in January 1944, but faced severe opposition from the foreign secretary, Anthony Eden, among others. Lord Moyne, however, was a strong supporter.

Tragically, the plan was before the Cabinet for final approval in the same week that Moyne was assassinated. Yet again, a political assassination achieved the opposite of its intent. Moyne's brutal murder caused the scheme to be immediately shelved, and the staunch opposition of Moyne's successor in Cairo, Sir Edward Grigg, to any form of partition meant that the British government never again seriously considered this type of compromise. Clement Attlee's Labour government of 1945, distracted by other priorities, witnessed two years of dreadful indecision over Palestine, as the British wavered about how to deal with the growing number of immigrant Jews and rising Arab–Jewish tensions. In 1947, Britain passed its mandate back to what was by now the United Nations, which voted for partition: immediately Arab states attacked the fledgling Israel. Sixty years on, the fruits of this bitter dispute are still convulsing the region and beyond.

'resettlement trains' to the Auschwitz death camps, where most were immediately gassed.

Yet the rejection of Eichmann's offer ultimately played little part in Moyne's assassination. The resident minister was instead chosen for disposal as a symbol of the British imperialism that was obstructing Jewish migration into the Arab-populated territory of Palestine. In 1940, with Nazi Germany in the ascendant, Irgun (the Jewish National Military Organization) abandoned its paramilitary struggle against British rule; but one disaffected adherent, Avraham Stern, formed his own 'Stern Gang' to continue operations, and this evolved into the Fighters for Israel's Freedom (sometimes known by the acronym 'Lehi'). One of their leaders, Nathan Yellin-Mor, later said they had considered assassinating the previous resident minister in 1941, but he had been Australian and was deemed insufficiently 'imperialist'. Moyne's appointment in 1944 was just what the terrorists had been waiting for. They now demonized him, unfairly, as an anti-semitic Arabist who had consistently followed an anti-Zionist line, and they sought his murder on the grounds that this would advertise the seriousness of the Zionist cause to the British government and the world.

After the assassination, Lehi announced: 'We accuse Lord Moyne and the government he represents, with murdering hundreds and thousands of our brethren; we accuse him of seizing our country and looting our possessions ... We were forced to do justice and to fight.' Meanwhile, Bet-Zuri and Hakim were tried in an Egyptian court and, in January 1945, found guilty of murder. Their appeals for clemency were dismissed, partly in response to pressure from Moyne's old friend, Churchill. Interestingly, Bet-Zuri and Hakim also enjoyed the support of many local Egyptians, who also resented British rule and saw the imminent end of the war as a chance to grasp genuine independence for their country. Nevertheless, the two men were hanged in Cairo on 23 March. Bizarrely, their eve-of-execution request was for a book of poems by the archetypal poet of Britain's empire – Rudyard Kipling.

Moyne's assassination was condemned by the Jewish establishment in Palestine, who began to cooperate with the British authorities in attempting to deal with both Lehi and Irgun. Chaim Weizmann, who subsequently became the first President of Israel, is reported to have said that Moyne's death was more painful to him than that of his own son.

Back in Britain, Churchill lamented to the House of Commons that 'If our dreams for Zionism are to end in the smoke of an assassin's pistol, and the labours for its future produce a new set of gangsters worthy of Nazi Germany, then many like myself will have to reconsider the position we have maintained so consistently and so long in the past.' The *Times* rightly declared that the assassins had 'done more by this single reprehensible crime to demolish the edifice erected by three generations of Jewish pioneers than is imaginable'.

Mohandas K. GANDHI

1869–1948, INDIAN POLITICAL LEADER

ASSASSIN	Nathuram Godse
DATE	30 January 1948
PLACE	New Delhi, India

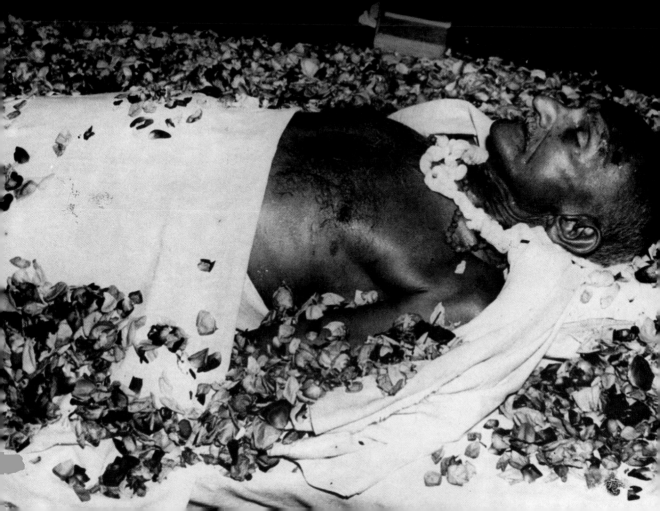

astuteness that was to serve him so well later in life. His devout mother, an adherent of the Jain religion, taught him the tenets of her faith: the sanctity of life, vegetarianism, abstinence from alcohol, fasting for self-purification, and mutual tolerance across creeds and sects. These principles helped to frame and guide his adult political career.

In 1888 Gandhi went to University College, London, to study law. Here, as a practising Jain, he joined the Vegetarian Society, was elected to its executive committee, and founded a local chapter. He later credited this experience as having given him valuable lessons in organizational behaviour.

Gandhi returned to India after being successfully admitted to the bar, but he had limited success establishing a law practice in Bombay (now Mumbai). He ended up returning to his home town of Rajkot to make a modest living drafting petitions for litigants. That, too, failed after he earned the enmity of a local British officer. Frustrated and dispirited, in 1893 Gandhi accepted a year-long contract from an Indian legal firm in Natal, South Africa.

South Africa, though, would be the making of Gandhi, and the experience opened his eyes to far more dramatic forms of racial discrimination than were evident to him in India. He was thrown out of a court in Durban for refusing to remove his turban; he was ejected from a train at Pietermaritzburg after refusing to move from the first-class coach to a third-class one, to make way for white passengers; he was savagely beaten by a stagecoach driver for refusing to travel on the footboard to make room for a European passenger. Such incidents stirred Gandhi to a realization of the racism and social injustice then endemic in South Africa.

> 'Non-violence is the first article of my faith. It is also the last article of my creed.'
>
> Gandhi, defending himself in court against charges of sedition, 1922

On the termination of his year-long contract, Gandhi prepared to return to India but was persuaded to stay and lead the legal fight against the Natal Legislative Assembly's proposed bill to deny Indians the right to vote. Although unable to halt the bill's passage, his campaign was successful in drawing attention to the grievances of Indians in South Africa, and it helped him to found the Natal Indian Congress in 1894, with himself as its secretary.

In 1896 Gandhi briefly returned to India in order to bring his wife and children back with him to South Africa. Once back in Africa, in January 1897, he was attacked by a white mob, which tried to lynch him. He refused, though, to press charges against any of the mob, stating that it was one of his principles not to seek redress for a personal wrong in a court of law. It was an early indication of the values that would shape his later campaigns.

As the Second Anglo-Boer War got underway in 1899, Gandhi argued that Indians should support the British war effort against the Afrikaners in order to legitimize their claims to full citizenship. Accordingly, he organized a volunteer ambulance corps of 300 Indians and 800 indentured labourers, which became one of the few medical units prepared to serve wounded Black Africans. Gandhi himself acted as a stretcher-bearer at the Battle of Spion Cop, one of many early disasters for the British forces – and he was subsequently decorated for it.

After the war, however, there was still much to do. In 1906 Gandhi announced a non-violent campaign against the Transvaal regional government's proposal to enforce registration of all Indians. Over the next eight years, thousands of Indians in South Africa were jailed (including Gandhi himself on many occasions), flogged, or even shot; they responded by striking, refusing to register, burning their registration cards and other forms of non-violent resistance.

Gandhi returned to India in 1914, joining the Indian National Congress – the principal political grouping in the struggle against British rule for Indian self-government. Here he initiated protests against social injustice. His first public success was won in 1918, in a campaign targeting Gujurati landlords (and their British protectors) who forced their tenants to grow indigo and other cash crops instead of the foodstuffs necessary for their survival (the result being famine and alcoholism in the affected villages). Gandhi organized a detailed study and survey of these villages, describing the atrocities and terrible episodes of suffering, and began a clean-up of the worst areas, building schools and hospitals. Unsurprisingly, he was soon arrested and ordered to leave the province, but hundreds of thousands of people protested outside his jails, police stations and courts demanding his release. Ultimately, the provincial government, prodded by the British, acceded to his demands, and it agreed to give the villagers control over their farming and compensation for their losses. By the end of the campaign, Gandhi was being addressed by the people as 'Bapu' (Father) and 'Mahatma' (Great Soul), and his fame was spreading nationally.

In April 1919 General Reginald Dyer ordered his troops to open fire on an unarmed religious celebration in Amritsar, in the Sikh province of the Punjab, where objections to British colonial policies were running high and where there had been some disturbances. While the official report declared that 379 Indians had been killed, the actual death toll was probably nearer 1000. In the aftermath of the massacre, leading politicians in Britain condemned the atrocity, and Indians rioted in the streets. (Years later, in 1940, Sir Michael O'Dwyer, Lieutenant Governor of the Punjab in 1919, was shot dead in London by an avenging Punjabi revolutionary.)

Gandhi was careful to criticize both Dyer and the retaliatory violence. He offered condolences to British

Gandhi in brief

1869 Born Mohandas Karamchand Gandhi in the Indian princely state of Porbandar, Gujarat, India, where his father is chief minister.

1888–91 Studies law at University College, and trains as barrister at the Inner Temple, both in London.

1893 Failing to find post as barrister in India, takes up one-year appointment with legal firm in Natal, South Africa.

1894–1914 Remains in South Africa, championing the legal and civil rights of the Indian community, adopting strategy of non-cooperation.

1914 Returns to India and joins the Indian National Congress and its campaign for civil rights and Indian self-government. Initiates protests against social injustice, which continue for the rest of his life.

1921–4 Now leading the INC, introduces 'non-violent' boycotts of British institutions: tried for sedition and imprisoned until 1924.

1924–7 Following two years in prison, withdraws from politics to travel around India promoting Indian crafts and the plight of the 'Untouchables' (Dalits), the lowest rank in India's caste system.

1930 Launches campaign against tax on salt, publicized by his 'Salt March'.

1939–42 Resolves not to support British India's wartime role, instead launching his 'Quit India' campaign.

1942–4 Jailed with other Congress leaders after negotiations for independence fail.

1947 Opposes the partition of India on independence.

1948 Assassinated (30 Jan.) by a Hindu extremist.

PARTITION

IT HAS BEEN ESTIMATED THAT over half a million people died as a result of the partition of India in 1947. This is just what Gandhi had feared; yet, as many Congress leaders pointed out, the death toll could have been immensely higher, and the duration of the inevitable civil war far longer, if Partition had been rejected.

The new northerly nation, defining itself through Muslim identity, comprised two separate enclaves, East Pakistan (now Bangladesh) and West Pakistan, separated geographically by India. Independent India was formed out of the majority Hindu regions of the subcontinent previously under British control. The many remaining semi-autonomous princely states negotiated to join either Pakistan or India between 1947 and 1950, their decisions based on geography and local circumstances. The border between India and Pakistan was to be determined by a commission headed by the British lawyer, Sir Cyril Radcliffe, but it split along partisan religious lines, leaving him the invidious task of making most of the decisions. The Labour-apppointed viceroy, Lord Louis Mountbatten, was accused (with some justification) of rushing the process of partition and independence, and also, less fairly, of influencing Radcliffe's awards in India's favour. In the event, the two nations were granted their independence before there was a properly defined boundary between them.

Anxious not to end up vulnerably on the 'wrong side' of a divide, there occurred massive population exchanges: about 7.25 million Indian Muslims headed to Pakistan, while a slightly larger number of Hindus and Sikhs left what was now Pakistan for India. It was one of the largest population movements in recorded history. And it was tragic, too, for in many areas there was a complete breakdown of law and order, replaced by riots and massacres. Today, the subcontinental neighbours, both armed with nuclear weapons, continue to argue over borders, in particular with regard to Kashmir.

civilian victims of the uprising and condemned the riots – to the rage of many within the Congress Party. However, Amritsar helped Gandhi to the conclusion that Indian independence was the only way forward. From December 1921 he helped to reorganize the party with this one goal firmly in mind.

Meanwhile, Gandhi expanded his non-violent protest to include a boycott of foreign-made (particularly British) goods. Homespun cloth should, he advocated, be the only fabric worn by Indians, and not British-made textiles; if feasible, this cloth should be spun at home. At the same time, Gandhi exhorted Indian men and women to boycott British educational institutions and courts, to resign from government employment, and to forsake British titles and honours.

Gandhi's policy of non-cooperation enjoyed widespread success. Violence in Uttar Pradesh in February 1922, however, encouraged Gandhi to call off the campaign of mass civil disobedience. Two weeks later he himself was arrested, tried for sedition, and sentenced to six years in prison. He was incarcerated until February 1924, when he was freed after an operation for appendicitis. During this period the Congress Party began to show ominous signs of a split along the religious fault line between Hindus and Muslims.

By December 1928 Gandhi was calling on the British government to grant India dominion status immediately (in the manner of Canada and Australia), or face a new campaign of non-violence aimed at achieving complete independence. The British did not respond, however, and on 31 December 1929 the new national flag of India was provocatively unfurled in Lahore. In March 1930 Gandhi launched a new campaign against the notoriously iniquitous tax on salt, which he publicized by his famous 'Salt March' to the sea at Dandy, where he proceeded to make salt himself. Thousands of Indians joined him on the march, and the subsequent unrest resulted in the imprisonment of over 60,000 people.

India's new viceroy, Lord Irwin (subsequently the Earl of Halifax), opted to negotiate with Gandhi, and in March 1931 agreed to free all political prisoners. In return, Gandhi agreed to call off the campaign for civil disobedience and to represent the Indian

National Congress at the Round Table Conference in London. The conference was a severe disappointment, and soon after his return to India Gandhi was arrested yet again. In protest, Gandhi embarked on a six-day fast in September 1932 and a 21-day fast of self-purification in May 1933.

When war broke out in 1939, Gandhi initially backed Britain in a qualified way, but other Congress leaders were offended by the viceroy's unilateral declaration of war on India's behalf. Gandhi eventually came to the conclusion that it would be nonsensical to support a war to preserve democracy if India did not have democracy itself. Momentously, he launched a campaign demanding nothing less than that the British 'Quit India'. As a result of this stand, Gandhi and the entire Congress Working Committee were arrested in Bombay by the British authorities on 9 August 1942. Gandhi was held for two years, during which time his wife and personal secretary died.

Gandhi was released in May 1944 because of his failing health. The following year in Britain, Clement Attlee's Labour government gave clear indications that it was prepared to grant India its independence, and Gandhi called off the struggle, encouraging the new viceroy, Lord Wavell, to release over 100,000 political prisoners.

In the subsequent negotiations, Gandhi was vehemently opposed to the partition of India along religious lines. However, Congress ignored his advice and approved the partition of the subcontinent into India and Pakistan as the only way to prevent a civil war between Hindus and Muslims. On the day of the transfer of power in 1947, Gandhi did not celebrate independence with the rest of India. Instead, he was alone in Calcutta, mourning Partition and working to end the appalling outbreaks of violence that accompanied it. He launched his last 'fast-unto-death' in Delhi, asking that all communal violence be ended once and for all.

In such an eventful life, Gandhi had made enemies among fellow Indians, especially among those who hated his ecumenical, inclusive respect for Muslims and Hindus alike. At various points since 1934, there were attempts (in some cases, inconclusively proven) to kill or harm him. On 30 January 1948, Gandhi was staying at the magnificent house of the wealthy Birla family in New Delhi. Here, the man described by India's Prime Minister Nehru as 'the father of the nation', finally fell victim to the kind of violence he had spent his life eschewing. Nathuram Godse, a Hindu radical who regarded Gandhi as an appeaser of Muslim Pakistan, shot and killed 'Bapu' as he was on his way to a prayer meeting. Godse and his co-conspirator Narayan Apte were tried, convicted, and executed in 1949.

Gandhi was buried in New Delhi. The majority of Gandhi's ashes were divided among all the major rivers of the world, from the Nile to the Thames, with a small portion being enshrined at the Mahatma Gandhi World Peace Memorial, within a thousand-year-old stone sarcophagus sent from China.

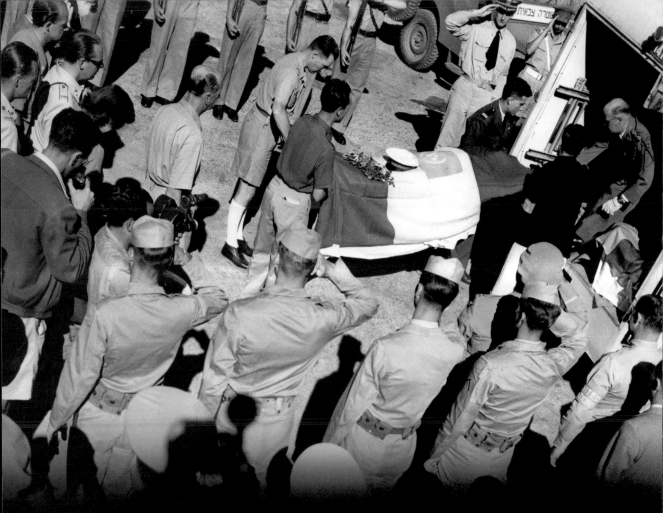

Folke
BERNADOTTE

1895–1948, SWEDISH UNITED NATIONS MEDIATOR

ASSASSIN	Yehoshua Cohen
DATE	17 September 1948
PLACE	Jerusalem, Israel

Folke Bernadotte, Count of Wisborg, officer and diplomat, lived to all intents and purposes a charmed life in the higher echelons of society. He was born in 1895, a nephew of Sweden's King Gustav V and a direct descendant of the French Marshal Bernadotte, who in 1818 had founded the current Swedish royal dynasty when he became King Charles XIV.

Bernadotte's first 50 years were serenely untroubled. He trained as a cavalry officer at the elite military school of Karlberg. He married an American heiress, Estelle Manville of Pleasantville, New York, with whom he had four children. He represented his country at the Chicago 'Century of Progress' Exposition of 1933 and the New York World's Fair of 1939 – surely two of the most interesting and unusual diplomatic commissions of the decade. He became head of the Swedish Scouts movement in 1937, and was appointed vice-chairman of the Swedish Red Cross in 1943. And in 1943–4 Bernadotte organized exchanges of prisoners-of-war from within Germany, managing to extricate 11,000 Allied prisoners from the Reich via Sweden.

In 1945, Bernadotte's life changed completely, in a manner that catapulted him onto the world's stage and exposed him to the full horrors of war. In his capacity as an officer of the Red Cross, he received an offer from the senior Nazi Heinrich Himmler: that Germany would surrender to Britain and the United States, provided it was allowed to continue the fight against the Soviet Union. The offer was passed to British Prime Minister Churchill and US President Truman without Hitler's knowledge, but was never accepted. Days later, Himmler was captured by the Allies and, in order to avoid interrogation, committed suicide.

Shortly before the end of the war, Bernadotte led a rescue operation transporting interned Norwegians, Danes and other Allied inmates from German concentration camps, including Ravensbrück, to hospitals in Sweden. Around 15,000 people were taken to safety in the mission's Red Cross 'White Buses', including many thousands of Jews. The rescue exposed Bernadotte and his Swedish Red Cross staff to significant danger from the disintegration of the Nazi state and the persistent Allied bombing. The White Buses continued in the late spring of 1945 to rescue more people.

Bernadotte recounted his wartime experiences in *The Fall of the Curtain: Last Days of the Third Reich*, published speedily in 1945. His achievement was subsequently publicized in the world's press, giving him international stature as a man of peace and compassion. Eight years later, however, his account of events was challenged by Himmler's former masseur, Felix Kersten, who had allegedly played an intermediary role in the Himmler negotiations but whom Bernadotte did not credit in his book. In an interview with British historian Hugh Trevor-Roper in 1953, Kersten alleged that Bernadotte had been no more than a transport officer and, most damagingly, that the count had privately sympathized with the Nazis' policy towards the Jews. Following the publication of his article, Trevor-Roper began to retreat from these charges, and gradually evidence began to appear suggesting Kersten was an unstable fantasist. (One of his most ambitious claims was that he had personally saved the whole Dutch population from deportation at the hands of the SS.) In 1995, Trevor-Roper told the journalist Barbara Amiel that he was no longer certain about the allegations. Other historians have been more definitive, however, with most concluding

> 'The provisional government of Israel is today exercising ... all the attributes of full sovereignty'
>
> Bernadotte's appreciation of Middle East realities, as quoted by Daniel Mandel in his *H.V. Evatt and the Establishment of Israel*, 2004

1895 Born Folke Bernadotte in Stockholm, Sweden, son of the Count of Wisborg and nephew to the Swedish king.

1918 Begins a military career, initially as lieutenant, before becoming a diplomat for Sweden.

1937 Becomes head of the Swedish Scouts movement.

1943—4 Appointed vice-chairman of the Swedish Red Cross, and secures exchange-release of 11,000 Allied prisoners from Germany.

1945 As war ends, leads Red Cross operation transferring inmates (including many Jews) from German concentration camps to hospitals in Sweden. Transmits offer of German surrender from Himmler to the Allies (24 April): it is rejected.

1948 Appointed UN's first mediator, as Arab countries fight with the fledgling Israel, and proposes two plans for resolving the conflict. Assassinated (17 Sept.) by member of the extremist Jewish Lehi group for his perceived pro-Arab inclinations.

that Kersten's account was based on forgery and distortion. However, the damage to Bernadotte's reputation from Trevor-Roper's article was considerable. As for its author, thirty years after his Kersten article Trevor-Roper was caught up in a far bigger scam when he 'authenticated' the newly discovered (but actually forged) 'Hitler Diaries' for the *Sunday Times*, a mistake that became more of a public event than his traducing of Bernadotte's good name in 1953.

Bernadotte's next mission after the war was an extremely problematic one: how to reconcile Jews and Arabs in what was then still Palestine, administered by the British under a League of Nations mandate. After 1945, hundreds and later thousands of Jews fled the European continent, where they had known only centuries of oppression, persecution and slaughter, and had journeyed to the Holy Land, their ancient Israel, to make a new life. Once here, however, they began to displace the Palestinian Arabs. Unrest followed, and in 1948, as the new United Nations voted to partition Palestine and allow Israel to come into being, all-out conflict erupted as neighbouring Arab countries launched attacks.

On 20 May 1948 Bernadotte was appointed UN mediator in Palestine – the first official mediator in the organization's history. In this capacity, he succeeded in achieving a truce in the war and laid the groundwork for the UN's relief agency for Palestinians. At the end of June 1948, Bernadotte submitted his first formal proposal, in secret, to the warring parties: that Palestine and Transjordan be reformed as a union of Arabs and Jews, with certain areas predominantly Jewish and others predominantly Arab (including Jerusalem), but also including free ports and airports. Both sides summarily rejected the proposal.

Bernadotte then suggested an arrangement of two separate states. Declaring, much to the Arabs' ire, that 'a Jewish state called Israel exists in Palestine and there are no sound reasons for assuming that it will not continue to do so', he called for the establishment of two adjacent nations based on 'the principle of geographical homogeneity and integration'. Jerusalem was to have special international status, and should not belong to either of the new nations. And Bernadotte defined a new border between the Jewish and Arab areas.

The rights of the territory's original inhabitants were not forgotten. Bernadotte proposed that the UN should establish a 'Palestinian Conciliation Commission', which would supervise the return of Arab refugees to their homes in Jewish-controlled areas where feasible, and (more controversially) the payment of compensation for those who chose not to return.

To the more extreme Jewish nationalists, Bernadotte had gone too far, with the fate of Jerusalem a particular bone of contention. In their eyes, he also compounded his partiality towards the Arabs when he declared in July that the main war appeared to be over and that the conflict now consisted primarily of 'incidents'. Somewhat unreasonably, the new Israeli government denounced the Swede's 'lack of sensitivity' in describing the continued loss of life in this manner, concluding that his role as a credible mediator was now in doubt.

The Israeli government's criticism of Bernadotte was interpreted by Jewish nationalist terrorists as a licence to remove him altogether, and as a way of derailing the peace process. (In fact, the Israeli government had already rejected the count's revised proposals by the time of his death.) An assassination plan was hatched by the splinter group 'Lehi' (Fighters for

Israel's Freedom), which used to be known as the Stern Gang and had a record of political killings, including the British administrator Lord Moyne in 1944. Three of its leaders – Yitzhak Shamir, Nathan Yellin-Mor and Yisreal Eldad – developed the plan. On 17 September, four men led by Meshulam Makover ambushed Bernadotte's motorcade in central Jerusalem, and Yehoshua Cohen fired directly into Bernadotte's car. The count and his aide, UN observer Colonel André Serot, were killed. Bernadotte's aide, General Aage Lundstrom, was in the same car, and afterwards gave a graphic description to the UN of the assassination:

> We were held up by a Jewish Army type jeep placed in a road block and filled with men in Jewish Army uniforms. At the same moment, I saw an armed man coming from this jeep. I took little notice of this because I merely thought it was another checkpoint. However, he put a Tommy gun through the open window on my side of the car, and fired point blank at Count Bernadotte and Colonel Sérot … Colonel Sérot fell in the seat in back of me, and I saw at once that he was dead. Count Bernadotte bent forward, and I thought at the time he was trying to get cover. I asked him: 'Are you wounded?' He nodded, and fell back …

On arriving at the hospital, Lundstrom described how he:

> … took off the count's jacket and tore away his shirt … I saw that he was wounded around the heart and that there was also a considerable quantity of blood on his clothes … When the doctor arrived, I asked if anything could be done, but he replied that it was too late.

The following day, the UN Security Council condemned the killing of Bernadotte as 'a cowardly act which appears to have been committed by a criminal group of terrorists in Jerusalem while the United Nations representative was fulfilling his peace-seeking mission in the Holy Land'. Lehi took responsibility for the killings, berating Bernadotte as a stooge of the British and their Arab allies, and therefore as a serious threat to the emerging state of Israel.

The Israeli government had no alternative but to take some action against Lehi, forcibly disarming it and arresting many members. Yet nobody was ever charged with the killings. Yellin-Mor and another Lehi member, Schmuelevich, were charged with belonging to a terrorist organization: they were found guilty, immediately released and pardoned. Yellin-Mor had meanwhile been elected to the first Israeli parliament, the Knesset. Years later, in October 1983, the former Lehi member Yitzhak Shamir became the seventh prime minister of Israel. In 1995, after the assassination had soured Israeli–Swedish relations for years, the Israeli government issued public regrets over Bernadotte's murder and gave thanks for his wartime rescue of thousands of Jews.

US DENIAL AND UN SUCCESSION

AFTER BERNADOTTE'S DEATH, his revised peace proposal and his status as 'honest broker' were undermined by reports in October 1948 that he had been in consultation with the British and American governments. Placed on the back foot, President Truman, who was facing a presidential election, backpedalled furiously and made pro-Zionist noises to reassure his Jewish American voters. Militarily, events had changed on the ground anyway to Israel's advantage. The Bernadotte plan was holed below the water, and unsurprisingly it failed to be voted through the United Nations.

The job of UN mediator now fell to Bernadotte's former assistant, the American Ralph Bunche. He eventually negotiated an Arab–Israeli ceasefire, which was signed on the Greek island of Rhodes in 1949. This achievement subsequently won Bunche the Nobel Peace Prize. In the eyes of many, this was an award that really belonged to the late Count Bernadotte.

Today, the Swedish government's Folke Bernadotte Academy is devoted to pursuing international conflict resolution: it constitutes a fitting memorial for the pioneer mediator.

FAISAL II

1935-1958, KING OF IRAQ

ASSASSINS	Iraqi coup plotters
DATE	14 July 1958
PLACE	Baghdad, Iraq

King Faisal of Iraq was very much a man of his era. On the one hand, he carried the Westernized sentiments of his class and background – he was, after all educated at one of the most traditional of Britain's schools and depended for his rule on British support. On the other hand he had a genuine desire to further the cause of Arab nationalism. Unable to square the circle, Faisal soon fell victim to a brutal coup, which saw both his murder (when aged only 23) and the end of the Iraqi monarchy.

The Hashemite Kingdom of Iraq was invented by the British at the end of the First World War, but it would last barely 40 years. It was carved out of the ruins of the old Ottoman Empire, using what had been known as Mesopotamia as its geographical basis. Faisal's grandfather, Faisal I, had fought for the Allies in the war at the head of the Arab Revolt, in which role he had become the patron of Lawrence of Arabia. A grateful Britain briefly installed him as King of Syria in 1920, and after his ousting by the French – who were keen to re-establish their influence in the Levant – he was compensated with the newly constructed Kingdom of Iraq in 1921.

In 1932 Iraq became the first of the former Ottoman territories to be accorded nominal independence, although it was tied to Britain in terms of her foreign policy and defence measures. Following Faisal I's death in 1933, his son, Ghazi succeeded to the throne: but he was killed in a car accident when his heir, Faisal, was aged only three. Thus, while Faisal II became king in 1939, his uncle Prince Abdallah ruled as regent until Faisal came of age in 1953. Iraqi army officers nevertheless remained suspicious of the pro-British stance of the royal family. It was widely rumoured that Ghazi's death had been engineered by British agents, or possibly by the Anglophile Iraqi prime minister, Nuri as-Said.

Middle Eastern politics grew even more complex with the advent of the Second World War. By 1941 the Allied powers of Western Europe were definitely on the defensive. France had already surrendered, and her possessions in the Levant, while technically ruled by the collaborationist Vichy regime, were available for use by the armed forces of Germany and Italy. Meanwhile, the British were being driven from Crete and Greece by superior German forces.

British resources in North Africa and the Middle East were already overstretched when, on 3 April 1941, Prince Abdallah was deposed in a coup by the pro-Nazi prime minister, Rashid Ali al-Gaylani, and Iraqi units besieged the British airbase at Habbaniya. An Iraq allied to the Germans was unthinkable for the British: it imperilled their valuable sources of Persian oil and threatened links with India (as road and air routes would be severed between India and Cairo). The British were also worried that nationalist insurrection in Iraq could spread to British-run Palestine and Egypt. As a result, in May 1941 General Wavell despatched a division of the Indian Army to Iraq to restore Abadallah to the regency, liberate Habbaniya and eject the pro-Axis members of the Iraqi government.

> 'Today, O my brothers ... we are stronger than ever before ... The same flag of freedom that flies over Baghdad today will be hoisted in Amman and Beirut'
>
> Egypt's President Nasser, welcoming the overthrow of Faisal II, as quoted in *Time* magazine, 28 July 1958

Vichy France offered to help the Germans by giving them safe passage through Syria, but by the time Hitler had declared that 'the Arab liberation movement is our natural ally', the RAF had annihilated the Iraqi air force while the British Army, having liberated Habbaniya, was occupying Basra. On 30 May British forces reached Baghdad, and the following day Abdallah was restored to the regency. Rashid, along with the Mufti of Jerusalem (who had called for a 'jihad' against the British), fled to Persia. By the middle of July 1941, the RAF and British Army, using Iraq as a forward base, had also overcome the Vichy French forces in neighbouring Syria and Lebanon, with Free French help.

Having safely guided Iraq to the conclusion of the war on the side of the Allies, Abdallah formally stepped down as regent in 1953. However, he continued to be a close adviser of the young king and a strong advocate of a pro-Western foreign policy.

During the war years, Faisal II was a long way from these events, at Harrow School in England, which he attended together with his cousin, Prince Hussein of Jordan – who in 1952 would accede to the Jordanian throne. The two boys were close, and reportedly they planned even then to merge their two realms to counter what they considered the threat of militant pan-Arab nationalism. Yet Harrow – the school of Winston Churchill and generations of British statesmen and civil servants – also instilled in young Faisal the habits of an English gentleman. Sadly, unfailing politeness and a devotion to the principle of fair play were of little help to the king in the volatile postwar world of the Middle East.

Iraq remained under British military occupation until late 1947. By then, the country was split between those who looked to the pro-British monarchy for a lead, and those who sought a radical nationalist alternative. In November 1946, an oilworkers' strike culminated in a massacre of the strikers by the police, and Nuri was brought back as prime minister. He briefly brought Liberals and National Democrats into the Cabinet, but soon reverted to a more repressive approach. He negotiated a new alliance with Britain in January 1948, prompting a violent response on the streets of Baghdad. Students and communists led the protests, and the Iraqi police reacted by killing many. The regent abrogated the treaty, but Nuri persisted in a policy of harsh repression of the protestors.

Faisal's coming of age in 1953 made little difference to Nuri's policies. In 1954 the Iraqi government signed up to the Baghdad Pact, a Cold War alliance tying Iraq closely with Britain and other pro-Western countries in the region (Iran, Turkey and Pakistan). But the anti-government protests were gathering strength. In 1956 they coincided with the watershed humiliation of Britain and France's attempted occupation of the Suez Canal region (effectively an attempt to topple Egypt's pan-Arabist leader General Nasser). So, in February 1957 the Iraqi opposition felt confident enough to broker a 'Front of National Union' made up of National Democrats, Independents, Communists and the pan-Arabist Ba'ath ('Renaissance') Party.

In February 1958, the Iraqi monarchy and its Hashemite ally King Hussein, in Jordan, declared a formal union ('Arab Federation') of their countries in reaction to the creation of the 'United Arab Republic' between Syria and Nasser's Egypt. Nuri became the first prime minister of the new Federation, but his triumph lasted only five months.

FROM COUP TO COUP

ONE OF COLONEL QASSIM'S FIRST ACTS as Iraq's new premier in 1958 was to dilute Iraq's relationship with Britain and United States. He withdrew Iraq from the pro-Western Baghdad Pact, and on 30 May 1959 the last British soldier left the Habbaniya airbase. At the same time, he dissolved the union of Iraq with the Anglophile King of Jordan. He also nationalized the assets of the British-owned Iraq Petroleum Company.

During the following years, Qassim supported the Algerian and Palestinian struggles against, respectively, France and Israel. He also demanded the annexation of Kuwait and the return of Iranian territory allegedly seized from Iraq. However, unlike his Ba'athist successor Saddam Hussein (who, with others, tried to assassinate Qassim in 1959), Qassim did not resort to unwinnable wars to enforce these claims.

On the home front, Qassim's actions were at first liberal and reformist. An interim constitution proclaimed the equality of all Iraqi citizens under the law, granting them freedom without regard to race, nationality, language or religion. The government freed political prisoners and granted amnesty to Kurds who had participated in uprisings in the 1940s. Qassim also lifted a ban on the Iraqi Communist Party. New housing was created for the poor, and the first steps were taken towards a genuine welfare state.

By 1961, however, Qassim's far-sighted reforms had begun to bear unwanted fruit. Increasing autonomy for the Kurds had merely stoked Kurdish claims for complete independence, resulting in considerable unrest. And for many pan-Arabists, Qassim's nationalist stance simply did not go far enough. Meanwhile, his pro-Arab foreign policy and firm support for the Algerian rebels earned him the enmity of Britain, France and the United States, while his suspicion of Nasser's Egypt left him relatively isolated on the international stage.

The 1959 attempt on his life led Qassim to implement a crackdown on political opposition. It was to no avail: in 1963 a coup staged by another colonel, Abdul Salam Arif, toppled Qassim, who was quickly tried and executed.

On 14 July 1958 Colonel Abdul Karim Qassim seized control of Iraq in a daring coup. Prince Abdallah calculated that, if the royal palace offered no resistance, there would be no bloodshed. The commander of the royal troops guarding the palace was accordingly ordered to cease fire. The king, Prince Abdallah and other members of the royal family were then captured and brought down to the main courtyard. There, allegedly on Qassim's orders, they were told to face the wall and were gunned down by troops under Qassim's protégé, Captain Abdus Sattar Assab.

King Faisal and Abdallah's wife, Princess Hiyam, were not killed instantly. The king died before reaching the hospital, but in the chaos of the coup Princess Hiyam was not recognized and managed to receive treatment, subsequently fleeing abroad.

Prime Minister Nuri was not among the royal party assassinated in Baghdad. He went into hiding, but was captured the next day as he sought to make his escape disguised as a woman. Nuri was executed and buried that same day, but an angry mob disinterred his corpse and dragged it through the streets of Baghdad, where it was hung up, burned and mutilated.

Qassim now had Iraq at his feet. Iraq was declared a republic, and the monarchy abolished. (The Balliol-educated successor to the Iraqi throne, Faisal II's uncle, Prince Zeid, was conveniently in London when the coup took place. He died in Paris in 1970.) Qassim assumed the posts of prime minister and defence minister, and took on executive and legislative powers. The years to come, however, were to demonstrate to the colonel that politics was a far more difficult and treacherous business than soldiering.

Medgar EVERS

1925-1963, US CIVIL RIGHTS WORKER

ASSASSIN	Byron de la Beckwith
DATE	12 June 1963
PLACE	Jackson, Mississippi, USA

Many murders and acts of violence were committed at the height of the civil rights unrest in America's Deep South in the 1950s and 1960s. Few were more resonant, however, than the assassination of African American activist Medgar Evers.

In 1994, almost thirty years after the tragedy (and two subsequent trials, which feebly failed to reach a verdict), police rearrested Byron de la Beckwith – a former fertilizer salesman and sometime member of the White Citizens' Council and Ku Klux Klan – for the murder. The body of Evers had been exhumed from his grave for an autopsy and found to be in a surprisingly excellent state of preservation as a result of embalming, and it yielded new evidence. Beckwith was convicted on 5 February 1994, after living as a free man for three decades after the assassination. His appeals against the decision were unsuccessful, and he died in prison in January 2001.

Following the retrial, Evers was reburied in a second funeral, enabling his grown-up children to say goodbye properly. Evers' life and death had already been the subject of one film, in 1983; now the new funeral was featured on HBO's TV series *Autopsy*, while the 1996 film *Ghosts of Mississippi* told the uplifting story of the 1994 trial itself.

Evers was born in Decatur, Mississippi, in 1925, and lived there until being drafted into the US Army, aged 18, in 1943. Arriving in France soon after D-Day, he fought courageously in Normandy and was demobbed in 1945 with an impressive war record. However, Evers soon found that the colour of his skin not only stopped him getting a job. When he and five friends attempted to vote in a local Mississippi election, they were forced away from the polling station at gunpoint.

Evers subsequently enrolled at Alcorn State University, majoring in business administration. He was a model student: a star of the university's football and track teams, he was keen debater and singer, and served as president of the junior class. He married classmate Myrlie Beasley on Christmas Eve 1951, completed work on his degree the following year, and moved to Mound Bayou, Mississippi, to sell insurance for Magnolia Mutual Life. More importantly, Evers also began to be involved in the Regional Council of Negro Leadership (RCNL), a Mississippi civil rights organization. He helped to organize the RCNL's boycott of service stations that denied African Americans use of their toilets: the boycotters distributing bumper stickers with the slogan 'Don't Buy Gas Where You Can't Use the Restroom'. And along with his brother, Charles, he attended the RCNL's highly popular annual conferences in Mound Bayou between 1952 and 1954.

> 'If he had to die to get us that far, he was willing to do it'
>
> Myrlie Evers, on her husband Medgar's struggle against racism, *Esquire* magazine, July 1991

Evers applied to the then-segregated University of Mississippi Law School in February 1954. When his application was rejected, he became the focus of a National Association for the Advancement of Colored People (NAACP) campaign to desegregate the university, using the US Supreme Court's recent ruling that segregation was unconstitutional.

The NAACP, one of the oldest and most influential civil rights organizations in the United States, was founded in 1909. Its mission, as enunciated in 1911, is:

To promote equality of rights and to eradicate caste or race prejudice among the citizens of the United States; to advance the interest of colored citizens; to secure for them impartial suffrage; and to increase their opportunities for securing justice in the courts, education for the children, employment according to their ability and complete equality before law.

In December 1954, Evers became the NAACP's first field officer in Mississippi. Desegregation was finally won at the University of Mississippi in 1962, when James Meredith became its first African American student.

In the years that followed, Evers found his profile rising, and by the early 1960s he was coming to the attention of a number of hostile constituencies. He pursued vocal and highly publicized investigations into two events: the murder of Emmett Till and the maltreatment of Clyde Kennard.

Till was an African American teenager from Chicago, who was murdered in the small town of Money in Leflore County, Mississippi. He was shot, beaten and thrown, weighted down, into the Tallahatchie River, where his body stayed for three days until it was discovered. His White assailants were acquitted, but they later admitted to the crime. Kennard had, like Evers, attempted to enrol at a segregated college, in his case Mississippi Southam. Despite offers from the state governor to pay for his tuition anywhere else in the state where he could gain acceptance, Kennard declined, pointing out that the college was the closest to his home. The all-White State Sovereignty Commission then conspired to have him framed for a crime: Kennard was arrested for reckless driving, police officers claiming to have found numerous bottles of whiskey under the seat of his car. Kennard was convicted on both offences, then rearrested on a trumped-up charge of stealing animal feed. On 21 November 1960 an all-White jury deliberated for only ten minutes before finding him guilty. Kennard was sentenced to seven years in prison, to be served at a high-security facility. In June 1961 the Mississippi Supreme Court overturned the conviction, but Kennard was only finally released seven months later, and he died of cancer before the end of the year.

As a result of these two cases in particular, Evers began to receive death threats. On 28 May 1963 a Molotov cocktail was thrown into the carport of his home. Five days before his death, he was nearly run down by a car on leaving the Jackson NAACP office. And the situation only got worse after he gave a pro-civil-rights speech to the local television station.

On 12 June 1963, Evers pulled into his driveway after returning from meeting with NAACP lawyers. Emerging from his car, he was shot in the back. He staggered thirty feet before collapsing, and he died at the local hospital fifty minutes later. Just the day before, President Kennedy had given a national address on television after the Alabama National Guard had intervened to uphold federal law and allow two students 'who happened to have been born Negro' to enrol at the University of Alabama. Kennedy's words were unequivocal: 'race has no place in American life or law'.

Evers, in death, became a national figure. Around 5000 people processed through Jackson to pay honour to Evers' body, including Martin Luther King (*see* photograph on p.140). He was buried on 19 June 1963 in Arlington National Cemetery, receiving full military honours

THE KU KLUX KLAN

THE KU KLUX KLAN (KKK) has long preached White supremacy, anti-semitism, racism, anti-Catholicism and homophobia. Its unusual name comes from the Greek *kyklos* ('circle'), combined with the Celtish term 'clan'.

Originally founded by veterans of the Confederate forces in 1866, the KKK's initial purpose was to violently resist the government's policy of Reconstruction in the South. This incarnation of the movement, however, was suppressed by President Grant's administration in the early 1870s.

In 1915, a second KKK was founded, inspired by D.W. Griffiths's overtly racist film *The Birth of a Nation* and the inflammatory, anti-semitic newspaper accounts of the trial and lynching of an alleged murderer, a Jewish factory manager. This incarnation soon comprised thousands of men organized in local chapters all over the country. At its peak in the early 1920s, the Klan's membership reached over 4 million. Extolling the virtues of segregation, anti-Catholicism, anti-communism and anti-semitism, many local groups took part in lynchings. Tainted by public scandals and their widespread support of Nazi Germany, however, Klan membership had declined sharply by 1940.

Although they were a prominent element in the opposition to desegregation and civilrights legislation in the 1950s and 1960s, their numbers were relatively small, and they relied heavily on fellow-travellers to support their cause and hide their crimes. These included the 1963 bombing of the 16th Street Baptist Church in Birmingham, Alabama, in which four children lost their lives.

The KKK still exists today. It is estimated that there are as many as 150 Klan chapters throughout the United States, largely – but not exclusively – based in the Deep South. Membership (which has perhaps dwindled to about 8000) is secret, as is the identity of the organization's titular head, the 'Wizard'. A member may use the acronym 'AYAK' ('Are you a Klansman?') in conversation to surreptitiously identify himself to another potential member; the required response is 'AKIA' ('A Klansman I am').

---

in front of a massive crowd of an estimated 20,000. The former chairman of the American Veterans Committee agreed to speak at the subsequent service, declaring that 'No soldier in this field has fought more courageously, more heroically than Medgar Evers.'

On 23 June 1963, Byron de la Beckwith was arrested for Evers' murder. But in the two separate trials he was given during 1964, the all-White juries could not agree to his guilt. During the course of his first trial, De la Beckwith was supported not only by a former Mississippi governor, Ross Barnett, but also by the retired army general and vociferous racist Edwin Walker.

Walker was an example of the kind of man Evers had been up against. After accusing various leading politicians of communist sympathies, he was relieved of his command in 1961. Embittered, he turned his attention to right-wing and racist politics. He lambasted the Supreme Court in its decision to desegregate the University of Mississippi as a 'conspiracy of the crucifixion by anti-Christ conspirators'. Walker had himself narrowly escaped assassination in April 1963 (strangely, at the hands of the Marxist-inspired Lee Harvey Oswald, the man 'credited' with killing President Kennedy). His career went on to include two arrests for 'public lewdness' in Dallas restrooms in the 1970s.

Gratifyingly, Evers' name still lives on. In 1970 Medgar Evers College was established in Brooklyn, New York, as part of the City University of New York. Evers' wife, Myrlie, became a noted activist in her own right, eventually serving as chair of the NAACP. Medgar's brother Charles also worked energetically for the cause of civil rights in Mississippi, and at the time of writing still lives in Jackson.

John F. KENNEDY

1917-1963, 36TH PRESIDENT OF THE UNITED STATES

ASSASSIN	Lee Harvey Oswald
DATE	22 November 1963
PLACE	Dallas, Texas, USA

In the modern media age, certain events register so shatteringly in the national or international psyche that they characterize an age. In the 21st century, the collapsing Twin Towers of the World Trade Center on 11 September 2001 have reconfigured the world in ways that are still unfolding. In 1963 it was the assassination of President 'Jack' Kennedy. Caught on television and replayed thousands of times since, it was a moment that seemed to symbolize the reaction of the old and outworn against the promise of the new.

Gone was the great white liberal hope, the youngest-ever president (and the first Roman Catholic one), the advocate of civil rights, the honorary *Berliner*, the defender of democracy, the man who saved the world from nuclear war over Cuba. He was glamorous (and partnered by a glamorous First Lady), clever, feted, mesmerizing, impossibly attractive to the opposite sex, and a dynamic embodiment of American self-confidence as the American Century reached its zenith.

Lee Harvey Oswald was none of these things. He never knew his father, who died shortly before Lee was born in New Orleans. As a result, his mother doted on him to excess. She also moved house a lot: young Lee attended 12 different schools. Unsurprisingly, then, her child became withdrawn and temperamental. He hit his mother, threatened his brother-in-law's wife with a knife, and after being caught for truancy was ordered to go for psychiatric observation, where doctors diagnosed 'personality pattern disturbance with schizoid features and passive-aggressive tendencies'.

Oswald never finished his high school education, yet as a teenager he decided to become a committed Marxist and to join the US Marine Corps. His time as a Marine was not a success: he was court-martialled twice, alienated from his fellow Marines by his pro-Soviet sympathies, and by the end of his Marine career (he was discharged early, having falsely claimed he had to care for his injured mother) he was on menial labour duties.

'The torch has been passed to a new generation of Americans'

From Kennedy's inaugural address as US president, 20 January 1963

In October 1959 Oswald emigrated to the Soviet Union, and announced that he wanted to renounce his US citizenship. When his application for Soviet residency was rejected (the Russians soon realized he had little of value to offer), Oswald feebly attempted to cut his wrists. This gesture persuaded the KGB to recommend his deportation, but surprisingly he was given a job as a metal lathe operator at the Gorizont Electronics Factory in Minsk and a rent-subsidised, fully furnished studio apartment in a prestigious apartment building. It was while he was there that he met the beautiful Marina Prusakova, a troubled 19-year-old student whom he married on 30 April 1961. Fourteen months later, Oswald, his wife and baby left the Soviet Union for the United States.

Settling back in Dallas, Oswald took a succession of low-paid jobs, and on 10 April 1963 he attempted to assassinate the extreme right-wing former general Edwin Walker, for which he was never apprehended. Interestingly, subsequent tests showed that the bullet that almost killed Walker was from the same cartridge manufacturer, and intended for the same type of rifle, as the two bullets which later struck Kennedy.

Oswald then returned to New Orleans, where, following the brinkmanship of the

Kennedy in brief

1917 Born in Brookline, Massachusetts, into a wealthy and influential family of Irish descent.

1936 After attending Choate School, Connecticut, enters Harvard University.

1938 Spends time in England, studying and working for the US Embassy (where his father Joseph is Ambassador).

1940 Joins the US Navy on graduation.

1943 Leads survivors to safety when his patrol torpedo boat is sunk by Japanese destroyer in the Solomon Islands, and is subsequently decorated for bravery.

1946 Elected as a Democratic Party Congressman for the 11th Massachusetts district (around Boston), and goes on to serve three terms in the House of Representatives.

1952 Elected to the US Senate.

1953 Marries Jacqueline Bouvier.

1955 Writes *Profiles in Courage*: it wins the Pulitzer Prize for biography (1957).

1960 Wins Democratic Party nomination to run as president.

1961 Inaugurated as US president. Establishes the Peace Corps. Authorizes CIA to support invasion of Cuba by anti-communist exiles (April): the 'Bay of Pigs' fiasco. Meets Soviet Premier Khrushchev, who demands Allies leave Berlin – in Aug. the Berlin Wall is built.

1962 First civil rights bill introduced in Congress. He resists the Cabinet hawks and succeeds in forcing a Soviet climbdown during the Cuban Missile Crisis (16–28 Oct.).

1963 Signs Nuclear Test Ban Treaty, the first disarmament agreement of the nuclear age. Asks economic advisers to prepare 'War on Poverty' programme for 1964. Assassinated (22 Nov.) in Dallas, Texas.

Cuban Missile Crisis, he became involved in pro-Castro demonstrations and activities. He even visited Cuba, declaring that he intended to travel from there back to the Soviet Union. Instead, he returned to Dallas.

On 16 November 1963, a local newspaper reported that President Kennedy's motorcade would be going through downtown Dallas in four days time, along a route that passed one block from the Texas School Book Depository, where Oswald was then working. Oswald was last seen there, by a co-worker, alone on the sixth floor about 35 minutes before the assassination.

Just before 12.30 p.m. on 22 November 1963, the open-top Lincoln Continental carrying President Kennedy slowly turned left, directly in front of the depository. As the car continued down Elm Street, shots were fired. (The majority of witnesses later recalled hearing three shots.) The first shot was generally assumed by onlookers to be a firecracker or a backfiring exhaust. In response, President Kennedy and his companion, Texas Governor John Connally, both turned to their right. Connally, though, recognized the sound of a high-powered rifle, and craned back to warn the president. He was too late: as Kennedy waved to the crowds on his right, a shot entered his upper back, penetrated his neck, and exited from his throat. He raised his clenched fists up to his neck and leaned forward and to his left, as his wife Jacqueline cradled him in her arms. Governor Connally was also hit, and yelled 'My God, they are going to kill us all!' The third and final shot took a large chunk out of the right side of Kennedy's head, covering the interior of the car and a nearby motorcycle officer with blood and brain tissue.

As Jacqueline Kennedy climbed onto the rear of the limousine (she later had no recollection of doing so), a nearby secret serviceman jumped onto the back of the car, pushed Mrs Kennedy back into her seat, and clung to the vehicle as it sped to Parkland Memorial Hospital. Shortly after the car arrived at the hospital, at 1 p.m., doctors pronounced the president dead. Vice-President Lyndon Johnson – who had been riding two cars behind Kennedy in the motorcade – took the oath of office as 36th President of the United States on board Air Force One at 2.38 p.m., just before it departed Dallas's inaptly named Love Field.

Governor Connally was critically injured but survived. Doctors later stated that after the governor was shot, Mrs Connally's swift action in pulling the Governor onto her lap saved him, protecting his front chest wound and his collapsed right lung.

As the motorcade had sped away from the plaza, police officers and spectators ran up the nearby grassy knoll towards the Triple Underpass, but no sniper was found. Howard Brennan, who was sitting across the street from the book depository, notified police that, as he watched the motorcade go by, he heard a shot come from above, and looked up to see a man with a rifle shoot from a corner window on the sixth floor of the depository. He had seen the same man, minutes earlier, looking out the window. Brennan's description of the sniper was immediately broadcast to all Dallas police, who quickly sealed off the entrances to the Depository.

Lee Harvey Oswald, reported missing to the Dallas police by his supervisor at the depository, was arrested in a cinema eighty minutes after the assassination for killing a Dallas police officer. Immediately after he had shot Kennedy, Oswald hid his rifle behind some boxes and descended via the depository's rear stairwell, leaving just before the police sealed off the building. He got a bus back to his home, then left, and while walking along the pavement was stopped by passing police patrolman, J.D. Tippit. As Tippit got out of his car, Oswald shot him four times with his revolver, then ran. Ducking into the entrance of a shoe store – whose owner quickly alerted the police – he scurried into the nearby Texas Theater without paying. Police entered the cinema, and Oswald – after exclaiming that 'it's all over now' – tried to shoot the arresting officer, but was successfully restrained. That evening, Lee Harvey Oswald was charged with the murders of Tippit and Kennedy. He denied all knowledge of the crimes, and then claimed he was merely a front for others.

Oswald's case never came to trial. Two days later, while being escorted to an armoured car for transfer from Dallas Police headquarters to the county jail, he was shot and killed by Jack Ruby, a Dallas nightclub owner, in front of live television cameras. Unconscious, Oswald was put into an ambulance and rushed to Parkland – the same hospital where JFK had died two days earlier. Doctors operated, but Ruby's single bullet had severed major blood vessels, and Oswald was pronounced dead. He was buried in Rose Hill Memorial Burial Park in Fort Worth, at a funeral in which there was no religious service and, fittingly, television and press reporters acted as pallbearers.

By now, President Kennedy's body had been brought back to the White House, and his flag-draped (and closed) casket was moved to the Capitol for public viewing. Hundreds of thousands lined up to view the coffin, and representatives from over 90 countries, including the Soviet Union, attended the funeral on 25 November. After the service, the president was buried in Arlington National Cemetery.

JACK RUBY

JACOB RUBENSTEIN, WHO IN 1947 (on his arrival in Dallas) changed his name to Jack Leon Ruby, was a Dallas businessman and nightclub owner. On 24 November 1963 he claimed his place in history by shooting and killing Lee Harvey Oswald as he was being transferred from Dallas police headquarters. As a manager of nightclubs and dancehalls, Ruby developed close ties to the many Dallas police officers who frequented his clubs. He was also loosely connected to the Mafia; many of his close friends were leading figures in the Dallas underworld.

Did organized criminals pay Ruby to murder Oswald, in order to eradicate evidence of an underworld conspiracy to kill the president? One of Ruby's friends, Joe Campisi, was an associate of Carlos Marcello, the Mafia boss who had reportedly talked of killing the president. The day before Kennedy was assassinated, Ruby was visiting Joe Campisi's restaurant.

After being arrested for Oswald's shooting, Ruby (also known as 'Sparky' on account of his notoriously short temper) announced he had shown the world that 'Jews have guts' and that he had shot Oswald to avenge Kennedy (and to spare Jackie Kennedy the ordeal of appearing at Oswald's trial). Ruby later claimed, though, that he shot Oswald on the spur of the moment when the opportunity presented itself.

On 14 March 1964 Ruby was convicted of 'murder with malice', i.e. premeditated murder, and sentenced to death. However, on 5 October 1966 his appeal was upheld. Arrangements were underway for a new trial to be held when, on 9 December 1966, Ruby was admitted to Parkland Hospital in Dallas, suffering from pneumonia. A day later, doctors realized he had advanced cancer. He died on 3 January 1967 and is buried in the Westlawn Cemetery in Chicago.

The 1964 Warren Commission report on the assassination concluded that Oswald acted alone, shooting at the president's car from the book depository. (His shots had also hit bystander James Tague, who received a minor facial injury.) Fifteen years later, the House Select Committee on Assassinations (HSCA) concluded that Kennedy had been assassinated as a result of a conspiracy. The committee criticized the performance of both the Warren Commission and the FBI for failing to investigate whether other people conspired with Oswald to murder the president. And the HSCA further suggested that an unnamed assassin from behind the grassy knoll opposite the depository had fired a fourth bullet. This theory was supported by acoustic evidence from a broadcast by a nearby police motorcycle, and was corroborated by 20 eyewitnesses in the plaza who claimed they heard a shot from the grassy knoll. Yet in 1981 a special panel of the National Academy of Sciences disputed the evidence of a fourth shot, concluding it was simply random noise. This was in turn rebutted in 2000 by government scientist D.B. Thomas, who supported HSCA's findings, while Thomas was debunked by a multi-author article in *Science and Justice* in 2005.

> 'The Commission has found no evidence that either Lee Harvey Oswald or Jack Ruby was part of any conspiracy, domestic or foreign, to assassinate President Kennedy'
>
> From the conclusions of The President's Commission on the Assassination of President Kennedy, better known as the Warren Commission, as delivered in September 1964. Rather than closing the debate, it fuelled conspiracy theories for years to come.

The debate goes on, spawning a distressingly large number of conspiracy theories. President Johnson, Fidel Castro, the CIA, the FBI and the Soviet government have all been implicated at one time. Worryingly, a 2003 poll found that 70 per cent of respondents suspected there was an assassination conspiracy.

To help defuse some of this speculation, a government Act of 1992 required that all surviving documents relating to the assassination should to be released to the public by no later than 2017. On 19 May 2044, the fiftieth anniversary of the death of the former First Lady, Jacqueline Kennedy Onassis – and assuming her last child, Caroline, has died – the Kennedy Library will release a 500-page transcript of her oral history of John F. Kennedy, which Jackie had dictated.

MALCOLM X

1925–1965, US CIVIL RIGHTS ACTIVIST

ASSASSINS Talmadge Hayer, Norman '3X' Butler
and Thomas '15X' Johnson

DATE 21 February 1965

PLACE New York City, USA

Malcolm X's life is a tale of astonishing metamorphoses: from Baptist to Muslim, from burglar to martyr, from shoe-shine boy to human rights activist, from drug dealer to one of the most prominent African American leaders in the United States. His life exemplifies the truth that circumstances of birth need not be an impediment to outstanding achievement.

Malcolm Little was born in 1925 the son of a Baptist minister in Omaha, Nebraska. His father was a civil rights activist; his uncles and his mother had suffered at the hands of White racists. According to *The Autobiography of Malcolm X*, three of his uncles had been murdered by Whites, while his mother had been threatened by Ku Klux Klansmen while she was pregnant with him in 1924. In 1931 his father committed suicide (Malcolm later claimed he had been murdered), and his mother, beset by the ensuing disputes over insurance claims, had a mental breakdown. She was declared legally insane in December 1938, and Malcolm and his siblings were split up and sent to different foster homes.

Malcolm graduated from junior high school at the top of his class, but he dropped out after a teacher allegedly told him that his aspirations of being a lawyer were 'no realistic goal for a nigger'. He was subsequently sent to a detention centre, became a shoe-shiner at a nightclub, and worked for the New Haven Railroad. On relocating to Harlem in New York, he also became involved in drug dealing, gambling, racketeering and robbery.

When examined for the military draft in 1941, doctors classified Malcolm as 'mentally disqualified for military service'. (He explains in his *Autobiography* that he put on a display to avoid recruitment.) In early 1946 he was arrested for a burglary after trying to sell stolen goods to a pawnshop, and was sentenced to ten years in prison.

While incarcerated, Malcolm began to read voraciously, and he converted to Islam after being sent literature by his brother Reginald. On his release from prison in 1952, Malcolm went to meet African American Muslim activist Elijah Muhammad in Chicago and began to work for Muhammad's 'Nation of Islam' (NOI) organization. He also changed his surname to 'X', which he explained as symbolizing his rejection of the new names (and the 'X'-brandings) that African slaves were given on their arrival in America.

> '1964 looks like it might be the year of the ballot or the bullet'
>
> Malcolm X, speaking in Detroit, 12 April 1964, showing that his brand of action never ruled out violence – if provoked

By 1954 Malcolm had become minister of the Nation of Islam's Temple Number 7 on Lenox Avenue in Harlem (renamed Malcolm X Boulevard in 1987), and had rapidly expanded its membership. He became a familiar figure in the local media and an eloquent public speaker, opened additional mosques, and was largely credited with increasing membership in the NOI from a mere 500 in 1952 to about 30,000 in 1963. In 1964 he even inspired the boxer Cassius Clay to join the NOI and to change his name to Muhammed Ali.

Nevertheless, Malcolm was growing apart from the NOI, and in particular from his former mentor, Elijah Muhammad. In his *Autobiography*, Malcolm explained that the initial cause of the rupture had been Muhammad's extramarital affairs with a series of young secretaries and widespread jealousy of Malcolm's popularity and high media profile. However, in reality the reasons for the breach were not so one-sided. Following the assassination of President Kennedy in 1963, Malcolm rashly claimed it was a case of 'chickens coming home to roost'. The subsequent public outcry led to a public censure from the NOI, and a ban on public speaking.

In March 1964 Malcolm announced his break from the Nation of Islam and the founding of his 'Muslim Mosque Incorporated'. This new organization moved away from the NOI's concentration on religious issues to advocate political and economic issues and Black nationalism. It was, at the same time, more explictly Islamic: Malcolm converted to orthodox Islam, and made his 'Hajj' – his pilgrimage – to Mecca in April 1964.

Malcolm's new international status was underlined when, in July 1964, he addressed the Organization of African Unity's first assembly of heads of state and governments, in Cairo. In his address he backed the utopian concept of a strong and non-aligned 'United States of Africa', which he declared would also be viewed as a sign of liberation for African Americans. At the same time he rejected the simplistic definition of racism by the NOI as a struggle of Blacks against Whites. Racism, he declared, was an international problem that transcended the battle lines being drawn in the United States. Speaking of his days in the NOI, he admitted that he had been 'pointed in a certain direction and told to march. Well, I guess a man's entitled to make a fool of himself if he's ready to pay the cost. It cost me twelve years.'

In 1964–5 Malcolm visited France and Britain. In England, he made a considerable impression by taking part in a debate at the Oxford Union and then visiting Smethwick in the West Midlands, a down-at-heel industrial suburb with a growing West Indian and Asian population, where racial tensions were at boiling point. In the recent British general election, Conservative candidate Peter Griffiths won the seat amid rumours that he had campaigned on the message that 'If you want a nigger for a neighbour, vote Liberal or Labour.' (Prime Minister Harold Wilson had already labelled Griffiths 'a parliamentary leper'.) Malcolm visited a 'Whites only' pub and council estate in Smethwick, and his forceful invective, comparing the treatment of British Blacks and Asians in the area to the 'Jews under Hitler', made for good television and helped raise his international profile. But it was to be his last television interview.

Malcolm X in brief

1925 Born Malcolm Little in Omaha, Nebraska, and moves to Lansing, Michigan while an infant.

1931 His father, the Rev. Earl Little, a Baptist minister, commits suicide.

1938 His mother is committed to an insane asylum.

1946–52 While in prison (for burglary) he undergoes a conversion and joins the Nation of Islam (NOI), which combines elements of Islam with black nationalism.

1952–64 On release from prison meets Elijah Muhammad, leader of NOI, and works for the organization, helping to greatly expand its size and influence. By 1954 has become minister of Temple No. 7 in Harlem.

1964 Breaks with the NOI, and during pilgrimage to Mecca adopts the Muslim name of El-Hajj Malik el-Shabazz. Founds Muslim Mosque Inc. and the Organization of Afro-American Unity (OAAU). Visits France and Britain.

1965 Assassinated (21 Feb.) by three renegade NOI members while giving a lecture in New York.

On 20 March 1964, *Life* magazine published a celebrated photograph of Malcolm X, clutching an M1 carbine, pulling back the curtains to peer out of a window. By this time, however, the implicit target was not just White racism. Malcolm had recently declared that he would defend himself from the daily death threats that he and his family were receiving. Undercover FBI informants were warning that Malcolm X had already been marked for assassination by enemies in the Nation of Islam.

The fears were not without foundation. In a spirit of senseless pettiness, the NOI sued to reclaim Malcolm's home in Queens, New York, which they claimed to have originally paid for. Not only did the Nation win, but the night before the house was to have been turned over to the NOI – making Malcolm and his family homeless – the property was mysteriously burned to the ground. Malcolm and his family escaped unhurt, but no charge of arson was ever successfully brought.

On 21 February 1965 Malcolm X was booked to give a speech at the Audubon Ballroom in the heart of Manhattan. He had only just begun when a disturbance broke out in the crowd. A man started yelling at his neighbour to 'get your hand outta my pocket! Don't be messin' with my pockets!' Malcolm's bodyguards moved to quiet the disturbance and Malcolm appealed for peace. This, though, was clearly just a diversion. A man rushed forward and shot Malcolm in the chest with a shotgun. Two other men then charged the stage and fired revolvers at Malcolm, who altogether was shot 16 times.

Angry onlookers in the crowd caught and beat one of the assassins, Talmadge Hayer, as he attempted to flee the ballroom. Meanwhile, Malcolm was rushed to New York's Columbia Presbyterian Hospital, where he was pronounced dead on arrival.

The police report on the shooting later disappeared, and the resulting investigation was inconclusive. Nevertheless, two suspects identified by witnesses — Norman '3X' Butler and Thomas '15X' Johnson – were eventually charged. Hayer himself confessed to having fired shots into Malcolm's body, but he testified that Butler and Johnson were not present and were not involved in the shooting. All three, however, were convicted. Butler (who also went by the name of Muhammad Abd al-Aziz) was paroled in 1985 and went to work once again for the Nation of Islam under the leadership of Louis Farrakhan. In 1998 he was appointed by Farrakhan as the head of the NOI's Temple Number 7 in Harlem, the very one Malcolm X had founded. Thomas '15X' Johnson changed his name to Khalil Islam, and was paroled from prison in 1987.

Fifteen hundred people attended Malcolm's funeral in Harlem on 27 February 1965 at the Faith Temple Church of God in Christ (now Child's Memorial Temple Church of God in Christ). He was buried at the Ferncliff Cemetery in Hartsdale, New York.

DR VERWOERD STABBED IN THIS BENCH

WHERE MEMBERS STRUGGLED WITH ASSASSIN

ASSASSIN ENTERED HOUSE FROM HERE

Hendrik
VERWOERD

1901–1966, PRESIDENT OF SOUTH AFRICA

ASSASSIN Dimitri Tsafendas

DATE 6 September 1966

PLACE Johannesburg, South Africa

Hendrik Frensch Verwoerd embodied the *apartheid* system of racial separation in South Africa, which he helped to perfect and sustain. To many people outside the country, he is a forgotten name from a despised past: Nelson Mandela, not Hendrik Verwoerd, is the figure many prefer to represent South Africa in the 20th century. Yet as recently as 2004, Verwoerd featured in the top twenty of the South African Broadcasting Corporation's poll of the top one hundred South Africans of all time.

Born in the Netherlands, Verwoerd had emigrated to South Africa by the time he was two. He studied at the University of Stellenbosch, where he completed his Masters degree in psychology in 1922 and his doctorate, on the psychological effects of fatigue, in 1924. He then spent several years in Germany – not yet in the grip of Hitler's Nazis, but run by the severely divided politicians of the shaky Weimar Republic. If any country influenced him at this time, though, it was the United States, where racial segregation was becoming the norm in many areas.

'We will stand like walls of granite'

Verwoerd, on the fortress of *apartheid*, 1 December 1960. The walls tumbled thirty years later.

After beginning an academic career in sociology in South Africa, Verwoerd grew attracted to Afrikaner politics and became editor of the nationalist newspaper *Die Transvaler* in 1937. He soon expressed political ambition himself. In the landmark 1948 election, which began the Afrikaner-dominated National Party's 45-year grip on power, he stood as one of its candidates. He failed to gain a seat, but he was appointed to the Senate instead, where he sat until chosen as prime minister in 1958.

Verwoerd was an unabashed believer in *apartheid*, which literally means 'apartness' but which to all intents and purposes was a figleaf for White supremacy. As Verwoerd said in 1960:

> We call ourselves European, but actually we represent the White men of Africa. They are the people not only in the [South African] Union but through major portions of Africa who brought civilization here, who made the present developments of black nationalists possible. By bringing them education, by showing them this way of life, by bringing in industrial development, by bringing in the ideals which Western civilization has developed itself.

The denial of civil rights to Blacks, Indians and other non-Whites ('Coloureds', 'Asiatics') had been developing over many years. But Verwoerd was instrumental in shaping and applying *apartheid*'s particularly comprehensive ideology after 1948 – notably as minister of 'native affairs' during the early 1950s. As such, he is often labelled the 'Architect of Apartheid'.

In 1950, the formal identification of South Africans by race, complete with identity cards, was introduced, and intermarriage between Whites, Blacks and Coloureds was forbidden. In 1951, the Bantu Authorities Act built on earlier legislation to formalize the separate areas where Blacks could legally reside, including the townships on the edge of cities. The most famous township would be the one outside Johannesburg, eventually called Soweto (standing for 'South Western Townships'), which by 1960 was home to over half a million Blacks.

A law of 1953 prohibited people of different races from using the same public amenities; and in 1954 Black immigration to the cities was banned. Beaches were segregated, as were cinemas and theatres. From 1957, churches in White areas were not allowed to admit Blacks. In 1959, in a similar vein, separate universities were set up for Blacks, Coloureds and Indians.

After Verwoerd became prime minister in 1958, his government enacted some crucial statutes of the *apartheid* system. The Promotion of Bantu Self-Government Act of 1959 set up separate Black tribal 'homelands' (*bantustans*), which were eventually destined for 'independence'. However, these artificial 'states' remained economically dependent on Pretoria. Verwoerd's policy, promoted under the innocuous banner of 'separate development', was not only to encourage relocation of Blacks to the homelands, but also to speed it up. These individuals would eventually be denied citizenship in South Africa, their rights then only recognized within their (economically wholly unfeasible) tribal homelands.

The policy of 'separate development' was now perfected. Verwoerd established the Bantu Investment Corporation to promote economic development and lure Black South Africans away from White South Africa. Blacks were now unable to operate businesses in 'White' South Africa without a permit – and could not employ Whites in their own homelands.

Some attempted to resist the establishment of *apartheid*. In March 1960, the Pan Africanist Congress (PAC) – a splinter group which had broken away from the larger, communist-inspired African National Congress (ANC) – called on Blacks to demonstrate against the imposition of homeland-registered 'pass books', symbols of their loss of South African citizenship. The biggest of these demonstrations occurred at Sharpeville, a black township outside Vereeniging. A large crowd – variously estimated at between 3000 and 20,000 – converged on Sharpeville police station, offering themselves up for arrest for refusing to carry their pass books. After the crowd demolished the station's perimeter fence, a force of about 300 armed police panicked and opened fire. Sixty-nine demonstrators were killed and over two hundred injured. All the victims were Black, and most of them had been shot in the back. The police chief in charge, Colonel J. Pienaar, subsequently noted that 'My car was struck with a stone. If they do these things they must learn their lesson the hard way.'

In the wake of the shooting, Black workers staged a general strike and demonstrations continued. Verwoerd responded by declaring a state of emergency, which allowed the security forces the right to detain people without trial. Over 18,000 were arrested, including much of the ANC and PAC leadership, and both organizations were banned.

Yet the Sharpeville Massacre proved, in some senses, to be the salvation of the ANC. Before Sharpeville, those ANC leaders advocating violent resistance, such as Nelson Mandela, had been marginalized as being far too radical. After Sharpeville, Mandela was allowed to launch a campaign of bombing and sabotage, which helped raise the ANC's profile both internally and internationally. The results for Mandela himself, though, were not so promising: in June 1964, he and seven others were sentenced to life imprisonment for terrorism.

International reaction to Verwoerd's legislative programme and the Sharpeville Massacre was, for once, swift and decisive. British Prime Minister Harold Macmillan used his celebrated 'Wind of Change' speech to South Africa's Parliament to publicly warn Hendrik Verwoerd's

Verwoerd in brief

1901 Born in Amsterdam, and emigrates to South Africa when very young.

1924 Completes his doctorate at the University of Stellenbosch, and becomes professor of applied psychology (1927) and sociology (1933).

1937–48 Becomes active in National Party politics. Appointed editor of the Afrikaner nationalist daily *Die Transvaler*.

1948–57 Following appointment as a Senator, becomes minister of native affairs (1950) and the chief architect of *apartheid*.

1958 Becomes National Party prime minister and continues policies of 'separate development'.

1960 Bans the Black oppositionist ANC and Pan Africanist Congress after anti-passbook demonstration results in the Sharpeville Massacre of Blacks by police. Narrowly escapes assassination.

1961 South Africa becomes a republic and withdraws from the British Commonwealth. Some opponents of the regime (including Nelson Mandela) turn to violent action.

1964 Mandela and others are imprisoned for terrorism.

1966 Assassinated (6 Sept.) in the all-White South African Parliament.

1995 President Nelson Mandela visits Verwoerd's widow, Betsie, for coffee, an action viewed as a symbolic healing of past wounds.

APARTHEID

SOUTHERN AFRICA, WHETHER UNDER British imperial or Afrikaner sway, had seen a progressive increase in racial segregation from the 19th century into the 20th. The term *apartheid* ('apartness') was first coined during a speech by the general and statesman Jan Christian Smuts, two years before he became prime minister of what was still the 'Dominion of South Africa' in 1919. Yet the formal creation of a rigid, enforceable, national system of *apartheid* was the work of the governments that followed the 1948 election, won by the National Party campaigning against Smuts's more moderate United Party.

The Population Registration Act (1950) classified South Africans racially, and the Group Areas Act (1950) dictated where people could live and work: these became the cornerstones of the edifice of *apartheid*.

The Separate Amenities Act of 1953 segregated most areas of public life, while the Pass Laws Act (1952) in effect introduced internal 'anti-passports', by which Blacks or Coloureds could be denied access to parts of the country: pass books became the notorious symbols of oppression. From 1953, a separate Black education system was designed to, in actuality, prepare Blacks for lives as working-class inferiors.

Notwithstanding the fact that White South Africa was dependent on Black labour to function, the ultimate goal of *apartheid* was to ensure a White future for the country by herding Blacks into the separate tribal *bantustans* or 'homelands'. Verwoerd's original term for them was 'native reserves', ominously recalling the reservations into which Native Americans were herded from the 1830s.

administration that an unstoppable 'national consciousness' in Black Africa was a 'political fact'. The United Nations denounced Mandela's trial and imposed economic sanctions. And after much heated negotiation, the British Commonwealth condemned South Africa. Verwoerd saw this as an opportunity, called a referendum, and rebranded South Africa a stand-alone republic, rejecting the British monarch as head of state. This was a happy development for Verwoerd and many others in the National Party and Afrikaner community, whose anti-British sentiments reflected traditional antipathies. For them, it was a final liberation from sixty years of subservience to Britain since defeat in the Second Anglo-Boer War (1902).

For the next thirty years, until the release of Nelson Mandela and the legalization of the ANC and PAC in 1990, South Africa turned its back on the international community and concentrated on making complete segregation a reality. Much of this was achieved, however, in the absence of the godfather of *apartheid*.

Verwoerd had already been the target of an assassination attempt in April 1960, when he was shot by David Pratt while opening the Rand Easter Show in Johannesburg. On this occasion he was merely injured; Pratt was declared insane and sent to a mental hospital, where he committed suicide a few months later. Six years later, on 6 September 1966, the assassin was more successful. Verwoerd was, with grim irony, stabbed to death in the apparent safety of the House of Assembly, the lower house of the nation's Whites-only Parliament.

Verwoerd's assassin was Dimitri Tsafendas, a parliamentary clerk. Tsafendas, whose mother was Black and whose father had been Greek, had dark skin, but was still legally defined as 'White'. However, he had recently applied for – and been denied – reclassification as 'Coloured' in order to legitimize his recently initiated relationship with a Coloured woman.

The motive Tsafendas declared at his trial, though, remains unique in the history of assassination: he asserted that a large worm in his stomach had told him to kill Verwoerd. As a result – surprisingly – the trial judge spared him the death penalty and sentenced him to life imprisonment. He died in prison in 1999, aged 81.

After the dismantling of *apartheid* began in 1990, and Black and White politicians negotiated the inevitable transition to Black-majority rule, South Africa began to erase much of Verwoerd's physical and legislative legacy. Roads, bridges and schools named after *apartheid*'s architect were renamed. His much-vaunted homelands were merged back into South Africa. And in 1994 the whole South African population was invited to vote in the country's first-ever general election based on the principle of universal suffrage – an epoch-making event, which surely had Hendrik Verwoerd shuddering in his grave.

Martin Luther KING

1929–1968, US CIVIL RIGHTS LEADER

ASSASSIN	James Earl Ray or another
DATE	4 April 1968
PLACE	Memphis, Tennessee, USA

Peace Prize. But in March 1968 he had embarked on a new campaign to combat poverty and was in Memphis, Tennessee, supporting striking African Americans.

In early April, Martin Luther King returned to Memphis as part of his 'Poor People's Campaign' launched at the beginning of the year. He addressed a packed crowd at the Mason Temple. Although only 39 years old, he reflected on mortality, proclaiming that 'it really doesn't matter what happens now':

> Like anybody, I would like to live a long life. Longevity has its place, but I'm not concerned about that now. I just want to do God's will. And He's allowed me to go up to the mountain! And I've looked over, and I've seen the Promised Land … And so I'm happy tonight. I'm not worried about anything. I'm not fearing any man.

The words seemed prophetic. One day later, King was dead, assassinated by a racist petty criminal in the same Southern city.

At the beginning of April, King was staying – as he had often done before – at Memphis's very modest Lorraine Motel, in his favourite room, 306. It was common knowledge that he generally stayed there when in the city, and anyone with a grievance in Memphis would have known where to find him.

At 6 p.m. on the fine, warm evening of 4 April, Martin Luther King was leaning over the motel's second floor balcony, outside his room, looking down. A minute later, he was shot from below, the bullet smashing his face and travelling into his spinal cord, eventually settling in his shoulder. Friends inside ran to the balcony to find King on the ground. Attempts to call an ambulance were delayed, because the motel switchboard operator was apparently suffering a heart attack from seeing King shot. Twenty minutes later an ambulance did arrive, but King was pronounced dead at St Joseph's Hospital at 7.05 p.m.

When news broke of King's assassination, outrage among African American communities prompted a nationwide wave of riots in more than sixty American cities. On 9 May, President Lyndon B. Johnson declared a national day of mourning for the lost civil rights leader. That same day, King 'spoke' at his own funeral, which took place at the Ebenezer Baptist Church in Atlanta, Georgia, where he had been (like his father before him) the pastor. It was the area he had grown up in. A recording of his 'Drum Major' sermon, first given on 4 February 1968, was played at the ceremony. In it, King asked that no mention be made at his funeral of his many awards and honours, but requested that he merely be remembered for trying to 'feed the hungry', 'clothe the naked' and 'love and serve humanity'. His good friend the gospel singer Mahalia Jackson sang his favourite hymn,

'I still have a dream. It is a dream deeply rooted in the American dream.'

From King's iconic 1964 address in the shadow of the Lincoln Memorial, a speech that deftly interwove African American aspirations and traditional White American ones

'Take My Hand, Precious Lord', as he had wished. Vice-President Hubert Humphrey attended the funeral in President Johnson's stead, Johnson controversially preferring to attend a pre-arranged meeting on the Vietnam War.

King's assassin was the 40-year-old habitual criminal James Earl Ray. He was a convicted thief with a prodigious arrest record, as well as an escaped convict who had broken out of the Missouri State Penitentiary a year before the assassination. On 4 May he fled from the scene and, astonishingly, was able to leave the United States soon afterwards on a transatlantic flight. However, early in July 1968 he was captured at London's Heathrow Airport while trying to leave the country on a false Canadian passport in the name of Ramon George Sneyd.

Ray was quickly extradited to Tennessee and charged with King's murder. On 10 March 1969 he finally confessed – but recanted his confession three days later. On the advice of his

THE MARCH ON WASHINGTON

IN 1963, MARTIN LUTHER KING'S Southern Christian Leadership Conference led US civil rights organizations in the March on Washington for Jobs and Freedom. President Kennedy initially opposed it, concerned that it would retard the passage of civil rights legislation, but King was adamant that the march would proceed. He did eventually acquiesce to presidential pressure, and the event ultimately took on a far less strident tone. But the campaign still demanded an end to racial segregation in schools; meaningful civil rights legislation, including a law prohibiting racial discrimination in employment; protection of civil rights workers from police brutality; a $2 minimum wage for all workers; and self-government for the largely black District of Columbia.

The march was a resounding success. More than 250,000 people of diverse ethnicities attended the event. At the Lincoln Memorial, King delivered his celebrated 'I Have a Dream' speech, electrifying the crowd and producing what has since been judged one of the finest addresses in American oratory. Using all his rhetorical skills as a Baptist preacher and all his knowledge of biblical expression, he took the European metaphors of the New World as a promised land for poor and oppressed Whites and applied them to African Americans:

I have a dream that one day this nation will rise up and live out the true meaning of its creed: We hold these truths to be self-evident that all men are created equal.

I have a dream that one day on the red hills of Georgia the sons of former slaves and the sons of former slave owners will be able to sit down together at the table of brotherhood.

I have a dream that one day even the state of Mississippi, a state sweltering with the heat of injustice, sweltering with the heat of oppression, will be transformed into an oasis of freedom and justice ...

I have a dream that one day every valley shall be exalted, and every hill and mountain shall be made low, the rough places will be made plain, and the crooked places will be made straight, and the glory of the Lord shall be revealed and all flesh shall see it together ...

This is our hope. This is the faith that I will go back to the South with. With this faith we will be able to hew out of the mountain of despair a stone of hope. With this faith we will be able to transform the jangling discords of our nation into a beautiful symphony of brotherhood. With this faith we will be able to work together, to pray together, to struggle together, to go to jail together, to stand up together, to stand up for freedom together, knowing that we will be free one day. And this will be the day when all of God's children will be able to sing with new meaning, 'My country 'tis of thee, sweet land of liberty, of thee I sing. Land where my fathers died, land of the Pilgrim's pride, from every mountainside, let freedom ring!' And if America is a great nation, this must become true.

Five years later, King sought to reproduce the event's success for his new 'Poor People's Campaign'; but he was assassinated before the new march could be staged. Five weeks after his death, demonstrators began to show up in Washington, D.C., for the campaign. However without King's energy to inspire it, the March never wholly took off. Only 7000 turned up – a far cry from the many thousands of 1963 – and the economic bill of rights that the campaign demanded was never enacted.

1929 Born Michael King Jr. in Atlanta, Georgia, but his Baptist father changes both their first names to honour the 16th-century German Protestant.

1948–51 After studying sociology at Morehouse College, Atlanta, studies divinity and is awarded a Ph.D. in theology from Boston University, earning the title 'Dr'.

1953 Becomes a Baptist minister in Montgomery, Alabama, one of the few leadership roles then available to African Americans.

1955–6 Leads the Montgomery Bus Boycott, which ends with the US Supreme Court's decision outlawing racial segregation on all public transport.

1957 Helps found the Southern Christian Leadership Conference (SCLC), a civil rights movement; serves as its first president.

1960 Becomes pastor of the Ebenezer Baptist Church in his home neighbourhood.

1963 Over a quarter of a million people hear his 'I have a Dream' speech in front of the Lincoln Memorial, at the end of the March on Washington for Jobs and Freedom. Spurred by the march, the Civil Rights Act (1964) and the National Voting Rights Act (1965) are passed.

1964 Becomes youngest person ever to receive the Nobel Peace Prize.

1967 Begins speaking out against US involvement in the Vietnam War.

1968 Comes to Memphis as part of the 'Poor People's Campaign'. Assassinated there (4 April) on the balcony of his motel.

2000 All US states observe the federal holiday of Martin Luther King Day in January.

attorney, Ray had pleaded guilty in a hearing, thereby evading the possibility that a full trial might end with his earning the death penalty. Ray later fired his attorney and claimed, somewhat incoherently, that he had been set up by a man he met in Montreal, Canada, whom he only knew as 'Raoul'. Ray was sentenced to a 99-year prison term, but spent the remainder of his life attempting to withdraw his guilty plea and go to trial.

As with the assassination of President Kennedy in 1963, the murder of Martin Luther King has long been the subject of conspiracy theories. Ray's confession was certainly extracted under duress, and while he was a well-established thief and burglar, he had no record of committing violent gun crimes. In 2004 the civil rights leader Jesse Jackson, who was with King on the balcony, declared that 'I will never believe that James Earl Ray had the motive, the money and the mobility to have done it himself.' Advocates of a wider conspiracy point out that the two separate ballistic tests conducted on the alleged murder weapon, a Remington Gamemaster, had neither conclusively proved Ray had been the killer nor that it had been the gun that actually killed King. Moreover, witnesses who were with King at the moment of his death say the shot came from another location, from behind thick shrubbery near the motel – shrubbery that was inexplicably cut away in the days following the assassination.

The FBI plays a prominent role in these conspiracy theories. The Bureau's paranoid director, J. Edgar Hoover, had long regarded King with deep suspicion, and King had been the focus of FBI surveillance since 1961 (sanctioned at the time by Attorney General Robert F. Kennedy). The Bureau placed wiretaps on King's home and office phones, and bugged King's hotel rooms as he travelled across the country in an attempt to prove that he was a communist.

By the mid-1960s, the focus of the Bureau's investigations shifted to an attempt to discredit King through public revelations regarding his colourful private life. The FBI distributed reports alleging extramarital affairs to friendly reporters, King's colleagues and even King's family. The Bureau also sent viciously racist anonymous letters to King threatening to reveal information if he did not cease his civil rights work. By the time of King's assassination, though, this shameful ploy had clearly failed, and the FBI's investigation had begun to focus on the leftward direction of King's campaigns and his potential links with the Black Power movement.

On the day King was assassinated, FBI agents were observing the Lorraine Motel from a deserted fire station across the road. (Ironically, this was located next to the rooming house in which James Earl Ray was staying.) The agents watched King, through papered-over windows with peepholes cut into them, until he was shot. Straight away, all six agents rushed out of the station and were the first people to administer first-aid to the stricken King.

To many, the FBI's presence at the scene of the crime suggests that they were centrally involved in the assassination. Certainly, Martin Luther King's son thought so: in 1997 Dexter King met with Ray in prison, and publicly he supported Ray's efforts to obtain a full trial. To this day the King family does not believe Ray had anything to do with the murder. However, the truth will remain buried for some years: in 1977 law officers ordered all known copies of the recorded audiotapes and written transcripts of the FBI's electronic surveillance of King between 1963 and 1968 to be sealed from public access until 2027.

On 10 June 1977, shortly after he had testified to the House Select Committee on Assassinations that he did not shoot King, James Earl Ray and six other convicts escaped from Brushy Mountain State Penitentiary in Tennessee. They were recaptured within a few days, but not before Ray had been stabbed. He lived for another twenty years, dying in prison of liver failure on 23 April 1998.

On 6 April 2002, the Rev. Ronald Wilson told the *New York Times* that it had been his father, Henry Clay Wilson, and not James Earl Ray, who had assassinated Martin Luther King. The motive, he suggested, was not racism, but anti-communism.

> ‘God didn't call America to do what she's doing in the world now. God didn't call America to engage in a senseless unjust war as the war in Vietnam.’
>
> From King's ‘Drum Major’ sermon, 4 February 1968, preached at his Ebenezer Baptist Church and reprised there via audiotape for his funeral three months later.

By this time, over 700 US cities had named streets after King. In 2007 King County, Washington, changed its logo to an image of his face. King's childhood neighbourhood in Auburn, Georgia, including the Ebenezer Baptist Church, has been a National Historic Site since 1980. And every year, Americans take a day of rest on Martin Luther King Day, celebrated on the third Monday of the month of January.

bert KENNED

1968, US POLITICIAN

ASSASSIN Sirhan Sirhan
DATE 5 June 1968 (died 6 June)
PLACE Los Angeles, California, USA

On 5 April 1968, the day after the assassination of Martin Luther King, US Attorney-General Robert Kennedy delivered a speech in Cleveland, Ohio. It was a sharply critical attack on the hatreds and prejudices that seemed to be tearing America apart. 'What has violence ever accomplished?' he asked. 'What has it ever created? No martyr's cause has ever been stilled by an assassin's bullet ... No one, no matter where he lives or what he does, can be certain whom next will suffer from such a senseless act of bloodshed.' But exactly a month later, Kennedy himself fell victim to an assassin's bullet. It seemed as if no political leader was safe in modern America.

Robert Fitzgerald 'Bobby' Kennedy was surely destined to be President of the United States. In March 1968 the incumbent, President Johnson, had finally announced that he was not standing for re-election, bowing out to make way for his vice-president, Hubert Humphrey. But by then Kennedy had already established a clear lead over his principal Democratic Party rival, Eugene McCarthy, in the early primaries, and his exciting, reformist ideas and comparative youth made Humphrey look leaden, old and very much the creature of the Establishment. The Republicans' front-runner, Richard M. Nixon, who had narrowly lost to John F. Kennedy in 1960, now seemed a tarnished and apparently broken figure from the past.

In June 1968, Kennedy defeated McCarthy in the critical California Democratic primary. The way seemed open for the Democratic nomination, and then the presidency. The exhilarating expectations that his brother John had raised on his election in 1960, prematurely dashed by John's assassination in 1963, could now be fully realized. Yet, moments after claiming victory, shortly after midnight on 5 June, the man many expected would be the next president was shot and killed. Four days later, his former political adversary, President Johnson, declared an official day of national mourning in response to the outpouring of public grief that had followed Kennedy's untimely death.

Robert Francis Kennedy was born on 20 November 1925, the seventh child of the ambitious Joseph P. Kennedy and his long-suffering wife, Rose. Robert was sent to Harvard, studied law, and began work in the US Department of Justice. In 1952 he resigned his post to manage his brother John's successful Senate campaign in Massachusetts. His success prompted John to recall him to run his presidential campaign, seven years later. In the meantime Robert ('Bobby') Kennedy had achieved a national profile as a dogged chief counsel for the Senate Labor Rackets Committee, where he had come head-to-head with the leaders of organized crime and corrupt union leaders, most notably Jimmy Hoffa and his Teamster union.

Following John's election victory in 1960, Robert was appointed US attorney-general. No holder of this post had previously enjoyed such a clear influence over all areas of policy as Robert did. Often, indeed, it was President Kennedy who sought the advice and counsel of his younger brother.

As attorney-general, Robert Kennedy pursued a relentless crusade against organized crime, often sharply disagreeing over policy with FBI director J. Edgar Hoover, who

> 'Let's dedicate ourselves to ... tame the savageness of man and make gentle the life of this world'
>
> From Kennedy's impromptu eulogy to Martin Luther King, assassinated that evening, Indianapolis, 4 April 1968

Kennedy in brief

1925 Born the seventh child of the wealthy and powerful Joseph and Rose Kennedy, in Brookline, Massachusetts.

1938 Spends year at school in England while his father is US Ambassador there.

1943—6 Trains as a naval officer at Harvard, and serves briefly as apprentice seaman.

1946—51 Studies government and law at Harvard College and Virginia University. Writes occasional foreign journalism for the *Boston Globe*.

1951—2 Begins work in the US Department of Justice, but resigns to manage JFK's successful election campaign for the Senate.

1952—7 Legal counsel for Senate Subcommittee on Investigations and chief counsel for the Democratic Party in the Senate.

1957—9 Achieves public profile as chief counsel to the Senate committee investigating labour racketeering, but resigns to run JFK's presidential campaign in 1960.

1961—4 Influential attorney-general under his brother's presidency, pursuing action against organized crime, supporting civil rights, and helping to end the Cuban Missile Crisis.

1965—8 Elected a US Senator for New York.

1968 Declares his candidacy for Democratic presidential nomination, and wins important primaries. Shot (5 June) after victory in California, and dies the next day.

continued to deny that the Mafia even existed. Convictions against major organized crime figures rose eight-fold during his term. But his campaign inevitably earned him the enduring enmity of crime kingpins and corrupt union bosses.

Kennedy was also energetic in his espousal and promotion of civil rights legislation. During his tenure as attorney-general, he undertook the most energetic and persistent desegregation of the administration that Capitol Hill had ever experienced. He demanded that every area of government begin recruiting realistic levels of black and other ethnic workers, going so far as to criticize Vice-President Johnson himself – who was never a fervent admirer of either Kennedy – for his failure to desegregate his own office staff. In September 1962, he sent US Marshals and federal troops to Oxford, Mississippi, to enforce a federal court order admitting the first African American student, James Meredith, to the University of Mississippi. The event sparked days of rioting, yet Kennedy refused to back down, asserting that African American students should be fully able to enjoy the benefits of all levels of the educational system.

Nine months after his brother's assassination in November 1963, Robert Kennedy left the government – now in the hands of his old foe Lyndon B. Johnson – to run for a seat in the US Senate, representing New York. Kennedy won by a landslide, and used the following years to launch campaigns to combat poverty, desegregate buses, increase voter registration, enforce human rights and – most controversially – stop the escalation of the war in Vietnam.

In January 1968, President Johnson began to run for re-election, prompting Senator Kennedy to announce that he would not be seeking the presidency. However, after Johnson won an astonishingly narrow victory in the New Hampshire primary against the little-known Senator McCarthy, Kennedy reversed his stance and declared his candidacy. On 16 March 1968 he declared that:

> I do not run for the presidency merely to oppose any man, but to propose new policies. I run because I am convinced that this country is on a perilous course and because I have such strong feelings about what must be done, and I feel that I'm obliged to do all I can.

McCarthy supporters angrily denounced Kennedy as an opportunist, but on 31 March Johnson stunned the nation by dropping out of the race. Vice-President Hubert Humphrey entered the race in his stead, relying on the support of the unions and of local and central government. He came too late to enter any primaries, but had the support of the president and many Democratic insiders. In reply, Robert Kennedy, like his brother before him, planned to win the Democratic nomination, and ultimately the presidency, by attracting popular support in the primaries – appealing directly to the people over the heads of the Establishment.

Kennedy's ticket was unapologetically liberal. He called for racial and economic justice, a non-aggressive stance in foreign policy (a sideswipe at Johnson's deep involvement in Indochina), the decentralization of government and for an ambitious programme of social improvement. He particularly praised and targeted the young, whom he publicly identified as representing the future of a reinvigorated American society based on partnership and equality. The implication was unambiguous: Kennedy epitomized the youthful potential of America's future, Humphrey (and Nixon) the failures and compromises of the past.

Kennedy's victory in the California primary effectively knocked McCarthy out of the race. The same day, his victory over Humphrey in the latter's home state of South Dakota suggested that Humphrey, too, would not prove a serious obstacle. All seemed set fair for the party's nomination at August's National Democratic Convention in Chicago, which he hoped would witness his peaceful coronation as Johnson's heir-apparent.

Around midnight on 4/5 June, Kennedy addressed his euphoric supporters in the ballroom at Los Angeles' Ambassador Hotel. He left the stage after his victory speech, and kept talking to reporters as he took a short-cut through the hotel pantry, in order to greet supporters working in the hotel's kitchen. Kennedy was standing in a crowded kitchen passageway when a 24-year-old Palestinian, Sirhan Sirhan, opened fire with a .22 calibre revolver and shot Kennedy in the head at close range. Bystanders immediately shouted 'We don't want another Dallas!' and Sirhan was pinned to a table and subjected to a number of attacks before security operatives rescued him. Kennedy, meanwhile, was rushed to the Good Samaritan Hospital, where he died the next day.

Five other persons in the kitchen were also were shot, but all five recovered. Auto Workers Union leader Paul Schrade was shot in the head, but miraculously survived; he was told that if the bullet had penetrated a millimetre further, he would have been dead.

Sirhan Sirhan was convicted to life imprisonment, and still lives. Inevitably, there have been many allegations that he was not acting alone and was the tool of organized crime or even the victim of a plot by renegade CIA operatives. None have so far proved convincing.

Kennedy's body lay in state at St Patrick's Cathedral in New York before the funeral, after which it was transported by special train to Washington. Thousands of mourners lined the tracks and stations, paying their respects as the train passed by. He was then buried near his brother, John, in Arlington National Cemetery – at his own request, at night, and with the bare minimum military escort and ceremony.

Kennedy was not the only one who died that night. For thousands of Americans, hope in a brighter, kinder, peaceful future died too. Many continue to ponder what might have happened if 'the best candidate we ever had' had gone on to run for the presidency.

CHICAGO 1968

THE DEMOCRATIC PARTY'S National Convention of 1968 met at a turbulent time, in the wake of the assassinations of Martin Luther King and Robert F. Kennedy. (Lyndon Johnson himself wisely decided not to attend.) The Democrats eventually settled on the compromise candidate of Hubert Humphrey, who would subsequently lose the presidential election to Richard Nixon. However, the voting process was confused, leading many people to suspect that the procedure had been rigged. Anti-war demonstrators protested throughout the convention, and while the protests were initially uneventful, tempers gradually heated as the night progressed, and soon police and protestors were clashing all around the convention centre and the surrounding streets.

Expecting protests, Chicago Mayor Richard Daley over-reacted and announced an 11 p.m. curfew in the city. He then unleashed the police, who responded with unnecessary severity. One observer described the convention hall as 'approaching a military installation: barbed-wire, checkpoints, the whole bit'. Police, live on television, roughed up renowned national journalists such as Mike Wallace and Dan Rather, while Mayor Daley shouted expletives at speakers from the floor.

Eight protestors were later tried, but all were acquitted. The subsequent Congressional report on the night's violence unambiguously assigned blame for the mayhem in the streets to Daley's police force, describing the violence as the result of a 'police riot'.

Georgi MARKOV

1929–1978, EXPATRIATE BULGARIAN DISSIDENT

ASSASSIN Unverified
DATE 7 September 1978 (died 11 September)
PLACE London, England

Thursday the day of 7 September 1978 was the birthday of Bulgarian Communist Party leader and Soviet stooge Todor Zhivkov. The Bulgarian Secret Police, assisted by the notorious Soviet secret service, the KGB, had already undertaken two failed attempts to kill the expatriate Bulgarian dissident Georgi Markov. Now they chose the occasion of Zhivkov's birthday to attempt once more – in possibly the most bizarrely conceived political murder ever conducted. It was a most unusual birthday present for the most ill-mannered and boorish of dictators.

The 7th of September was a pleasant, early autumn day. In fact, London was enjoying lingering summer weather, and the realities of the Cold War seemed a long way away. Markov had arrived by train at Waterloo Station on his way to work at the BBC's World Service. He had just walked north across the Thames via Waterloo Bridge and was heading towards the World Service's home nearby, housed in Harvey Corbett's bombastic Bush House. As he was passing the bus stop on the north side of the bridge, he was needlessly jabbed in the thigh by a man holding an umbrella. The man apologized – in, Markov later recalled, a thick foreign accent – and swiftly walked away.

Markov immediately felt a sharp, stinging pain where his skin had been punctured by – it seemed – the umbrella tip. When he arrived at work at Bush House, he noticed a small red scab had formed, and that the pain was, if anything, increasing. As a result, he told at least one of his colleagues at the BBC about the bus-stop incident and about his injury. That evening, he developed a high fever and was admitted to hospital. He died there three days later.

Before he died, Markov repeatedly told doctors that he thought he might have been poisoned. Accordingly, the police ordered a thorough post-mortem examination of Markov's body. The results were startling: forensic pathologists discovered a spherical metal pellet, the size of a pinhead, embedded in Markov's calf. The platinum pellet (*see* p.166) contained a cavity which, following an examination by experts from the British Army's chemical warfare research establishment at Porton Down, contained traces of the lethal toxin ricin. There was, and is, no known antidote to ricin poisoning.

> 'I can't believe people go 'round stabbing other people with umbrellas'
>
> An incredulous Annabel Markov, Georgi's widow, at the time of his death

Georgi Ivanov Markov was born in a suburb of Bulgaria's capital, Sofia, in 1929, and he originally worked as a writer there. By his adulthood, Bulgaria was firmly behind the Iron Curtain in the Soviet sphere of influence, administered as a one-party communist state. In 1962 Markov published a novel, *Men*, which both won him the annual award of the Union of Bulgarian Writers and membership of the Union – a crucial prerequisite for a professional career in literature in communist Bulgaria. Markov then combined writing novels, plays and television screenplays with a job at one of the state-controlled publishers. While his prose was very successful, most of his plays were stillborn: the state censors banned their performance. His ambitious novel *The Roof* was also censored, dramatically halted mid-printing by government officials when they grasped that its story of the collapse of a factory roof was a thinly veiled assault on Leninism and official incompetence.

The premier that Markov ridiculed, Todor Zhivkov, was one of the least inspiring of all the postwar puppets of the Soviet 'empire'. Born in 1911, Zhivkov exaggerated his wartime

Markov in brief

record as a partisan leader to ingratiate himself with the invading Soviets. As a result, he profited by the Soviet-engineered coup of 9 September 1944, which installed the communist government and made him head of the capital's police, now restyled the People's Militia. Establishing himself as a hardline Stalinist, he was appointed the party's First Secretary in 1954. Two years later Zhivkov – having performed a wily U-turn and converted himself into a fervently anti-Stalinist supporter of Nikita Khrushchev – became the effective prime minister, abrogating to himself presidential powers in 1971.

Zhivkov would happily bend whichever way the wind was blowing. When Khrushchev was toppled and Leonid Brezhnev came to power in the Soviet Union in 1964, Zhivkov rapidly adjusted his rhetoric to suit the new Kremlin line. He then went on to develop a very close personal relationship with Brezhnev himself. He slavishly supported Brezhnev over the political split between the communist giants of China and the Soviet Union in 1966. In 1968 he volunteered Bulgarian tanks to help crush the liberal reforms of the 'Prague Spring' in Czechoslovakia. By the early 1970s he was even proposing that Bulgaria be integrated into the Soviet Union as one of its republics. There was no better friend to the Soviet government than the Bulgarian premier.

Zhivkov was rude, clumsy and notoriously stupid. He became a caricature dictator, promoting his appalling family to key party positions, building a motorway to link the capital with his tiny birthplace, and populating the country's towns and villages with execrable statues of himself. His country accent, pig-like face, dog-like devotion to the Soviets and unapologetically brusque public conduct frequently became the butt of (privately expressed) Bulgarian jokes.

However, life under Zhivkov's rule was not particularly amusing. In 1972, all Muslim Bulgarians – the country was for centuries part of the Ottoman Empire – were forced to Christianize their names. Twelve years later, after Markov's death, the same policy was applied to all Bulgarian nationals that were ethnically Turkish, resulting in riots and in considerable loss of life at the hands of the security forces. By 1978, too, the influence of the secret police had permeated every facet of daily life, and informing on one's friends and colleagues had become a commonplace activity.

In 1969 Markov could stand no more, and he defected from Zhivkov's repressive Bulgaria. Having moved to the West, he eventually settled in London and worked as a broadcaster and journalist for the BBC World Service, the CIA-funded Radio Free Europe and Germany's world service radio network, Deutsche Welle. He also managed to have some of his plays published and produced.

Markov's 'In Absentia' broadcasts frequently criticized the Bulgarian communist regime in general and the ludicrous Zhivkov in particular. Inevitably, then, it was not long before he was swiftly promoted to the top of the Bulgarian government's 'to do' list. Soon, too, the Bulgarians were requesting the assistance of the highly experienced KGB in order to devise a method of quietly disposing of this stubborn irritant.

BY THE LATE 1980S, the sophisticated Soviet architect of *glasnost*, Premier Mikhail Gorbachev, had developed a deep personal antipathy for Bulgaria's crass and overbearing Todor Zhivkov. And without Soviet backing, Zhivkov – who had built his regime on unquestioning support for his Soviet masters – was doomed. On 10 November 1989, just as the Berlin Wall was coming down, Zhivkov was forced to resign as leader of the Bulgarian Communist Party and as head of state, following ominous signals from Gorbachev to senior Bulgarian party officials.

After Zhivkov's fall, Bulgaria's one-party communist state was swiftly dismantled. In June 1990, Bulgaria held its first democratic election for over fifty years. In the same year the authorities arrested Zhivkov on charges of fraud and nepotism, and in 1992 he was convicted of embezzling government funds and sentenced to seven years in prison. Allowed, on account of his age, to serve his term under house arrest, he was acquitted in 1996: he was now an embarrassment to a Bulgarian government that preferred to look forwards rather than backwards. He died of pneumonia in 1998, aged 87.

Meanwhile, Markov's membership of the Union of Bulgarian Writers had, predictably, been suspended, and he was sentenced in his absence to six years in prison for his defection. Consequently, his works were withdrawn from libraries and bookstores, and he became an invisible 'non-person', never to be mentioned in the official Bulgarian media, until the collapse of the communist regime in 1989.

Ten days before Markov's murder, another Bulgarian dissident, Vladimir Kostov, was shot in Paris while waiting on the platform of a Metro station. Under Kostov's skin, doctors found a pellet similar to that which subsequently killed Markov. However, in Kostov's case the pellet's coating had been damaged before firing. This saved Kostov from the full effects of the ricin inside, and instead of Markov's fate he merely suffered a fever.

Kostov reported to the Paris police that he had been shot by a man carrying a small bag but made no mention of an umbrella. This has led many to suggest that Markov mistook his assailant's umbrella for the murder weapon, which must have been a small pistol or similar firing device concealed inside. Whatever the weapon's size and nature, forensic experts declared that the 'gun' that killed Markov was of a very sophisticated design. Accordingly, the finger pointed once more to the KGB.

Since 1978, several high-profile KGB defectors, including Oleg Kalugin and Oleg Gordievsky, have asserted that the KGB was indeed behind Markov's assassination, which was carried out by an agent codenamed as 'Piccadilly'. Apparently, the ricin-impregnated bullet was not the only form of delivery that was considered by the KGB. One of the more bizarre alternatives was a poisonous jelly, which would be smeared on Markov's skin – though how exactly this would be applied remains a matter for bar-room conjecture.

No-one was ever charged with Markov's murder, and the circumstances remain murky, with many of those who may have known something now dead themselves. There have even been accusations that Markov was initially an agent for the Bulgarian regime but then started working for the British Secret Intelligence Service (MI6), so earning Zhivkov's fatal disapproval. (Markov's relatively kid-glove treatment by the regime while he was in Bulgaria is cited as evidence for this.) In 2005, the journalist Hristo Hristov published convincing reports in a Bulgarian newspaper containing newly unearthed documents. These confirmed the assassin was a Dane of Italian origin, one Francesco Gullino: he was the only Bulgarian government agent in London at the time, the aforementioned Agent Piccadilly. Gullino was even interviewed by British police in Denmark in 1993, but the evidence available then was too slim for extradition. He has since disappeared.

Markov's grave, meanwhile, lies in a peaceful Dorset churchyard, in his adoptive country, while post-communist Bulgaria has publicly honoured its lost son for his contribution to literature and his opposition to Zhivkov's tyranny.

George MOSCONE
and Harvey MILK

ASSASSIN Dan White
DATE 27 November 1978
PLACE San Francisco, California, USA

George Moscone was a San Franciscan who rose to be mayor of his city – and one of the most able, tolerant and liberal leaders the city of San Francisco has ever boasted. His life story is an impressive and typically American tale of rags-to-riches success. Tragically, today he is remembered largely for the fact that he met his death along with his city official Harvey Milk, who was the victim of the world's first anti-gay assassination.

George Moscone began his political rise in 1966. As a State Senator in the early 1970s he helped to pass legislation liberalizing homosexual rights in California (he was heterosexual himself). In 1975 he decided to run for the office of Mayor of San Francisco and succeeded in winning a desperately close race on behalf of the 'progressives'.

In office, Moscone was the first mayor to appoint large numbers of women, gay men and lesbians, as well as racial minorities, to official city positions. His new police chief, Charles Gain, encouraged ethnic minorities to join the city's police force. Not all Moscone's appointments were unqualified successes, however. The Rev. Jim Jones, appointed to the Housing Commission, would achieve notoriety thousands of miles away in Guyana, when he and the cult he led expired in an act of mass murder-cum-suicide. This happened on 18 November 1978, just a few days before Moscone met his own violent death.

To the surprise of many in San Francisco, Moscone adamantly opposed the construction of a proposed convention centre, arguing presciently that such massive, modernist monoliths would destroy traditional neighbourhoods and displace hundreds of residents. Nevertheless, the giant structure was ultimately built and, in a grotesque irony, it now bears the name 'Moscone Center'.

San Francisco's district elections for the city's board of supervisors took place in November 1977. Among those elected was one Harvey Milk, who succeeded on his third attempt to join the board. He had lived in San Francisco since 1972, after stints in the US Navy and behind the scenes on Broadway, running a camera store with his partner in The Castro's gay village. Here he soon emerged as a community leader, founding the Castro Valley Association of local businesses, and becoming known as the 'Mayor of Castro Street' – a title that he himself coined.

> ## 'If a bullet should enter my brain, let that bullet destroy every closet door'
>
> Milk's hope (from a tape played at his memorial service) that his potentially violent death might help liberate gay men and women

In 1976, Mayor Moscone (in the left of photograph, p.170) appointed Milk (centre of photograph) to the powerful board of permit appeals. The following year, and now on the board of supervisors, Milk had become the first openly gay elected official of any large city in the United States. In his 11 months as a supervisor, Milk sponsored a gay rights bill for the city – as well as an ordinance requiring all dog owners to carry a scoop and clean up their dog's faeces from public areas. The latter issue was seized on by the local press, and Milk was widely feted (and ridiculed) as the author of the 'pooper-scooper' reform. He was also instrumental in defeating Proposition 6, which would have allowed openly gay and lesbian teachers to be fired from their jobs on account of their sexual orientation.

Already on the board by the time Milk joined it was the conservative former police officer and part-time fireman Dan White, who in subsequent meetings frequently clashed with its more liberal members, notably Milk. The new liberalism of the board in 1977 depressed White, who resigned. However, White then changed his mind about resigning after his supporters, including fellow supervisor Dianne Feinstein – Moscone's successor as mayor, and currently the senior US Senator for California – lobbied him to withdraw his resignation and seek re-appointment. Yet Moscone refused.

Enraged by Moscone's attitude, White stormed to City Hall on 27 November 1978 and demanded a meeting with the mayor. He took care to enter the building through an open basement window, in order to avoid detection of the gun he was carrying – and the ten extra rounds of ammunition he had in his pocket. (Astonishingly, White claimed at his trail that the double murder was not premeditated.) After making his way to the mayor's office, he confronted Moscone about what he saw as his 'betrayal'. Moscone once again refused his request for re-appointment; in response, White pulled out his gun and shot and killed the mayor where he sat.

White then reloaded his weapon and made his way to the opposite side of City Hall, where he entered the office of Supervisor Harvey Milk. White later alleged that Milk 'smirked' at him, and said that it was 'too bad' about the mayor's decision. White's answer was to shoot Milk five times, in the chest and head. He then left City Hall and quietly turned himself in at the precinct police station where he had formerly been an officer.

At his trial, White's defence lawyers argued that their client had been mentally incapacitated at the time of the killings because of his depression, and that the killings had not been premeditated. Among the factors cited as evidence of White's allegedly depressed state was his high consumption of sugary junk food – a bizarre argument, which the press (reporting that sugar had caused his depression) seized on eagerly and labelled the 'Twinkie defense', after the much-loved and sugar-packed cake bar. Swayed by White's lawyers, the jury – to widespread incredulity – found White guilty of voluntary manslaughter rather than first-degree murder.

White's sentence was immediately denounced as overly lenient and the jurors as homophobic. The city erupted on the City Hall and the Castro district, where the police proceeded to attack innocent bystanders as well as presumed rioters. Thankfully, though, no-one died in the disruption. By then, thousands had attended a spontaneous, candlelit memorial vigil on the night of Milk's funeral. Milk had even assumed that he might be assassinated, and had recorded several audio tapes to be played in that event. They were duly brought out.

White eventually served five years of his seven-year sentence and was paroled on 6 January 1984. He served a year's parole in Los Angeles, but then unwisely decided to return to San Francisco, despite Mayor Feinstein's public plea for him to stay away. Back in his home city, however, White became increasingly depressed, and on 21 October 1985 he committed suicide. His brother Tom found his body in his garage the following afternoon; White had run a garden hose from the exhaust pipe to the inside of his car, and had died of carbon monoxide poisoning.

Moscone and Milk in brief

1929 George Moscone is born in San Francisco, California (24 Nov.). He goes on to receive a law degree from Hastings College.

1930 Harvey Milk is born in Woodmere, New York (22 May). He goes on to graduate from State College at Albany, New York (1951), before service in the US Navy, work on Wall Street and eventually co-directing Broadway musicals.

1963 Moscone wins seat as a Democrat on San Francisco's board of supervisors and then a seat in the California State Senate (1966) – and becomes a staunch supporter of gay rights.

1972 Milk settles in San Francisco, running a camera retail business and getting involved as community and business spokesman.

1976 Moscone elected Mayor of San Francisco.

1977 After San Francisco shifts to a system of district elections, Milk is elected the first gay member of the board of supervisors, supporting Moscone and advocating gay-rights measures.

1978 Moscone and Milk are assassinated (27 Nov.) at the City Hall by disgruntled ex-board member Dan White.

THE CASTRO

SAN FRANCISCO HAS, SINCE THE HIPPY HEY-DAY of the mid-to-late 1960s, become renowned as the United States' gay and lesbian capital. It currently boasts the highest percentage of same-sex households of any American county, and it has been estimated that one in five male city residents over the age of 15 is gay.

The gay community in the city is centred on the Castro district. The area's nomenclature has nothing to do with Cuba's president. Rather, Castro Street at the district's heart was named after José Castro, a Mexican politician who led the opposition to US rule in California in the mid-19th century. From 1910 to 1920, the Castro Street area was known as 'Little Scandinavia', after the origins of its recent immigrants. By 1940 it was better known as a rough Irish neighbourhood.

Castro's reputation as a gay centre stems from the aftermath of the 'Human Be-In' and subsequent 'Summer of Love' of 1967, which took place largely in the neighbouring Haight-Ashbury district. Some of the Flower Children who stayed on after 1967 had, by the mid-1970s, metamorphosed into 'Castro Clones', dressed in stretch-fit denim trousers, black combat boots and tight T-shirts, a mode usually complemented by a bravura moustache. By 1985 the stretch of Castro Street between 18th Street and Market Street had become known as 'Clone Canyon'.

In 1998 Frank Falzon, a detective with the San Francisco police, claimed to have met with White in 1984. At this meeting, reported Falzon, White allegedly confessed not only that his assassination of Moscone and Milk was indeed premeditated, but that he had also planned to kill another supervisor, Carol Ruth Silver, as well as state assembly member Willie Brown.

As for the victims, today Harvey Milk is widely regarded as a martyr for the gay community and the gay rights movement. Mayor Moscone is remembered largely through the Moscone Center – the ungainly edifice whose construction he so abhorred.

Oscar ROMERO

1917–1980, ARCHBISHOP OF SAN SALVADOR

ASSASSIN Unverified
DATE 24 March 1980
PLACE San Salvador, El Salvador

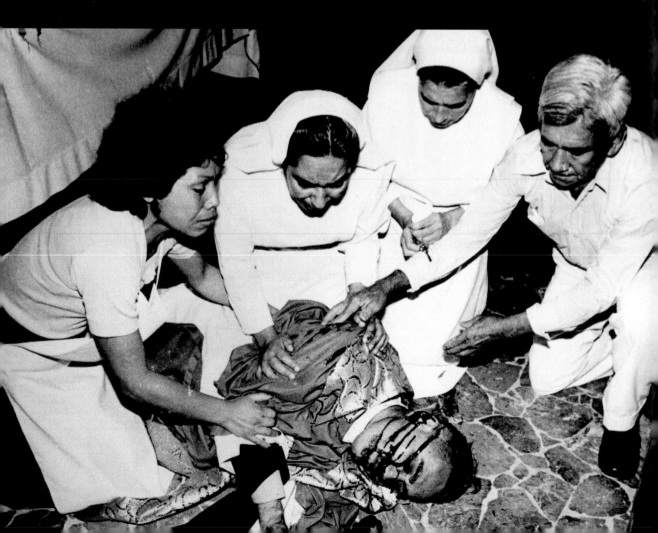

Monsignor Oscar Arnulfo Romero y Galdámez, better known as Archbishop Romero, has been called the unofficial patron saint of Latin America. He is one of the ten 20th-century martyrs from across the world depicted in stone above the Great West Door of London's Westminster Abbey. In 1997 his passage to sainthood began, when he was proposed for beatification and canonization. One of the most widely admired religious figures of the last century, he dared to speak out against oppression and torture. His death at the hands of gunmen, though widely predicted, eventually took place while he was celebrating Mass in his cathedral in San Salvador.

Romero was born in 1917 to a poor Salvadoran family. As a boy he showed a prodigious talent for carpentry. However, at the age of 13 he entered a minor religious seminary run by the Claretian order in San Miguel. Seven years later he graduated to the national seminary run by the Jesuits in the country's capital, San Salvador; here his promise was quickly recognized, and he was despatched to Rome. Despite Italy's ill-judged entry into the Second World War in 1940, and the consequent social and economic dislocation, Romero managed to stay in Rome long enough to complete his theology degree in the summer of 1941 and to be ordained as a Catholic priest in April 1942.

> ## 'I too have to walk the same path'
>
> Archbishop Romero's momentous decision to join those pursing social justice for the oppressed of El Salvador

Returning to El Salvador, Romero worked as a parish priest in San Miguel for over twenty years. There he proved an exemplary, but hardly radical, community priest, though he did start a chapter of Alcoholics Anonymous. He also played a part in promoting the construction of San Miguel's new cathedral. By 1966, when he was appointed secretary of the episcopal conference for El Salvador and editor of the newspaper for the archdiocese (*Orientación*), he was known – if at all – as a staid, conservative figure who was unlikely to challenge papal or governmental authority.

In 1970 Romero became 'auxiliary bishop' to San Salvador's Archbishop Luis Chávez y González. More radical elements in the priesthood protested at the promotion of such a traditionalist, establishment figure. However, this proved no impediment to his rise through El Salvador's Catholic hierarchy. In 1975 he succeeded to the bishopric of Santiago de María. Two years later – to the dismay of liberal circles all over Central America – Oscar Romero donned the robes as the new Archbishop of San Salvador.

Barely three weeks after his installation as archbishop, Romero confronted what was a turning point in his life. Father Rutilio Grande was a close personal friend, despite also being a Jesuit priest of a progressive disposition. This was a time of burgeoning support for 'liberation theology' in Latin America, whereby priests were becoming actively involved in politics and campaigns for social justice, in defence of the downtrodden masses living under the continent's military regimes. But progressive views were dangerous things to have under the president-generals who ran El Salvador in the 1970s. On 12 March 1977, Rutilio was assassinated on his way to celebrate Mass.

His death had a profound impact on Romero. For him it was a Damascene moment, opening his eyes to the plight of those whom Rutilio had been trying to help. That evening he went to view the body, and he later famously told César Jerez, the Jesuit Provincial, that 'When I looked at Rutilio lying there dead, I thought "if they have killed him for doing what he did, then I too have to walk the same path".' Romero urged the government of President Arturo Molina to investigate the crime, but it studiously ignored his pleas, while the government-controlled press remained ominously silent.

Father Rutilio's murder both radicalized Romero and galvanized him to speak out. In the next few years he evolved into a high-profile opponent of the appalling poverty and endemic social injustice around him. He also lashed out at the political corruption, widespread torture and the all-too-frequent assassinations (including churchmen) that characterized the political life of the country. His speeches and writings became well known internationally, and in 1979 he was even nominated for the Nobel Peace Prize. In February 1980, shortly after receiving an honorary doctorate by the Catholic University of Leuven, he met Pope John Paul II and expressed his concerns about El Salvador's governmental terrorism and its increasing prevalence.

By then, actual civil war had erupted in El Salvador following the 1979 coup of the 'Revolutionary Government Junta', a left-wing putsch which had ousted the government of President Carlos Romero. The junta itself fell a few months later, and El Salvador embarked on 12 years of bloody anarchy. The period saw a (sometimes three-way) conflict between an impotent government, right-wing death squads often acting in cahoots with (or, indeed, staffed by) the official military, and the left-wing guerrillas of the Farabundo Martí National Liberation Front (FMLN). The victims in all this, perhaps as many as 80,000, were of course mostly civilians.

The highest-profile victim of the death squads was Romero himself. In 1980, the archbishop warned US President Jimmy Carter that increased military aid to El Salvador

THE SCHOOL OF THE AMERICAS

MANY OF THE SALVADORAN ARMY OFFICERS who led the death squads were trained at the notorious School of the Americas (SOA). The institution was first established by the Truman government in the Panama Canal Zone in 1946 as the Latin American Ground School, with the avowed purpose of training Latin American officers to resist communism and promote democracy. In 1949 it was renamed the US Army Caribbean School. By 1956 it began to focus its training exclusively on Latin Americans, and it has conducted its classes solely in Spanish ever since. In 1963 it was renamed again, as the School of the Americas, while the focus of its curriculum was changed from nation-building skills to anti-communist counter-insurgency. Now located at the huge US army base of Fort Benning at Columbus, Georgia, in 2000 the school was renamed yet again, adopting the less provocative (but possibly more Orwellian) title of the Western Hemisphere Institute for Security Cooperation.

Today, approximately 1000 students a year attend the institute, whose official remit is 'to provide professional education and training' while 'promoting democratic values, respect for human rights, and knowledge and understanding of United States' customs and traditions'. The institute claims it has now installed a vetting system aimed as preventing human-rights abusers from gaining a place there. However, critics claim that its graduates have perpetrated many of the worst human rights violations in recent Latin American history, and have repeatedly demanded its closure. In 2007 a Congressional amendment to cut off its funding failed by just six votes.

Undeniably, the list of the School's alumni reads uncannily like a rogue's gallery of Latin American dictators and murderers, including such notorious names as Argentina's military dictator and death-squad leader Leopoldo Galtieri (1926–2003), Panama's dictator-cum-drug-trafficker Manuel Noriega (b.1934), Guatemalan hardman Efraín Montt (b.1926) – and Roberto D'Aubuisson. But several governments have now withdrawn their nationals from the school. In 2004, the anti-US Venezuelan president, Hugo Chávez, was the first to do this, and in 2006 the governments of Argentina and Uruguay followed suit, as did the Costa Rican president, Oscar Arias.

would 'undoubtedly sharpen the injustice and the repression inflicted on the organized people, whose struggle has often been for their most basic human rights'. However, the vacillating Carter – worried that El Salvador would become 'another Nicaragua' in the run up to the US presidential elections – ignored Romero's pleas.

Romero's end came on 24 March 1980. What are believed to be right-wing assassins murdered him as he celebrated Mass at a small chapel near his cathedral. The day before, his sermon had called for soldiers to disobey orders that violated basic human rights. As he concluded the homily, unidentified men in fatigues burst in and shot him repeatedly. Unsurprisingly, the murderers were never caught. In 1993 a UN report identified the man who ordered the killing as Major Roberto D'Aubuisson. His driver, Rafael Alvaro Saravia, was indicted for his role in the assassination by a US court in 2004.

Romero was buried in the crypt of his own cathedral. The funeral on 30 March 1980 was attended by more than 250,000 mourners, an enormous show of support for Romero and all he stood for – and a challenge to the army. During the ceremony, government security forces threw bombs into the crowd while army sharpshooters, dressed as civilians, fired into the chaos from the balcony or roof of the National Palace, causing panic. Forty-two civilians died that day, and hundreds were wounded.

Romero's death provided the world with a luminous example of principle and courage, but sadly did nothing to stem the violence in El Salvador. Atrocities culminated in the rape and murder of Jean Donovan, an American lay missionary and follower of Romero, by a government death squad in December 1980, and the El Mozote massacre of December 1981, when Salvadoran armed forces killed an estimated 900 civilians – including women and children – in two villages as part of an anti-guerrilla campaign.

1982 saw the creation by the very same Major D'Aubuisson and other right-wing officers of a new political party, the Nationalist Republican Alliance (ARENA), as a response to the increasingly well-organized FMLN. In 1989 ARENA's candidate Alfredo Cristiani, who had deliberately sought the support of business groups – as well as of moderate US opinion – triumphed in the Salvadoran presidential election. Three years later, now that generous US funding and *matériel* had vastly improved the size and quality of the government's armed forces, his adminis-tration was able to claim that it had successfully terminated the civil war. ARENA still dominates El Salvador's politics, while Archbishop Romero's murder continues to remain unpunished.

Romero in brief

1917 Born in Ciudad Barrios, El Salvador, near the Honduran border (15 Aug.).

1930–7 Attends seminary of the Claretian Order, San Miguel.

1937–43 Studies theology at San Salvador's Jesuit seminary, and then in Rome, earning degrees and doctorate. Ordained as priest in Rome (1942).

1944–66 Parish priest in San Miguel, El Salvador.

1966 Appointed secretary of the episcopal conference for El Salvador and editor of the church's newspaper *Orientación*.

1970 Becomes 'auxiliary bishop' to San Salvador's Archbishop Luis Chávez y González.

1975 Appointed Bishop of Santiago de María.

1977 Chosen as the new Archbishop of San Salvador. Spurred by the political killing of a Jesuit friend, abondons political conservatism and campaigns on social, religious and human-rights issues.

1979 El Salvador's new ruling junta fragments, and years of what amounts to civil war begin.

1980 Travels to Europe to receive honorary doctorate, and discusses El Salvador's plight with Pope John Paul II. Assassinated (24 March) while celebrating Mass near his cathedral.

1997 A process of beatification for him begins.

Anwar al-SADAT

1918–1981, PRESIDENT OF EGYPT

ASSASSIN Khalid Islambouli
DATE 6 October 1981
PLACE Cairo, Egypt

By 1981 Mohammed Anwar al-Sadat had seemingly achieved the impossible. Having united and strengthened Egypt in the aftermath of the death of President Nasser, the father of modern Egypt, he concluded a peace treaty with the nation's implacable enemy, Israel. It was an achievement that astonished and delighted the non-Arab world. Shunned, however, by his former Arab allies, he became a prime target for Arab radicals, and he ultimately fell victim to one of the most bizarre and bloody assassinations of modern times.

Sadat was born in 1918 to a poor Egyptian–Sudanese family, one of 13 brothers and sisters. He graduated from the Royal Military Academy in Cairo in 1938, joined the army as a second lieutenant and was posted to the Sudan. There, he met with Nasser and the other junior officers then plotting to overthrow the British-backed Egyptian government. Sadat was imprisoned intermittently during the Second World War for secretly negotiating with the Germans to expel the hard-pressed British forces from Egypt, but he finally escaped.

In 1952, having rejoined the army and absorbed the influence of the 'Free Officers' revolutionary movement, he participated in Nasser's dramatic and successful coup, dethroning the Anglophile Egyptian king, Farouk I. It was Sadat who seized the radio networks and announced the outbreak of revolution to the Egyptian people. During the next 18 years, Sadat was one of Nasser's trusted lieutenants. Minister of state in 1954, he rose to become president of parliament in 1960 and, in 1964 and again in 1969, the Egyptian vice-president. When Nasser died of a heart attack in 1970, it was Sadat's voice that informed the nation of the tragic news.

In the wake of Nasser's death, Sadat acted quickly and decisively to establish his personal power base. Initially, his rivals believed he could be easily manipulated and would act as a convenient figurehead for the time being (press and politicians even called him 'donkey'). However, they seriously underestimated Sadat's political skills and gritty determination. In what became known as the 'Corrective Revolution', Sadat replaced office-holders across the country with his own nominees. He purged all officials loyal to the memory of Nasser and promoted individuals who owed their livelihoods to Sadat's own patronage.

> 'We accept to live with you in permanent peace based on justice'
>
> From Sadat's historic speech to Israel's Knesset, 20 November 1977

In foreign affairs, Sadat soon demonstrated that he did not necessarily intend to pursue the implacably anti-Israeli policy of his predecessor. Egypt's longstanding enmity against its Jewish neighbour, exacerbated by the stunning Israeli triumphs of the Six Day War of 1967, appeared unshakeable. However, in a letter of 1971 that surprised the world, Sadat endorsed the Arab–Israeli peace proposals formulated by UN negotiator Gunnar Jarring, based on Israel's withdrawal to its pre-1967 borders. However, when neither Israel nor its perennial benefactor, the United States, was even willing to discuss the terms, Jarring and Sadat's peace initiative failed.

Over the next two years, Sadat balanced on a precarious tightrope. He took care not to give unnecessary offence to the United States, while in 1972 he expelled 20,000 Soviet military advisers from Egypt and began to woo the governments of Britain and France. At the same time he began to build up his armed forces to a state where, in contrast to the humiliations of 1967, they would be able to present a credible challenge to Israel's formidable military might. Arab allies such as Jordan, Lebanon and Iraq were reluctant to commit themselves to another risky war against Israel (though both Jordan and Iraq were eventually to send military assistance). However, Colonel Gaddafi's Libya was willing to fund Egyptian rearmament. At the same time, while ostensibly loosening his ties with the Soviet Union, Sadat was happy to receive large quantities of Soviet tanks, aircraft and missiles.

Revenge for the Six-Day War was unleashed on 6 October 1973 when, in the midst of both the Jewish Yom Kippur and the Muslim Ramadan festivals, Egyptian forces invaded Israeli territory in the Sinai peninsula while Syria struck in the Golan Heights. The Israeli prime minister, Golda Meir, had been warned of an impending Syrian attack, but both she and her intelligence services dismissed the claims. They had believed that the Egyptian army – the backbone of any credible Arab threat – had been too seriously weakened by the loss of its Soviet military advisers. In the event, the complacent Israeli forces, as surprised by events as the Arabs had been in 1967, fell back, and for a time it seemed as if they were beaten. However, Israel's British-made Centurion tanks regrouped to repel the seemingly inexorable advance of the Arab armour, and then switched to the offensive. By 22 October, three divisions of the Israeli army, led by General Ariel Sharon, had crossed the Suez Canal and encircled the Egyptian Third Army. Prompted by action from both the United States and the Soviet Union, the UN Security Council demanded an immediate ceasefire.

Israel had ostensibly won, and now held more territory on the Golan Heights than it had at the beginning of October. However, in the aftermath of the war it was Sadat and his Arab allies who appeared to be invigorated. The myth of Israeli invincibility, created by the wars of 1948–9 and 1967, had been shattered. The Israeli government purged its armed forces of many of the senior officers, blamed for the country's pre-war unpreparedness. Finally, Golda Meir's government, its reputation in tatters, itself resigned in April 1974.

Emboldened by their strong negotiating position, and enraged by the unequivocal US support for Israel during the war, the Arab members of the oil-producing cartel OPEC had already resolved to reduce oil production by 5 per cent per month on 17 October. The result was a sharp rise in the worldwide price of oil, and an international energy crisis.

In Egypt, the army's initial successes greatly increased Sadat's popularity. He himself was feted by the government-controlled media as 'the Hero of the Crossing', after the Egyptian armour's early victories. While his opposite number in Israel was forced to resign, Sadat was able to impose much firmer control of the Egyptian state apparatus and took the opportunity to initiate many long-planned reforms.

By 1977, Sadat felt secure enough at home and abroad to launch a peace initiative aimed at healing the bitter Arab–Israeli divide. In November of that year, Sadat took the unprecedented step (and without US or Soviet backing) of visiting Israel, becoming the first Arab leader to do so. His speech before a special session of the Knesset in Jerusalem implicitly assured Egyptian recognition of the state of Israel, an act that comprehensively redefined the politics of the Middle East. Encouraged by this immensely brave and risk-laden decision, US President Jimmy Carter invited Sadat and the Israeli prime minister, Menachem Begin, to a summit at the presidential retreat of Camp David in September 1978. To worldwide astonishment, the talks were successful, and in 1979 Israel and Egypt signed a historic peace treaty. Israel withdrew its troops and settlers from Sinai by April 1982, in exchange for the establishment of normal diplomatic and social relations with Egypt and, it was hoped, a lasting peace. Both Sadat and Begin (pictured together on p.178, Sadat to the left) were rewarded with the Nobel Peace Prize for 1978.

Unsurprisingly, the treaty outraged much of the Arab world. Nasser had made Egypt an icon of Arab nationalism and the focus of pan-Arab resistance to the establishment of the state of Israel. Many hopes were placed on Egypt to help extract concessions from Israel for the displaced Palestinians and others in the Arab world. By signing the accords, Sadat seemed to have left the other Arab nations to fend for themselves, destroying hopes for a united Arab front. Accordingly, in 1979 the Arab League suspended Egypt's membership and moved its headquarters from Cairo to Tunis – actions that were not reversed until 1989.

By 1981, the prosperity that Sadat had promised Egyptians in the wake of the peace accord had failed to materialize. There was widespread unrest both at the deteriorating economic situation and at the nation's bleak diplomatic isolation in the Arab world. In September 1981 Sadat lost his patience and imposed a draconian crackdown on 'intellectuals and activists' of all ideological persuasions, imprisoning 1600 assorted communists, Nasserist diehards, Islamists and university types – but also, for good measure, Coptic Christian clergy, selected journalists and campaigners for women's rights. Predictably, though, the hamfisted clampdown merely served to incite his domestic opponents, while the worldwide condemnation of his actions served to emphasize his international isolation.

THE ROAD TO AL-QAEDA

SADAT'S VICE-PRESIDENT, HOSNI MUBARAK, whose hand had been injured during the attack that killed Sadat, succeeded to the presidency. The transition was relatively smooth, and Mubarak reacted swiftly to stamp out Sadat's opponents. The blame for the assassination was laid at the door of radical Islamist groups, who, since the founding of the Muslim Brotherhood in 1928, had long been a thorn in the side of Egyptian governments. Recently they had been taking advantage of Sadat's unpopularity and the deal with Israel to woo army officers. Over three hundred radicals were indicted during the trial of Sadat's assassin, Islambouli, particularly those connected with Egyptian Islamic Jihad, which was thought to be the group behind the killing.

The accused included the Jihad leader Ayman al-Zawahiri, who, during the trial's proceedings, became a spokesman for the defendants (he knew English) and achieved an international profile. He was to turn this notoriety to good use after his release from prison in 1984, when he travelled to the Afghan–Pakistani border and introduced himself to the radicalized Saudi tycoon Osama Bin Laden, who was then helping bankroll the fight against the Soviet occupation of Afghanistan. The two men soon established a close relationship. In 1989 Zawahiri and others persuaded Bin Laden to found and finance his own Islamic terrorist group, which by the mid-1990s was being termed 'al-Qaeda'.

Meanwhile, the plot to murder Sadat was never fully uncovered. It may never be. On 31 October 2006 Sadat's nephew was sentenced to a year in prison for defaming Egypt's armed forces, less than a month after he gave an interview accusing Egyptian generals of masterminding his uncle's assassination.

Rumours of assassination plots multiplied, while Sadat compensated for his inner anxieties by ordering ever more festive military uniforms for himself.

The end for President Sadat was all too public. While reviewing his armed forces in the annual military parade of 6 October 1981, designed to commemorate the early victories of the 1973 war, total mayhem erupted. As the air force's Mirage jets roared overhead, a Russian-made troop carrier halted before the presidential reviewing stand and an artillery lieutenant, Khalid Hassan Shafiq Islambouli, strode forward. Sadat stood to receive his salute in the sweltering heat, whereupon assassins rose from the truck, throwing grenades and firing their assault rifles. Islambouli, shouting 'Glory to Egypt' (some sources say 'Death to the pharaoh'), shot Sadat in the head. At first many onlookers believed the firing was all part of the review's entertainment, until the prostrate form of Sadat convinced them otherwise. Two of the attackers were killed on the spot, while military police arrested the others. Sadat was rushed to a hospital, and early radio reports downplayed his life-threatening injuries; however, his death hours later was finally announced to the nation that evening.

> **'Any life lost in war is the life of a human being, irrespective of whether it is an Arab or an Israeli'**
>
> Sadat, quoting his words to Israel's Knesset, as he accepted the Nobel Peace Prize in 1978

Sadat was not the only victim of the assassins' assault. In the confused firefight that accompanied Islambouli's execution of the president, several others were killed, including the Cuban ambassador and a Coptic Orthodox bishop. A further 28 people were wounded, including James Tully, the Irish minister for defence, and four US military liaison officers.

The principal assassin, Islambouli, was subsequently found guilty and executed in April 1982. Meanwhile, Sadat's funeral was attended by a record number of dignitaries from around the world, including three former US presidents: Gerald Ford, Jimmy Carter and Richard Nixon. Significantly, though, no Arab leaders attended the funeral apart from Sudan's embattled president, Gaafar Nimeiry. Sadat himself was buried in the Unknown Soldier memorial in Cairo.

Benigno AQUINO

1932–1983, FILIPINO POLITICIAN

ASSASSIN	Unverified
DATE	21 August 1983
PLACE	Manila, Philippines

On 21 August 1983 Benigno Simeón Aquino, popularly known as 'Ninoy', stepped cautiously through a plane door and into the bright sunlight at Manila International Airport. The aircraft had just brought Aquino, the *de facto* leader of the political opposition, back to his native Philippines for the first time in three years. News that the country's dictator, President Ferdinand Marcos, was ailing had encouraged him to return. Aquino's aim was to try and secure the Philippines' return to democracy should the autocrat finally expire.

Tragically, Aquino got no further than the airport tarmac. He was accompanied by several foreign journalists – invited along partly to ensure his safety – plus a nearby convoy of security guards, all assigned to him by the Marcos government. In addition, there was a contingent of 2000 military and police personnel at the airport. Despite all the security, Aquino was shot in the back of the head as he descended the steps from the aircraft.

Government investigators later claimed that Aquino was gunned down by one Rolando Galman, a lone figure who had been conveniently shot dead by airport security seconds after Aquino was shot. (The mayhem at the airport is depicted in the photograph on p.183) No-one actually identified who pulled the trigger; one of Aquino's fellow-passengers did, though, later testify that she had seen a man in military uniform behind Aquino on the stairs point a gun at the back of his head, followed by the sound of a gunshot.

As President Marcos was reportedly gravely ill, most people assumed that the assassination had been engineered by the hugely powerful First Lady, Imelda Marcos, a former beauty queen who had survived a televised assassination attempt herself in 1972. She was, after all, a shrewd and ruthless political operator in her own right.

> 'I have returned to join the ranks of those struggling to restore our rights and freedom'
>
> From Aquino's last statement to the press, on board his fatal flight to Manila, August 1983

When the president recovered he ordered a government commission to investigate the assassination. The result was a predictable whitewash: a number of the middle-ranking military officers who had arrived to greet Aquino on the tarmac were found guilty, and they are still serving life sentences at the National Bilibid Prison in Manila. A recent appeal against their sentences claimed that a business partner of the Marcos family, Eduardo Cojuangco, ordered the assassination, even though he had been cleared by the official investigation.

At first it seemed as if Marcos's government had got away with yet another gross abuse of power. However, the aftershock of Aquino's murder was to sweep both Marcos and his despised spouse completely away, and to transform Filipino politics.

Aquino's family background was a controversial one. His grandfather had been a general in the revolutionary army that fought against Spain at the end of the 19th century. His father, however, had been a prominent official in the puppet government assembled after the fall of the Philippines to Japanese forces in 1941, and had died in mysterious circumstances after the Second World War.

Young Ninoy became a journalist, and used his media contacts – and his family's name – to enter the political arena. Aged only 21, he became a close adviser to Defence Secretary

Ramon Magsaysay; by 1955 he was Mayor of Concepción, and six years later was appointed governor of the province of Tarlac. In 1967, aged 34, he became the youngest elected senator in the country's history and proceeded to assume the mantle of the increasingly authoritarian Marcos government's principal critic. His personal attacks on the extravagant and notoriously ambitious First Lady outraged the president and secured Aquino's public reputation as a fearless opponent of Marcos's drift towards dictatorship.

Aquino's warnings were vindicated when, in August 1971, government agents bombed a public platform on which many of the leaders of Aquino's Liberal Party were speaking. Marcos accused communist insurgents of perpetrating the assault and used the attack as an excuse to round up political opponents. Despite his promises, however, the bombers were never tried. (One of the bombers was allegedly captured and identified as a police sergeant, but then snatched by military personnel and never heard of again.)

Worse was to come. On 21 September 1972 Marcos declared martial law and arrested Aquino and other opposition politicians. Five years later, the government's military commission sentenced Aquino to death by firing squad. Aware of growing foreign impatience with Marcos's tactics, however, the sentence was suspended – although Aquino remained in prison, where in March 1980 he suffered two heart attacks.

Aquino was clearly now in failing health, and the Marcoses did not want a martyr on their hands. Accordingly, on 8 May Imelda Marcos made a bizarre personal visit to Aquino's cell and offered him immediate evacuation to the United States on condition that he would not attack the Marcos regime while abroad, and that he would return at some future date. Aquino jumped at the opportunity of freedom, and agreed. He was then bundled into a waiting van and taken back to his home, where his whole family were collected and put on an American-bound plane the very same day.

Having arrived in the United States, Aquino underwent a heart operation at a Dallas hospital and recovered quickly. Renouncing his pact with the Marcoses, he settled with his wife, Cory, and their children in a Boston suburb and repeatedly criticized the Marcos regime, warning that the president's repression would only serve to radicalize his many opponents. The Filipino government, meanwhile, tried to frame Aquino as the author of a series of bombings that plagued the capital after 1981.

By early 1983, having learned of the deteriorating political situation in the Philippines and of the declining health of the – supposedly – terminally ill president, Aquino decided to return home. Filipino consular officials in the United States were ordered not to issue any passports for the Aquino family, while Marcos's government warned all international airlines that they would be denied landing rights if they tried to fly the Aquinos to the

Aquino in brief

1932 Born in Tarlac, the Philippines, into an influential political–military family.

1950–4 Works as journalist and begins political career as adviser and fixer of Defence Secretary (later President) Magsaysay.

1955 Elected Mayor of Concepción; later deputy governor for Tarlac province (1959) and governor (1961).

1967 Elected youngest-ever member of the Philippine Senate.

1968 Achieves leadership of the Liberal Party, opposing the regime of Ferdinand Marcos.

1972–80 Imprisoned with other politicians as Marcos announces martial law: he goes on hunger strike, is sentenced to death for (probably manufactured) offences, but remains a political figurehead.

1980 Now very ill, is released from prison to travel to USA for heart surgery.

1980–3 Lives near Boston with wife Corazon ('Cory') and family, campaigning against the Marcos regime.

1983 Returns to the Philippines, contrary to the wishes of the weakening Marcos regime. Assassinated on arrival (21 Aug.) at Manila Airport, which is later renamed Ninoy Aquino International Airport in his memory.

1986 After 'losing' a disputed election to Marcos, Cory Aquino becomes President of the Philippines when a popular revolution forces Marcos into exile.

IMELDA MARCOS: LIFE AFTER DEATH

IMELDA MARCOS, THE LADY MACBETH of modern Filipino history, achieved her own immortality by providing the 20th century with a unique symbol of despotic excess: her personal collection of 888 handbags and 1060 pairs of shoes, which was discovered in the presidential palace after she and her husband were toppled.

In 1990 Imelda Marcos was acquitted of racketeering and fraud in the United States, in a trial that garnered worldwide attention and starred the actor George Hamilton as witness for the defence. The following year she was finally allowed to return home to the Philippines.

Astonishingly, the indefatigable Imelda then proceeded to demonstrate nerves of steel – and the hide of a rhinoceros – by attempting a political comeback. She stood for president in the 1992 election, but came only fifth. Persevering with immense determination in the face of universal derision, in 1995 she was elected Congresswoman for the district of Leyte. In 1998 she made yet another bid for the presidency, and while finishing only ninth out of eleven candidates, she cannily managed to cement a friendship with the victor, Joseph Estrada. During President Estrada's administration, many of the cases filed against Mrs Marcos by the Aquino government were dismissed on technicalities.

She still keeps going. In 2007 Imelda's daughter announced that her mother was considering running for the post of Mayor of Manila. Later that year, however, she was indicted for ten cases of graft.

Philippines. Aquino therefore chose a circuitous route home, flying from Boston to Los Angeles, Singapore, Hong Kong and Taiwan's capital Taipei – Taiwan having already severed diplomatic links with Manila. In the event, his precautions were in vain. His route had been discovered, and his assassin must have been already planted on his final plane.

Two million people lined the streets at Aquino's funeral on 31 August 1983, and the nationwide protests did not go away. Cory Aquino, Ninoy's wife, campaigned tirelessly across the country in a bid to vindicate her late husband's brave stand. Pressured by his US allies, Marcos was forced to reintroduce the semblance of democracy. In the general election of 1986, Cory Aquino – to the Marcoses' incredulity – won a sizeable victory. Marcos's rigged electoral commission attempted to reverse the result, but much of the Filipino electorate had witnessed countless undeniable instances of blatant electoral fraud. Marcos's attempt to cling to power was condemned by the US Senate and by the Filipino church, and the population took to the streets and demonstrated. Most crucially, the Filipino army gradually began to defect from its erstwhile master. The Marcoses, recognizing that their grasp on power was fatally undermined, fled to exile in Hawaii, where Ferdinand Marcos, indicted for embezzlement but never tried, died of kidney failure in 1989.

The Marcoses having thrown in the towel, Cory Aquino was duly declared the 11th President of the Philippines. The apparatus of the Marcos government was dismantled and the constitution rewritten. However, the Aquino administration was plagued by repeated coup attempts – fomented by communist groups and by the army – and a series of punishing natural disasters. Exhausted, Cory Aquino refused to offer herself for a second term and stood down as president in 1992.

Manila International Airport has now been renamed the Ninoy Aquino International Airport, Ninoy's image is printed on the country's 500-peso bill, and the day of his assassination is now a public holiday. His memory is now revered by political factions across the country, and his bronze memorial in Makati City has become the customary venue for anti-government rallies and demonstrations – a development Ninoy would surely have applauded.

Indira GANDHI

1917–1984, PRIME MINISTER OF INDIA

ASSASSINS Satwant Singh and Beant Singh
DATE 31 October 1984
PLACE New Delhi, India

Indira Gandhi was one of India's most remarkable and controversial political leaders as well as the daughter of the country's first prime minister, Jawaharlal Nehru. She was also the mother of its seventh prime minister, Rajiv Gandhi; but by 1991 both mother and son had fallen victim to determined assassins. Indian politics had claimed two more of its brightest stars.

Indira's maiden name was, of course, Nehru. She was thus no relation to the 'Mahatma' Gandhi who was so shockingly assassinated in 1948. She took her married name (a common one in India) from her husband, Feroze Gandhi, a Congress Party radical whom she wed in 1942. The Nehru family, from the highest echelon in India's caste system, the Brahmins, was a dynasty of well-educated and wealthy lawyers, who had all been prominent members of the Indian National Congress (INC, or Congress Party) struggling for India's independence from Britain. Indira followed the family tradition and joined the Mahatma's 'Quit India' movement, for which wartime activism she and her husband were briefly imprisoned in 1943.

Following Indian independence in 1947, Indira moved with her children to New Delhi to assist her father, now prime minister. She became her father's confidante, secretary and nurse, managing his re-election campaign in 1951. Her absence from the marital home, however, prompted the effective end of her marriage; Feroze himself, after a brief career as an anti-corruption crusader, died of heart failure in 1960.

'My father was a statesman, I am a political woman. My father was a saint. I am not.'

Gandhi's astute self-observation, quoted by Oriana Fallaci in the *New York Review of Books*, 8 September 1975

In 1959 Indira Gandhi was elected president of the INC. Five years later, following the death of her beloved father, she was appointed to the government as minister for information. Her rapid political ascent was complete when, in the confused aftermath of the Indo-Pakistani War of 1965, she became the fourth person (and the only woman to date) to lead India as prime minister.

In office, Gandhi soon established a reputation as a determined hawk on both foreign and domestic issues. With Pakistan a Cold War ally of the United States, she tweaked India's traditional 'non-aligned' status by signing a treaty with the Soviet Union. She accelerated the country's nuclear programme, ostensibly to combat the perceived threat from Mao's China with whom India had humiliatingly lost a border war in 1962. As a result, in 1974 India was able to conduct her first successful underground nuclear test, thus joining the select club of the planet's nuclear powers. She also launched an ambitious programme of agricultural reform, aimed at ending India's reliance on food imports from the West and the nation's seemingly endemic series of regional famines. The outcome was astonishing: by the mid-1970s, India's chronic food shortages were a thing of the past, and India had been transformed into a net exporter of its surplus production of wheat, rice, cotton and milk.

Her controversial style, however, had already split the party, with her supporters now constituting the 'Congress (I) Party' (I = Indira). Following a landslide election victory in 1971, Gandhi increasingly resorted to authoritarian means in order to achieve her political ends. Using her unassailable parliamentary majority, she stripped power from the regional states and concentrated it in central government. And as she had been her father's closest adviser, now she in turn began to lean heavily on her son Sanjay in preference to elected Congress Party leaders.

In June 1975 Gandhi suffered her first major political setback. Allahabad's High Court found her guilty of employing a government servant in her election campaign – which technically constituted election fraud. Gandhi appealed against the decision, while opposition parties called for her resignation and fomented strikes and protest rallies. Gandhi had lost much popular support since 1971, and the global oil crisis of 1973 had helped to plunge the economy into recession and prices were now spiralling.

Faced with public unrest, Gandhi asked the Indian president (constitutionally the servant of the prime minister) to declare a state of emergency on 26 June 1975, whereby she would be able to rule by decree. The police and the army had already been called out to break up the strikes and protests; now, on the night of the declaration, almost all opposition leaders were imprisoned. In the days that followed, all elections were indefinitely postponed and all the regional state governments controlled by the opposition were dismissed.

Even the most fervent admirer of Indira Gandhi had to admit that her actions were outrageously arbitrary and blatantly undemocratic. Yet her swiftness and utter ruthlessness stunned the country. As India's cowed citizens braced themselves for more represssive measures, the economy recovered dramatically now that the country was strike-free. Accordingly, Gandhi's personal rule – the 'Indian Emergency' – lasted for almost 21 months and earned the truculent support of business and agriculture.

Civil liberties, though, continued to be flouted. Thousands of political activists were arrested and tortured, and thousands were killed – with many hundreds of thousands of people made homeless – as a consequence of Sanjay Gandhi's brutal slum-clearance campaign in Delhi, ostensibly initiated to combat disease and poverty but also having the effect of stifling urban protest. At the same time, Sanjay's bluntly efficient family-planning programme, which imposed vasectomies on thousands of fathers, enraged families and communities across India.

Indira Gandhi's totalitarian experiment had warped her political judgement. In 1977, vastly misjudging both the strength of her position and her own popularity, Gandhi called a general election. The result was a resounding defeat at the hands of the Janata Party alliance, led by a former Congress Party minister, Morarji Desai. It was the first time the Congress Party had lost a national election since India's independence.

The new Janata government swiftly ordered the arrest of both Indira and Sanjay Gandhi. However, the administration's disparate membership was deeply divided over how to proceed, and even about how to prosecute the Gandhis. Indira, ever the consummate politician, made public apologies for the excesses of her personal rule and thus managed to garner support from both the Left and Right. When the last Janata administration collapsed in disarray in 1980, Mrs Gandhi, in one of the most accomplished (and most rapid) political comebacks in history, won a landslide victory and returned to power.

Gandhi in brief

1917 Born in Allahabad, India, the only child of lawyer Jawarhalal Nehru. Attends university in West Bengal and Oxford.

1943 Briefly interned for supporting the 'Quit India' campaign.

1947 Moves to New Delhi to assist her father, now independent India's prime minister: manages his re-election campaign in 1951.

1959 Elected president of the Congress Party.

1964 Following the death of her father, appointed minister for information.

1966–71 Becomes prime minister. Goes on to sign treaty with Soviet Union, defeat Pakistan to ensure Bangladesh's independence in 1971, and initiates agricultural reforms.

1972 Wins a landslide election, but is accused of malpractice.

1974 India's first successful underground nuclear test.

1975–7 Declares a state of emergency, after the High Court finds against her regarding the 1972 election and after popular unrest. Rules by decree, then calls election but loses (1977).

1980 Returns to power.

1984 Authorizes army to end the occupation by Sikh Punjabi separatists at their Golden Temple in Amritsar, but hundreds of Sikhs die as a result. Assassinated (31 Oct.) by two Sikh members of her bodyguard.

AFTER INDIRA

RAJIV GANDHI BECAME PRIME MINISTER with no political reputation whatsoever. He used that to his advantage, dismantling corrupt government bodies and tackling inefficiency. He also reversed many of his mother's policies, improving relations with the United States, reducing import quotas, taxes and tariffs, and vastly increasing government support for science, technology and higher education. Abroad, he sent troops to aid the neighbouring government of Sri Lanka to help in its fight against the separatist Tamil Tigers.

Unfortunately for Rajiv, his much-admired anti-corruption drive soon engulfed him, as he became personally implicated in a scandal involving alleged payoffs to senior government officials by the Swedish arms manufacturer Bofors. With his reputation as India's 'Mr Clean' shattered, he resigned in 1989, and the Congress Party was heavily defeated in the ensuing election.

Loss of office did not, however, keep him safe from the consequences of previous actions. Now leader of the parliamentary opposition, he was assassinated on 21 May 1991 at Sriperumbudur, in the southeastern state of Tamil Nadu, while campaigning for the local Congress candidate. The assassin was a female suicide bomber sent by the Tamil Tigers, who detonated a beltful of bombs hidden beneath her dress.

It was not, though, quite the end of the Nehru–Gandhi dynasty. Immense pressure was put upon Rajiv's widow, Sonia, to lead the Congress Party, and after much resistance she eventually acceded. The victory of her coalition of parties in the 2004 general election effectively handed her the prime ministership – but in the face of (among other things) nationalistic grumblings over her foreign birth, she passed the role to a respected colleague, Manmohan Singh. She remains politically active, though in recent years eyes have turned to her son, Rahul, now an elected Congress Party politican.

The economic achievements of Gandhi's second ministry were overshadowed by the seemingly insuperable problem of the Punjab, the northwest province which Sikh extremists sought to transform into the independent state of Khalistan. Following his brief incarceration in September 1981, the Sikh separatist leader, Jarnail Singh Bhindranwale, retreated to Sikhism's holiest shrine, the Golden Temple in Amritsar, and began securing and fortifying the site against any potential government incursion. Gandhi, as always, urged a tough response, and on 3 June 1984 she ordered her army to storm the temple and remove Bhindranwale and his followers. In the event, the army operation was badly bungled: Bhindranwale was killed – becoming a martyr to his faith in the process – and hundreds of innocent Sikh pilgrims also died.

The Sikh community was outraged at the desecration of their most sacred temple. And the response, when it came, was swift and terrible. On 31 October, Indira Gandhi left her official home in New Delhi in order to be interviewed by actor Peter Ustinov for an Irish television documentary. As she was crossing the residence's garden, two Sikh members of her bodyguard, Satwant Singh and Beant Singh, opened fired on her with their hand-held machine-guns. The surrounding bodyguards returned fire, killing Beant and wounding Satwant (who was later convicted and hanged). But Mrs Gandhi died in her car on her way to the hospital.

After Gandhi's death, India erupted in a series of massive anti-Sikh riots. Countless Sikh temples – *gurdwaras* – were burned to the ground, and many people identified as a Sikhs were assaulted or murdered. (Many Sikh men hastily shaved off their turbaned hair and beard, traditionally left uncut, to preserve themselves and their families.) It has been estimated that up to 20,000 Sikhs died in the ensuing violence; however, not a single person was ever successfully prosecuted for these offences. Some years later, officials of the Delhi Congress Party were tried for incitement to murder and arson, but the cases were all dismissed for lack of evidence.

Indira Gandhi's son Sanjay had been her closest political adviser and companion. Indeed, many traced her most flagrant abuses of power between 1975 and 1977 to his malign influence. However, Sanjay was killed in a plane crash in 1980 and, distraught, his mother turned to her eldest son, Rajiv. He had lived in relative obscurity as an airline pilot and married an Italian national, Edvige (Sonia) Maino. Browbeaten by his imperturable mother, and with great reluctance, Rajiv finally agreed to take the place of his dead brother and continue the dynasty. On his mother's assassination, the Congress Party proclaimed him as prime minister in her place. Aged only 40, Rajiv Gandhi was the youngest person ever to assume that post.

Yitzhak RABIN

1922–1995, PRIME MINISTER OF ISRAEL

ASSASSIN	Yigal Amir
DATE	4 November 1995
PLACE	Tel Aviv, Israel

Despite its origin as a country born out of violence, Israel had until 1995 remained blessedly free from internecine political murders. While in much of the Middle East assassination had become commonplace, Israelis were able to boast that though their political landscape might be riven with deep faults, internal disputes had never escalated into premeditated murder.

Sadly, that reputation was shattered in 1995, when one of the most honourable and farsighted Israeli politicians – a man who had given the embattled state a genuine prospect of peaceful coexistence with its Arab neighbours – fell victim to an assassin's bullet.

Yitzhak Rabin was born in 1922 to Ukrainian immigrants in what was then Palestine, a League of Nations mandate administered by the British after the Ottoman Empire imploded in 1918. Never academically gifted, Rabin yet showed promise as a military strategist. In 1941 he joined the Palmach, the Jewish force created jointly by the British occupation forces and the irregular Jewish army, the Haganah, to resist the German forces then threatening to overrun Palestine from Egypt in the south and Syria in the east.

The Haganah had itself originated as an anti-Arab militia in 1920, and by 1936 it comprised 10,000 mobilized soldiers plus 40,000 reservists. During the Arab Revolt in Palestine of 1936–9, the Haganah had cooperated with the British army to crush the Arab rebels. However, after the threat of German invasion evaporated in 1942, following Montgomery's victory at El Alamein and the Torch landings in the western Maghreb, the Haganah and the Palmach both chafed under British restrictions, and by 1945 were primarily involved in facilitating large-scale yet illegal Jewish immigration to Palestine.

> 'It is time to put an end to the decades of confrontation and conflict'
>
> From the Oslo Accords agreed by Rabin, 19 August 1993

Rabin showed himself an excellent military administrator, and he rose to become the Palmach's chief operations officer by 1947. The following year war broke out, as neighbouring Arab countries attempted to stifle the controversial birth of the new Israeli state. During this Arab–Israeli War (also known as Israel's War of Independence), Rabin fought with distinction against the Egyptian army in the Negev Desert and helped to construct the armistice agreement of 1949. He stayed in the Israeli army, and in 1964 was appointed chief of staff of the Israeli Defence Forces. In this role he is credited as being the architect of Israel's lightning victory over its Arab neighbours during the pre-emptive Six Day War of 1967 – and despite the fact that the mounting strain beforehand had brought him to the verge of nervous collapse. However, it was the stunning Israeli territorial acquisitions of this war – notably the West Bank from Jordan and Sinai's Gaza Strip from the Egyptians – that would exacerbate the political challenges to come.

Having resigned from the army, Rabin was appointed to the plum post of Ambassador to the United States in 1968. Five years later, he joined the Labour Party, was elected to the Israeli parliament, the Knesset, and soon joined the Cabinet as minister of labour. And in June 1974 he reached the summit of his rapid political career. Golda Meir's administration was under constant attack over its alleged unpreparedness for the 1973 Yom Kippur War, when coordinated Egyptian and Syrian attacks nearly led to disaster. On 2 June Prime Minister Meir finally bowed to the inevitable and resigned. In her place, the proven military hero Rabin was elevated to the premiership.

THE RAID ON ENTEBBE

ON 27 JUNE 1976 AIR FRANCE Flight 139, carrying 248 passengers and crew from Athens to Paris, was hijacked by two Palestinians from the Popular Front for the Liberation of Palestine (PFLP) and two German terrorists from the self-styled 'German Revolutionary Cells'.

At their behest, the pilot flew first to Benghazi in Libya, then on to Entebbe in Uganda. Here the four hijackers were joined by three additional terrorists, supported by Uganda's dictatorial and notoriously unstable but pro-Palestinian president, Idi Amin. The hijackers then demanded the release of around forty Palestinians held in Israel and elsewhere. Failure to adhere to these demands would result, they declared, in the murder of all the aircraft's Jewish passengers.

Having negotiated to extend the hijackers' deadline, on 3 July Yitzhak Rabin and his government approved a rescue mission. That night, Israeli Special Forces landed at Entebbe an hour before midnight, their aircraft cargo bay doors already open. Posing as an official motorcade for President Amin, the soldiers' vehicles made straight for the main hall of the airport building, where the hostages were being held. Jumping from their cars, the soldiers ordered the hostages to lie down while they opened fire on the terrorists, eventually killing them all. (One hostage stood up and was shot by the Israelis, who mistook him for a hijacker; two others were killed in the crossfire.) The Israeli assault team then returned to their aircraft and began loading the hostages on board, while returning fire at the Ugandan soldiers who were attempting to stop them leaving. Meanwhile, soldiers from three other Hercules transport planes had destroyed 11 Ugandan MiG fighters on the ground, in case these pursued the departing rescuers.

All aircraft then took off for Nairobi and, after refuelling, flew on to Israel. The main operation had lasted less than thirty minutes. It delivered a huge political fillip to Rabin, and it remains a landmark in the history of counter-terrorist operations.

Two principal milestones marked Rabin's first term in office. In the first, Rabin ordered Israel's Special Forces to rescue almost 100 hostages (mostly Jewish) from Uganda's Entebbe Airport, where they had been taken from a hijacked Air France plane. In a daring raid, the Israelis whisked away the hostages, killed the hijackers and those Ugandan soldiers who intervened, and destroyed much of Uganda's air force capability on the runway. One Israeli soldier died and three hostages were caught in crossfire. (Notoriously, the Ugandans later killed the elderly hostage Dora Bloch, who was being treated in a Kampala hospital.)

The second milestone was, in fact, the manner in which Rabin's term in office ended, when two unfortunate coincidences undermined him. The fact that some new US fighter planes had been delivered to Israel on the Jewish Sabbath was a red rag to the more fundamentalist religious bulls among the opposition parties. In addition, it was discovered that Rabin's wife, Leah, continued to hold a US dollar account from the time that Rabin had been Ambassador to the United States – a technical breach of Israeli currency regulations. Although this amounted to a relatively minor misdemeanour, Rabin handed in his resignation in the wake of this disclosure – a noble act that earned him worldwide praise as a man of integrity.

Rabin's political resurrection was not long in coming, though. From 1984 to 1990 he served as minister of defence in the governments of Yitzhak Shamir and his longtime sparring partner Shimon Peres. In 1992 he succeeded Peres as the chairman of the Labour Party, and in the subsequent general election led Labour to a narrow victory over Shamir's incumbent administration.

Rabin's second term was marked by substantial advances in the quest for a lasting peace for the region. Out of the glare of the media spotlight, Norway's government hosted secret Israeli–Palestinian negotiations. At a conference in Washington, D.C., the participants signed an agreement in September 1993 by which Israel would recognize Yasser Arafat's Palestinian Liberation Organization (PLO) as the official Palestinian voice, while the PLO in turn renounced violent action and accepted Israel's right to exist as a sovereign nation. These accords were accompanied by the so-called Gaza–Jericho Agreement (also of September 1993), which laid out a basis for Palestinian self-rule, including the withdrawal of Israeli

Rabin in brief

troops from the West Bank, and created the partially autonomous Palestinian Authority to run the West Bank and Gaza Strip. Encouraged by these developments, Israel's neighbour Jordan negotiated a lasting peace treaty with Israel in 1994. With Yasser Arafat, Rabin was awarded the Nobel Peace Prize in 1994.

These achievements suggested that an over-all solution to the coexistence of Palestinians, Israelis and the Arab states was within reach. However, to many on the right wing of Israeli politics, Rabin's concessions to the PLO and to the Jordanians was treachery, and Rabin was excoriated by some for 'giving away' land that, they held, now rightfully belonging to the Israeli state.

Dissatisfaction exploded into appalling violence on 4 November 1995. As Rabin was leaving a political rally in Tel Aviv, held to celebrate the Oslo Accords, an Orthodox Jew, Yigal Amir, shot Rabin twice with a Beretta 84F semi-automatic pistol, just before the prime minister reached his official car. Rabin was rushed to the nearby hospital, where he died on the operating table from massive blood loss and a punctured lung. Upon hearing that the premier was dead, Amir – who had been caught at the scene of the assassination – merely told police he was 'satisfied'.

Hundreds of thousands of grieving Israelis thronged the square where Rabin was assassinated – a site soon renamed Rabin Square – to mourn his death. His funeral was attended by an astonishingly eclectic selection of world leaders, including US President Bill Clinton and the leaders of the two regional neighbours who had made peace with Israel: Egyptian President Hosni Mubarak and King Hussein of Jordan. Clinton delivered the funeral eulogy, and Rabin was buried alongside his wife on Mount Herzl.

At his 1996 trial, Amir attempted to defend his assassination on religious grounds. However, the court found him guilty and sentenced him to life imprisonment, plus six additional years for injuring Rabin's bodyguard. In a subsequent retrial, Amir was sentenced to an additional five years – and after an appeal on behalf of the state, eight years – for conspiring to commit the assassination. Meanwhile, the Knesset passed a law expressly forbidding the future pardoning of any assassin of an Israeli prime minister.

Amir remains in prison, and to a minority of Israelis he is a hero. He has never expressed regret for his actions, and sees himself as a martyr who was merely attempting to reverse what he saw as the fatal erosion of Israeli's sacred destiny and regional status. In recent years, his controversial divorce and remarriage to a prison visitor, and their attempts to conceive a child via in-vitro fertilization and conjugal visits – they had a son in 2007 – have kept him in the headlines. In 2007 Amir's family even launched the audacious, if not outright offensive, 'Campaign for Democracy' to press for Amir's release.

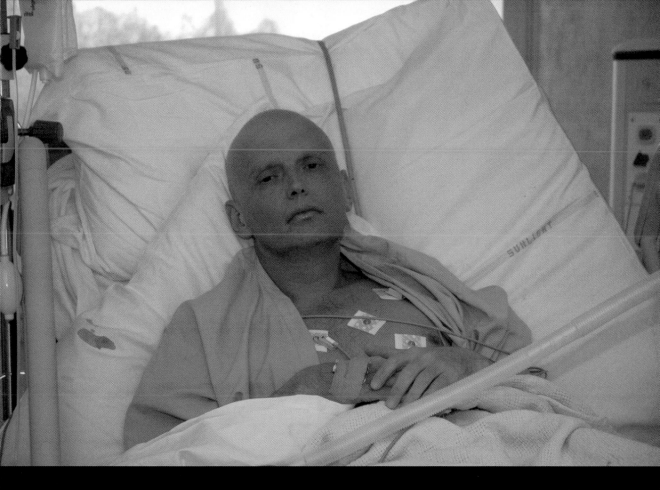

Alexander
LITVINENKO

1962–2006, EXPATRIATE RUSSIAN DISSIDENT

ASSASSIN Unverified

DATE 1 November 2006 (died 23 November)

Cold War was supposed to be over, a Russian agent-turned-political-refugee was murdered using a method most would have thought outlandish even if it had appeared in the pages of Ian Fleming: the secret application of a radioactive poison. It was no slick Bond-style operation, however, but a clumsy yet chilling crime that caught the world's headlines.

Alexander Litvinenko carved out a classic career path for a bright young man in the last days of the Soviet Empire. After being drafted into the army, in 1985 he joined the KGB security service and rose rapidly in its ranks. In 1991 – just as the Soviet Union was dissolving into its constituent republics – he was promoted to the 'Central Staff', specializing in counter-terrorism and the Chechen War, and in 1997 to senior operational officer and deputy head of the so-called 'Seventh Section'. By now, the KGB had been renamed the FSB, and in 1998 its head was Vladimir Putin.

By this time, though, disenchantment had set in. In November 1998, Litvinenko, now a lieutenant-colonel, joined with four other senior officers in publicly accusing his superiors of ordering the assassination of maverick tycoon Boris Berezovsky. Litvinenko was fired from his job and twice arrested by Russian authorities, yet he was swiftly released on both occasions. He subsequently fled to Britain, where he was granted political asylum and citizenship. (In 2001 Berezovsky himself followed suit.) He initially settled as far away from attention as possible, in the Cumbrian industrial town of Whitehaven, before moving to the North London suburb of Muswell Hill.

'You may succeed in silencing me, but that silence comes at a price'

The dying Litvinenko, from a statement released posthumously on 24 November 2006

Litvinenko now carved out a career in exile as a professional thorn in the side of the Russian authorities and the regime of Russian premier Vladimir Putin, who came to power in 2000. He gave television and radio interviews and lectures. He published a book, and the Russian authorities unsurprisingly attempted to pulp incoming copies. He delineated the FSB's alleged bombing campaign against civilian targets in Russia, most seriously that the 'apartment bombings' of 1999, which killed over 300 people, were a plot to incriminate Chechens and justify the renewed Russian onslaught on Chechnya that began soon afterwards. (It is a view shared by other Russian commentators and dissidents.) He even declared that Putin had personally ordered these events.

In later years Litvinenko's claims grew more outrageous. In 2005 he stated that 'all the bloodiest terrorists of the world', from the pro-Palestinian 'Carlos the Jackal' to the 9/11 bombers, had been connected to the KGB/FSB. The following year he even alleged in an article that Putin was a paedophile. He also accused Putin of personally ordering the assassination of the intrepid Russian journalist Anna Politkovskaya, and declared that the Italian politician and former president of the European Commission, Romano Prodi, had long been an agent of the KGB/FSB. Some began to dismiss his claims as paranoid exaggerations. It is a bitter irony that photograph showing, presumably unwittingly, a Russian Special Forces unit using pictures of Litvinenko for their target practice.

On 1 November 2006 Litvinenko suddenly fell seriously ill and was swiftly hospitalized in London. After a short time, his mystery illness became the stuff of national and international news as, through his friends, Litvinenko accused Putin's regime of poisoning him. The early rumours were that he was infected with a form of the poison thalium. On 22 November, medical staff at University College Hospital reported that the deteriorating Litvinenko had suffered a 'major setback' due to a heart attack. He died the following day, on 23 November.

Litvinenko's death was, to general astonishment, ultimately attributed to a rare and highly toxic radioactive element: polonium-210. Litvinenko had met with two former KGB agents-turned-businessmen, Dmitry Kovtun and Andrei Lugovoi, on the day he fell ill. They shared drinks in a bedroom of the Millennium Hotel and at its Pine Bar – Litvinenko apparently drank green tea. On the same day he had also had lunch at Itsu, a Japanese suchi restaurant in London's Mayfair, with an Italian, Mario Scaramella, who was investigating FSB activity in Italy. (Scaramella was initially also thought to have been poisoned, but later tests proved negative.)

Traces of polonium-210 were later found at all these locations – and plenty of others. Bar staff at the hotel – which didn't reopen until a year later – were found to be contaminated, as were Litvinenko's wife, two of the police officers investigating the case and the medical staff treating Litvinenko. However, no one other than Litvinenko has, thus far, become seriously ill.

By December 2006, London's Metropolitan Police were treating Litvinenko's death as murder, and on 20 January 2007 the *Times* even suggested that the police had identified the man they believed had added the poison to Litvinenko's drink. The suspected killer was, said the report, captured on cameras at Heathrow as he flew into Britain with Kovtun to carry out the murder. His name was 'Vladislav Sokolenko', an alias used as he entered Britain using a fake EU passport. It has since been suggested that Sokolenko was a Hamburg-based Chechen hitman employed by the FSB.

Several months of further investigations, however, shifted the focus. In May 2007, having received all of the police's evidence, the director of public prosecutions announced that there was sufficient evidence to charge Andrei Lugovoi in connection with the murder, and the British authorities formally asked Russia for his extradition. Lugovoi – a self-made millionaire who was evidently close to Putin – continued to publicly dismiss the claims against him as 'politically motivated' and emphasized that he did not kill Litvinenko, even claiming that he himself may have been an intended victim. And on 4 July 2007 the Russian prosecutor general's office declined to accept the extradition. Moreover, in what looked like obvious tit-for-tat tactics, the Russian authorities announced that they wanted to send their own team to Britain to investigate the events.

Litvinenko in brief

1962 Born in Voronezh, near Moscow, Soviet Union, the son of a doctor.

1980 Drafted into the Soviet army as a private.

1985 Joins the KGB and moves to Military Counter Intelligence in 1988.

1991 Promoted to the central staff of the KGB, concerned with counter-terrorism.

1997 Promoted to senior operational officer and deputy head of the 'Seventh Section' of what is now the FSB.

1998 Now a lieutenant-colonel, he and four other senior officers accuse the FSB (headed now by Vladimir Putin) of ordering the assassination of tycoon Boris Berezovsky: he loses his job and is arrested twice.

2000 Claims political asylum while stopping over in Britain: it is granted in 2001. He continues thereafter to criticize Putin's regime.

2001–3 Publishes two books: *The FSB Blows up Russia* and *The Criminal Group from the Lubyanka*.

2006 Poisoned with radioactive polonium-210 in his drink (1 Nov.) and dies in hospital three weeks later (23 Nov.).

2007 Russian authorities reject a British extradition request for Andrei Lugovoi, who is the only named suspect in the murder.

THE NEW KGB

THE FEDERAL SECURITY SERVICE of the Russian Federation (FSB) is the successor organization to the Soviet Union's notorious KGB. Renamed by President Yeltsin in 1995, it is engaged mostly in domestic affairs. Foreign espionage duties are supposedly now the province of the Russian foreign ministry.

Critics claim that it is engaged in suppression of internal dissent, and to that extent is little different from the old KGB. Indeed, some observers have noted that the FSB is more powerful than KGB was, since it is now directly responsible to the state president. FSB officers have responsibility for the country's 6000 nuclear weapons, and now even manage the strategic oil industry. The FSB has the right to electronically monitor the population, control political groups, run the country's borders, search homes and businesses, infiltrate the federal government, create its own front enterprises, investigate cases and to run its own prison system.

Vladimir Putin was appointed director of the FSB in 1998, in which post he was allowed by Yeltsin to increase the organization's powers and broaden its remit. On Yeltsin's retirement, it was relatively easy for Putin to vault from the FSB directorship to the state presidency, and in the eyes of some (such as Litvinenko) this amounted to an FSB coup. What is clear is that in today's Russia, former FSB individuals hold many key positions in politics and business.

In a susbequent twist to the story, Lugovoi was elected as a member of Russia's parliament, the Duma, in December 2007. He thus acquired parliamentary immunity from prosecution or extradition. On 10 December, the British Ambassador in Moscow regretted Lugovoi's election, noting that 'it does Russia no good at all to have Lugovoi there in the parliament' and warning that 'if he steps a foot out of Russia he will be arrested'.

Despite Lugovoi's consistent denials, the forensic trail of polonium-210 is consistent with his movements. It was found in the passenger aircraft used by Lugovoi to fly from and to Moscow. Traces were also discovered in all three hotels where Lugovoi stayed after flying to London in October 2006, and in the Pescatori restaurant in Mayfair, where Lugovoi dined.

The details of the police file on Lugovoi remain undisclosed, and there are various views as to the ultimate sponsor of the murder. Putin himself, the FSB, the Spetznaz (the Russian Special Forces), rogue security agents and nationalists, even prominent Russian oligarchs have all been blamed in the media. One thing is clear: if the intention was to despatch Litvinenko quietly via an untraceable mystery illness, then the result was a PR disaster. And, it has been noted, Lugovoi's high profile as an MP might not just be an insurance against the British authorities: whatever he knows about Litvinenko's death could, in the future, make him an embarrassing liability to others in Russia.

Meanwhile, Litvinenko's widow, Maria, continues to try and force the Russian government to admit responsibility. In December 2007 a recently released Russian prisoner, the ex-FSB Colonel Mikhail Trepashkin, told the European Court of Human Rights that a former FSB colleague had tried to hire him to remove Litvinenko on three separate occasions after 2002. His refusal to cooperate had, he alleged, led to trumped-up charges against him and four years in a Russian prison.

Others connected with the case have fared even worse than Trepashkin. Andrei Limarev, a former FSB agent and a colleague of Litvinenko, disappeared in the French Alps on 12 December 2006. He had reportedly told friends he felt he 'would be next'. And in the United States, on 2 March 2007, Paul Joyal, a former director of security for the Senate Intelligence Committee, was shot near his Maryland home. The previous weekend he had alleged on national television that the Kremlin was involved in the poisoning of Litvinenko. Joyal survived, and the FBI has become involved in the police investigation.

As for Alexander Litvinenko, he was buried in Highgate Cemetery in North London. A *Times* report of his funeral, of 1 December 2006, noted that his coffin must not be opened for 22 years, owing to the high dosage of polonium in his body. His killers continue to evade justice, while British–Russian relations remain at their lowest ebb for years.

Benazir Bhutto

On 18 October 2007, the Pakistani politician Benazir Bhutto – twice Prime Minister of Pakistan, and the first-ever woman premier of a Muslim state – returned to Karachi after eight years of exile in London and Dubai. The country's president, General Pervez Musharraf, had agreed to waive the corruption charges still outstanding against her and guarantee her safety on Pakistani soil. Nevertheless, barely had Bhutto left Karachi Airport on 18 October when a bomb targeted directly at her killed 136 people and injured at least 450 more.

This savage attack seemed to vindicate the suspicions of Bhutto's Pakistan People's Party that the country's intelligence agencies were, with or without the president's support, determined to prevent the charismatic Bhutto from regaining power in the imminent general election. After all, she was widely known for her secular and pro-American political agenda, and was loathed by fundamentalist Muslim militants; she also opposed Musharraf's increasingly authoritarian rule and suspension of civil liberties.

On 27 December 2007, barely nine weeks after her return to Pakistan, Bhutto was travelling back from a campaign rally in Rawalpindi. As she was standing to wave at supporters through the sunroof of her bulletproof car, a gunman shot at her from close range, while accomplices detonated charges close by the vehicle. Bhutto was rushed to a nearby hospital but was declared dead forty minutes later.

The recriminations, denials and conspiracy theories surfaced almost immediately. Bhutto's husband refused to permit a post-mortem examination, while the country's interior ministry said the bomb blasts had driven Benazir's head against the sunroof, fracturing her skull. A hospital spokesman protested that she had actually died from shrapnel wounds to the head. In February 2008, British detectives who had travelled to Pakistan concluded that it was, indeed, the bomb blast that was the cause of death. Al-Qaeda claimed 'credit' for the attack, describing Bhutto as 'the most precious American asset', while Musharraf denied any government complicity. For many of her supporters, it was all too much, and nationwide riots followed.

To many would-be assassins today, as much as to the original Assassins of the 12th-century Levant, political murder can be both sanctioned and exonerated by God or by government. In this sense, humankind has not, it appears, progressed much in nine centuries. As Mohammed Bouyeri, the 2004 killer of the radical and proudly atheist Dutch film-maker Theo Van Gogh, declared to a shocked passer-by: 'Now you know what you people can expect in the future.'

Such chilling prophesies will be of small comfort to Benazir Bhutto's declared heir, her 19-year-old son Bilawal Bhutto Zardari. At the time of her assassination he was quietly enjoying student life amid Oxford's dreaming spires. He must hope that the words of British Prime Minister Gordon Brown – that 'this atrocity strengthens our resolve that terrorists will not win there, here or anywhere in the world' – will prove to be a more prescient prediction for the 21st century than Bouyeri's menacing forecast.

Roman Empire 9, 11, 15; invasion of Britain 15
Roman Republic 9–11
Romero, Archbishop Oscar 174–7
Roosevelt, President Franklin D. 110, 112
Roosevelt, Theodore 88
Rosecrans, General William 74, 75
Rubens, Pieter-Paul 45
Ruby, Jack 147
Rudolf, Crown Prince 82, 83, 94
Rudolf II, Emperor 41
Russia 57–8, 70, 96, 115; assassinations in *see* Alexander II, Paul of Russia, Rasputin; attack of by Germany during Second World War 108; and Napoleonic Wars 59; reforms under Alexander II 70–1; serfdom 70, 71; war with Sweden 49; *see also* Litvinenko; Soviet Union; Trotsky
Russian Revolution (1917) 98, 100, 114
Russo-Turkish War (1877–8) 71
Rutilio, Father 175–6

Sadat, Anwar al- 178–82
Saddam Hussein 139
St Bartholomew's Day Massacre (1572) 34, 35, 39
Saladin, Sultan 21–2, 23
Salian Franks 40
Salic Law 37, 39, 40
Salisbury, Bishop of 19
Saltykov, Sergei 57
San Francisco 171, 173
Santiago de Cuba, Battle of (1898) 88
Sarajevo 94, 96
Saravia, Rafael Alvaro 177
Sattar, Dahmane Abd al- 198
Scaramella, Mario 201
School of the Americas (SOA) 176
Schrade, Paul 165
Schuschnigg, Kurt 103–4
Scotland 25–6
Scribe, Eugène 50
SD (*Sicherheitsdienst*) 119, 120, 121
Second World War 108, 133, 137
Seljuk Turks 21–2
Separate Amenities Act (1953) 156
'September massacres' (1792) 53, 55
Serbia 94, 96
Serbian Radical Party 107
Serot, Colonel André 135
Seven Years War 57
Seward, William 66
Seyss-Inquart, Arthur 104
Shakespeare, William 11
Shamir, Yitzhak 135, 193
'Share our Wealth' scheme 110, 112
Sharon, General Ariel 180
Sharpeville massacre (1960) 155
Sherman, John 75
shootings: Alexander of Yugoslavia 107; Aquino 184; Bernadotte 135; Canalejas 92; Evers 142; Faisal 139; Franz Ferdinand 96; Gandhi (Indira) 190; Gandhi (Mohandas) 131; Garfield 75–6; Gustav III 50; Kennedy (John F.) 146; Kennedy (Robert) 163, 165; King 158; Lincoln 66; Long 110, 112; McKinley 87–8; Malcolm X 152; Milk 172; Moscone 172; Moyne 124; Perceval 63–4; Rabin 194;

Rasputin 100; Romero 177; Sadat 182; William I 29, 31, 32
Sikhs 190
Singh, Beant 190
Singh, Manmohan 190
Singh, Satwant 190
Sirhan, Sirhan 165
Six Day War (1967) 179, 192
Sixtus V, Pope 35, 37
slave trade/slavery: abolition of 63, 67
Smith, Tommie 152
Smuts, Jan Christian 156
Soloviev, Alexander 72
Solway Moss, Battle of (1542) 25
Somerset, Earl of (Robert Carr) 43
South Africa 128; *apartheid* 154–6; Indians in 128–9
Soviet Union 168, 196, 197; *see also* Russia
Soweto 154
Spain 40, 86–7, 88, 90–2
Spanish Armada (1588) 36
Spanish Civil War 92
'Spanish Fury' 31
Spanish–American War (1898) 86–7, 88, 90
Special Operations Executive (SOE) 120
Speidel, Hans 108
Spencer, Earl 78, 80
Spion Cop, Battle of (1900) 129
Sri Lanka 190
stabbings: Becket 19; Buckingham 43, 46; Caesar 10–11; Caligula 15; Cavendish 78; Conrad of Montferrat 22–3; Elisabeth, Empress 82, 84; Henry, Duke of Guise 37; Henry III 37; Henry IV 39, 41; Marat 54–5; Paul, Tsar 57; Verwoerd 156
Stalin, Joseph 114, 115, 116
Stalwarts, the 75
Standard Oil Company 110, 111
Stephens, James 80
Stern, Avraham 126
Stern Gang *see* Fighters for Israel's Freedom
strangulation: Darnley 26–7
Suetonius 13
Suez crisis 138
suicide bombings: Alexander II 70, 72; Gandhi, Rajiv 190; Massoud 198
Sully, Duke of 39, 40, 41
Suursari, Battle of (1788) 49
Svenskund, Battle of (1790) 49
Sweden 48–9, 50, 133
Swedish Red Cross 133
Syria 138, 180
Szokoll, Major Carl 104

Taft, William Howard 110
Taliban 197–8
Tamil Tigers 190
Theobald, Archbishop of Canterbury 17
Thirty Years War 43, 45, 48
Thomas, D.B. 148
Tiberius 13
Till, Emmett 142
Tippit, J.D. 147
Tooke, John Horne 62
Tracy, William de 19
Trafalgar, Battle of (1805) 61
Treml, Franz 122
Trepashkin, Colonel Mikhail 202
Trevor-Roper, Hugh 133, 134

Tripoli, Count of 23
Trotsky, Leon 113–17
Trotskyism 115, 116
Truman, President 133, 135
Tsafendas, Dimitri 156
Tully, James 182
Tyre 21, 22

Uganda 193
Union, Edict of (1588) 36
United Nations 134
United States, assassinations in *see* Evers; Garfield; Kennedy (John F.); Kennedy (Robert); King (Martin Luther); Lincoln; Long; McKinley; Malcolm X; Moscone and Milk
Ustashe 106, 107, 108
Utrecht, Union of 31

Värälä, Treaty of (1790) 49
Verdi, Giuseppe 50
Versailles, Treaty of (1919) 102, 106
Verwoerd, Hendrik 153–6
Vetsera, Baroness 83
Villiers, George *see* Buckingham, 1st Duke of
Voltaire 52

Walker, Edwin 143, 145
Wannsee Conference (1942) 119, 120
War of the Austrian Succession 40
War of the Spanish Succession 48
'War of the Three Henries' 35
Warren Commission (1964) 148
Wars of Religion 34, 35–6, 37, 39, 40
Wavell, General 137
Weiss, Dr Carl 112
Weizmann, Chaim 126
Wellington, Duke of 61, 63
Westphalia, Treaty of (1648) 31
White, Dan 171–3
Wilberforce, William 63
Wilhelm II, Kaiser 94
Wilkes, John 52
William I, 'the Silent' 28–32
William II of the Netherlands 59
William V of Montferrat, Duke 21
Wilson, Henry Clay 161
Wright, Richard 152

Yellin-Mor, Nathan 126, 135
Yom Kippur War (1973) 180, 192
Young Bosnia 95
Yugoslavia 106–7, 108
Yusupov, Prince Felix 100

Zawahiri, Ayman al- 181
Zeid, Prince 139
Zhivkov, Todor 167–8, 169
Zinoviev 115, 116
Živković, Petar 107
Zubov, General Nicholas 57

This book is dedicated to Rachel

Picture Credits
2 Bettmann/Corbis UK Ltd; 8 Hulton-Deutsch Collection/Corbis UK Ltd; 12 Mary Evans Picture Library; 16 Bettmann/Corbis UK Ltd; 20 akg-images; 24 Mary Evans Picture Library; 28 akg-images; 33 Château de Blois/Gianni Dagli Orti/Art Archive; 38 Bettmann/Corbis UK Ltd; 42 TopFoto; 47 Mary Evans Picture Library; 51 Bettmann/Corbis UK Ltd; 56 Mary Evans Picture Library; 60 Mary Evans Picture Library; 65 Bettmann/Corbis UK Ltd; 69 Corbis UK Ltd; 73 Bettmann/Corbis UK Ltd; 77 Mary Evans Picture Library; 81 TopFoto; 85 Corbis UK Ltd; 89 George Grantham Bain Collection/Library of Congress; 93 Bettmann/Corbis UK Ltd; 97 Fortean/TopFoto; 101 TopFoto; 105 TopFoto; 109 Bettmann/Corbis UK Ltd; 113 akg-images; 118 TopFoto; 123 Hulton Archive/Getty Images; 127 Hulton-Deutsch Collection/Corbis UK Ltd; 132 TopFoto; 136 Bettmann/Corbis UK Ltd; 140 Flip Schulke/Corbis UK Ltd; 144 CPL/Everett/Rex Features; 149 Bettmann/Corbis UK Ltd; 153 TopFoto; 157 Bettmann/Corbis UK Ltd; 162 TopFoto; 166 Keystone/Getty Images; 170 Roger Ressmeyer/Corbis UK Ltd; 174 Bettmann/Corbis UK Ltd; 178 Bettmann/Corbis UK Ltd; 183 TopFoto; 187 AP/TopFoto; 191 Eldad Rafaeli/Corbis UK Ltd; 195 Yassukovich Sygma/Corbis UK Ltd; 199 Natasja Weitsz/Getty Images.

Publishing direction: Richard Milbank
Project management & additional text:
    Mark Hawkins-Dady
Proofreading & additional text: Rosie Anderson
Design & setting: Jane McKenna
Picture research: Zooid Pictures Ltd
Index: Patricia Hymans

Quercus Publishing Plc
21 Bloomsbury Square, London, WC1A 2NS

First published in 2008

Copyright © 2008 Steven Parissien

A catalogue record of this book is available from the British Library

Printed case edition:
ISBN 978-1-84724-190-0
Paperback edition:
ISBN 978-1-84724-703-2

Printed and bound in China

10 9 8 7 6 5 4 3 2 1